D0909141

Torah From Dixie

Intriguing Thoughts on
the Weekly Torah Portion
and Jewish Festivals

Edited by Benyamin Cohen
& Michael Alterman

Torah from Dixie

ISBN:0-87306-907-2

Published by:
B.C. Publishing
1490 High Haven Court
Atlanta, Georgia 30329
Phone: (404) 636-HOLY
Fax: (404) 320-6501
www.tfdixie.com
editor@tfdixie.com

Distributed by:
Feldheim Publishers
200 Airport Executive Park
Nanuet, NY 10954

Designed and produced by:
Bottom Line Design/NY

Printed in the United States of America

To order additional copies of this book, please call (404) 636-HOLY.

"... and the glory of children are their parents"
(Proverbs 17:6)

———❦———

This book is lovingly dedicated to
Ida Pearle & Joseph Cuba
of blessed memory by
Philip & Allison Cuba

This book will serve as an eternal memorial to their
lives which epitomized the love of Torah and
furtherance of Jewish education. They will always
be an inspiration to their family and to the Jewish
community in whose hearts their memory
will live on forever.

∞ Table of Contents

Deuteronomy

Jewish Festivals

בס"ד

YESHIVA
ATLANTA
The High School with a Higher Purpose

Rabbi Herbert J. Cohen, Ph.D
Dean

Resa S. Davids
Assistant Administrator

Philip G. Cuba
President

Barbara Gottlieb
First Vice President

Beverly Beard
Marilyn Feingold
Jonathan A.S. Freedberg
Diane Levy
Vice Presidents

Zahava Berkowitz
Recording Secretary

Michael Robinowitz, M.D.
Corresponding Secretary

Alexander S. Katz
Financial Secretary

Arthur M. Kurtz
Parliamentarian

Rabbi Emanuel Feldman
Honorary Secretary

Past Presidents
Ben Rabinowitz
Edwin J. Galler, M.D.
Daniel Burke
Benjamin Hirsch
George Kaplan
Eleanor Bogart
Charles D. Lowenstein
Larry Bogart
Dr. Robert Rush
Dr. Sheldon May
Jeffrey M. Ram
Arthur M. Kurtz

To the reader:

The publication of *Torah from Dixie* gives me great personal pleasure. As Dean of the Yeshiva High School of Atlanta for the past 21 years, I have been privileged to witness the spiritual/Torah growth of many of our students, who after graduating our school, continue to regularly study and teach Torah in various institutions both in the United States and in Israel. Among the schools where our graduates are currently learning are the Lakewood Yeshiva, Ner Israel, Yeshiva University, and the Mir in Jerusalem. These students are the primary contributors to this volume of Torah novellae.

Having read each of these *divrei Torah* when they first appeared in the weekly edition of *Torah from Dixie*, I am now even more impressed with the high quality of the authors' writing and the inherent Torah wisdom which they reveal. These brief essays continue to instruct and inspire when read yet again as this volume goes to press.

It is a great credit to the editors of *Torah from Dixie*, young men of vision and energy, to have brought this book from dream to reality. Their goal of spreading Torah is now fulfilled not only through a weekly newsletter on the Torah portion and through the Internet, but through the publication of this volume as well. Moreover, this book is a tribute to the many *rabbeim* of the Yeshiva High School of Atlanta, who over the years have inspired and motivated their students to choose a life of Torah living and learning.

May Hashem continue to bless the efforts of all those involved in the production and dissemination of *Torah from Dixie*.

Rabbi Herbert J. Cohen

∞ Introduction

The book you are about to read is the product of nearly three years of devoted effort by dozens of people. The articles inside have been culled from the weekly issues of *Torah from Dixie*, a non-profit publication dedicated to presenting inspirational thoughts on the weekly Torah portion. Over the past few years, we have been asked many questions about our journal, but, without a doubt, the one raised most often has been a simple, "Why?" What motivated a group of students, rabbis, and laymen from Atlanta, Georgia to produce a weekly publication on the Torah portion?

The answer is very simple. *Torah from Dixie* was conceived in order to satisfy a significant need. Thank G-d, there are many quality publications in circulation on the weekly Torah portion, each with its own style and approach. However, most of them are clearly addressed to audiences with advanced backgrounds in Torah study. We wondered if we could successfully produce a quality weekly newsletter discussing the Torah portion on a level that people, even with limited Torah knowledge, would appreciate and enjoy. We decided to give it a try, all the while assuming that it would be a short-lived venture.

Now, almost three years later, thousands of copies are printed each week and distributed to individuals and synagogues across the country. In addition, with the inception of our own website (www.tfdixie.com), people from all over the world with little or no access to any form of Torah study use the resources of *Torah from Dixie* to get their weekly dose of inspiration. In our wildest dreams we could never have imagined that *Torah from Dixie* would become so widely accepted and enjoyed, and we thank Hashem for providing us this opportunity to disseminate the words of His Torah.

We have tried to make this book as user-friendly as possible. In it you will find a brief summary of the major points of every Torah portion, and each summary is followed by several essays selected from the first two years of the *Torah from Dixie* weekly publication. Hebrew terms are *italicized* and translated either in the text or in the glossary. A short biographical sketch of the commentators quoted in this volume can be found in the back.

This book could not have come to fruition without the help and support of many people. First and foremost, we owe a tremendous debt of gratitude to Mr. Phil Cuba, a man with a vision, whose generous financial support and insightful guidance helped produce this volume. As President of Torah from Dixie, Phil has helped solidify our place in the Atlanta Jewish community and has positioned us for continued growth. In addition, we would like to thank Dr. S. Perry Brickman, Mr. Geoff Frisch, Mr. Egon Petschek, and the rest of the Torah from Dixie Board of Trustees who have supported *Torah from Dixie* from its inception and without whose dedicated devotion to Torah Judaism, this project would not exist.

Perhaps more than any other person, the remarkable growth of Atlanta as a center of Torah can be attributed to Rabbi Emanuel Feldman. His dedication is truly an inspiration to anybody who has seen the fruits of his labor.

We owe a tremendous debt of gratitude to all of our rabbis and teachers from whom we have had the privilege to learn throughout the years. They have a profound effect on every person who comes in contact with them.

It goes without saying that *Torah from Dixie* would not be possible without its wonderful group of writers whose volunteer efforts have surpassed our wildest expectations and from whose wit and wisdom we glean each week. Special thanks also to Rabbis Shlomo Freundlich and David Silverman whose rabbinic advice and guidance has served as a moral compass to keep *Torah from Dixie* on the proper Torah course.

The impeccable editing and beautiful design of the book is of crucial importance, and for that we would like to thank Mrs. Ethel Gottlieb, Mr. Yitzchok Saftlas, and Mr. Yaakov Gerber.

Sincere appreciation goes to our Sunday crew who, week in and week out, spend their free time stuffing envelopes and ensuring that the weekly mailings go out on time.

Special thanks to our families – Mommy, Daddy, and Leslie; Abba, Meryl, Dani, Elie, Rachel, Ezra, Chanie, Marty, and Joel – whose love and support through the good times and bad have helped us succeed and have enabled us to see our dreams fulfilled.

And finally, a world of thanks to the Atlanta Jewish community and to all of our loyal readers across the globe who have witnessed our growth and have helped nurture us to where we are today. Each and every one of you is a critical link in the venerable chain of Torah study.

It is our hope that this book will serve as a source of inspiration to its readers. May it motivate us to continually strive towards a greater relationship with our Creator and His Torah.

On behalf of the entire *Torah from Dixie* staff,

Atlanta, Georgia   Benyamin Cohen
Elul 5757   Michael Alterman

CS **Foreword**

by Rabbi Emanuel Feldman

When Moses says farewell to his people, he describes G-d's Torah as "*Tizal katal imrati* – My doctrine shall drop as the rain" (Deuteronomy 32:32). On which the Sifri comments:

"Just as the rain is one entity, and yet provides each tree with what it requires – to the grape according to its needs, to the olive according to its needs, to the fig according to its needs – so also are the words of the Torah; they are all one entity, but there is found in them Scripture, *Mishnah*, Law, and Lore."

This volume will surely provide each reader with an occasional insight, or inspiration, or understanding, or perception, "according to his or her needs." But above all else, the very fact that an entire volume of Torah thoughts could issue forth from a single community in the American South is a significant phenomenon, and provides its own measure of inspiration and encouragement.

For if anyone even twenty years ago would have dared prophesy that in 1997 there would be countless young people from Atlanta, Georgia, committed to Torah and *mitzvot*, and who were learning Torah in advanced *yeshivot* and *kollelim* in America and Israel – and that these young people would be able to issue a weekly pamphlet on the Torah portion and then to produce a volume of these thoughts – that prophet would have swiftly been consigned to the nearest hallucinatory specialist. But then again, the same fate awaited anyone in those days who dared express any confidence in the future of Torah in America, much less the South.

Of course, it is not only Atlanta that has witnessed such revolutionary change. Atlanta is but a microcosm of the astonishing revival of Torah consciousness throughout America.

In this revolution, Orthodox Judaism has been in the vanguard. With its emphasis on day schools, *yeshivot*, *kollelim*, and intensive Jewish living even before such things became fashionable, and often in the face of stubborn opposition from the Jewish establishment, it clung tenaciously to Torah living and Torah learning as the only avenue towards genuine Jewish revival. This little volume is a small manifestation of that tenacity, reflecting as it does the remarkable changes that have overtaken us. At a time when intermarriage, assimilation, and Jewish ignorance are at all-time highs, this collection makes a statement: When Jews have the courage and faith to return to their sources, Judaism will flower.

Note carefully the contributors to this volume. While there are some rabbis and teachers, the contributors are primarily young people who are engaged in advanced study of Torah. What they have in common is a commitment to Torah study and Torah living, a mature understanding of what that involves, and the ability to articulate that commitment and understanding. They also share something else – they each know one another, for at some crucial point in their lives they resided in Atlanta, Georgia.

Atlanta is not just another southern city; it can fairly be called the Torah jewel of the South, and with G-d's help will soon become one of the crowns of Torah in America. It already can boast of day schools, Jewish high schools, a *kollel*, and serious *beit midrash* study for adults – and it is the home of *Torah from Dixie*.

The weekly *Torah from Dixie* began as a fledgling weekly Torah portion sheet produced out of the Yeshiva University dormitory room of Benyamin Cohen and Michael Alterman some three years ago. Gradually, it blossomed into a stimulating weekly brochure eagerly read every *Shabbat* by thousands of Jews far and wide. This volume is a tribute to the vision and talents of the founders of *Torah from Dixie* – and of the individual writers, the supporters of the project, and to the Atlanta Jewish community which nurtured it over the years.

* * *

"*Harotzeh lehachkim yadrim,*" says the Talmud in Baba Batra 25b: "He who would be wise should face south [when he prays]." This is because in the *Beit HaMikdash*, the *menorah* was at the south of the chamber, and the *menorah* represents the light of wisdom. In addition, the sun in its daily march across the heavens traverses the southern skies, giving greater light and warmth to the southern portions of G-d's world.

May the light of Torah wisdom emanating from this southern community light up the lives of the readers of this collection. May it help bring to fruition the words of Moses in the very next verse of Deuteronomy cited above: "For I have called unto the Lord, let us bring glory to our Master."

Jerusalem   Emanuel Feldman
Elul 5757

GENESIS

PARSHAT BEREISHIT

arshat Bereishit (Genesis 1:1-6:8), the first portion of the Torah, begins with Hashem's creation of the world in six days and His "resting" on the seventh. Everything, from the separation between light and darkness on the first day, to the establishment of the heavenly spheres on the fourth, to the climactic fashioning of Man (Adam) and Woman (Eve) in Hashem's image and their placement in the Garden of Eden on the sixth, is created and arranged in its proper place during this first week. Humans are given dominion over the entire world with only one restriction – to refrain from consuming the fruit of the Tree of Knowledge. Eve is enticed by the serpent to partake of the forbidden fruit, and she offers some to her husband as well. Hashem responds by punishing them for their transgression, and additionally they are banished from the paradise of Eden.

After the expulsion, their first two sons, Cain and Abel, each bring an offering to Hashem. Abel's superior offering is accepted by G-d, while Cain's inferior offering is rejected. Cain jealously responds by killing his brother, and Hashem sends him into exile to wander the face of the earth. The Torah then gives a genealogy of the first ten generations of the world, beginning with Adam, his third son Seth, and leading up to the birth of Noah and his three sons. Disgusted by Man's wickedness, the portion ends with Hashem expressing His "regret" for creating the world and His decision to destroy every living thing, except for the righteous Noah and his family.

∽ **From Top to Bottom**
by Rabbi Shlomo Freundlich

We are introduced to Hashem's Torah with the fundamental principle of faith that it was G-d Who brought the universe into being by creating heaven and earth. This opening verse, however, communicates more than just the Jewish position on the Genesis vis-à-vis Darwinism. The *Midrash's* comment on this verse enlightens us to what can be considered the defining standard for authentic Jewish living.

The *Midrash* relates that when humans endeavor to construct an edifice, they begin at the bottom and build upward. Hashem, on the other hand, begins with the heavens above and proceeds downward, as indicated by the language of the Torah that first heaven and then earth was created.

It is not reasonable for us to assume that the *Midrash* calls Man to task for not building our skyscrapers beginning with the 85th floor and working downward. One does not need to be Newton to recognize the folly of such a project. What message, then, does the *Midrash* seek to impart regarding how we can best emulate Hashem's formula for creation?

Rabbi Shmuel Alter offers an illuminating insight that speaks to us with great urgency. He notes that young people are consumed with plans for building their future. They have grandiose dreams which include an exquisite home, the need to gain social and professional prominence, and whatever they consider essential to their security and material well-being. To be sure, religious life is not ignored. A kosher kitchen, Jewish education, and *mitzvah* observance are hallmarks of the Jewish home. But somehow the major part of their energies are directed toward the pursuit of the material, whereas the spiritual component of their lives, although paid generous lip service, is relegated to a secondary tier of importance. Daily *minyan* is attended if they have time, and Torah classes are attended if their schedules do not include prior commitments. They are obsessed with upgrading their hard drives, but how often do they entertain the thought of upgrading their Jewish value system.

This is what the *Midrash* exhorts. When the Torah says that Hashem created the world starting with the heaven, it means Hashem desires that the heavenly and spiritual realm be Man's focus in creation and life. However, all too often we construct the edifices of our lives from the bottom, making earthly pursuits and material successes the foundation of our lives. May we merit that the foundations we lay for ourselves and our families follow the blueprint of the greatest of all architects.

Marriage Counseling
by Rabbi Ariel Asa

In the Milchamsky household. . .

"Hi honey, I'm home," Dave said to his wife as he walked through the door.

"How was your day, dear?" Mrs. Milchamsky asked.

"Just awful. My co-worker is impossible to get along with, and this project is going to last another two months. I feel horribly frustrated. I'm in the mood to really stir up a scene at work tomorrow."

"I'm sorry to hear that," she responded. "I definitely think you should march into the boss' office first thing in the morning and give him an ultimatum – either the co-worker goes or you go. Don't let yourself be pushed around. You have to stick up for your rights."

The conversation (or rather the tirade) continued in this vein for several minutes.

Meanwhile, in the Shalomsky household, a very similar scenario was unfolding. As Mrs. Shalomsky was thinking how best to reply to her husband's problem, she stopped to think about the impact of her words. . .

"Hmm," she started, "it sounds like you're really disenchanted with your co-worker. Perhaps you should sit down with him and have an open discussion about the things he does that frustrate you."

Within a few minutes, a look of relief crossed Mr. Shalomsky's face as he considered what he would say on the morrow. Then he thought how lucky he was to have a wife who always knew precisely how to tactfully oppose him and help him keep his cool.

When Hashem was preparing to create the first female, He said, "It is not good for the Man to be alone. I will make for him a <u>helpmate opposed to him</u>" (Genesis 2:18). We don't usually perceive of a helpmate as someone who is going to be on the opposition. However, as is clear from the scenario above, a true helpmate knows when to constructively disagree with her spouse, saving him from untold hardship and pain. Thus, we derive a deeper meaning of Rashi's words on the above verse: "If he merits, she is a helpmate. If he doesn't merit, she is opposed to him." If he merits, then her <u>opposition</u> will help him. If he doesn't merit, even her <u>support</u> will be the ultimate opposition to him.

Based on the commentary of the Netziv.

Excuses, Excuses
by Michael Alterman

"Cain said to his brother Abel, and it happened when they were in the field that Cain rose up against his brother Abel and killed him" *(Genesis 4:8).*

An immediate question arises upon reading this verse. The Torah writes that "Cain said to Abel," and then there seems to be an obvious gap, a pause which strikes us, because the Torah does not tell us what Cain said. The entire congregation is sitting on the edge of their seats, listening carefully to the Torah reading, waiting for the climactic moment when they will hear what Cain has to say, and then, as if an entire line had been erased, the narrative skips forward to tell us that Cain killed his brother! But what happened? What did the two brothers talk about that caused Cain to react so drastically?

The Targum Yonason addresses this question by relating a fascinating argument which took place between the two brothers that led directly to the murder. Cain complained to Abel that there is no justice and ultimate judge in the world; there is no World to Come, and therefore the righteous will not be rewarded and the wicked will never be punished. Abel disagreed, and as a result of this argument, Cain decided to kill his brother Abel.

However, even after hearing this explanation of the conversation, the passage still remains unclear: If they were truly having a disagreement over such a fundamental subject, wouldn't it have been informative for the Torah to directly relate it to us?

It has been suggested that the Torah omitted any explicit mention of the subject of their argument because, in truth, it is totally insignificant to the story at hand. Cain had no right to take the life of his brother, end of story, no matter how much he justified his actions. The fact that Cain had a supposed excuse for his behavior (their difference of opinion) was irrelevant, because whatever his reasoning was, it remained merely a rationalization formulated by the human mind to allow itself to pursue its base desires. In truth, Cain was jealous that Abel's offering had been accepted by Hashem and that his own had not, so he wanted to kill his brother. But he had only one problem – his conscience. Cain couldn't simply destroy his own flesh and blood. He needed an excuse, a rationalization to make himself feel better about what he was going to do. He therefore instigated an argument, "discovered" that his brother disagreed, and proceeded to use that as his excuse for murder. However, because it was merely an excuse, the Torah deemed it to be immaterial and therefore chose to omit it from the narrative.

How often do we create excuses to justify our actions – fabricating rationalizations which, if we would simply take the time to analyze them, we would find that they are totally unfounded? Are we really honest with our friends, our families, Hashem, and ourselves, or do we simply search for the best excuses so that we can satisfy our conscience? As we begin this new year, let us strengthen our commitment to pursue the truth and beware of the dangerous rationalizations which inevitably will impede our quest for a good, moral life.

PARSHAT NOACH

*P*arshat Noach (Genesis 6:9-11:32) begins by describing Noah's superior character, contrasted with the wickedness of his generation. As a result of Mankind's evil, Hashem brings a flood to destroy every living creature, sparing only Noah, his family, and at least one pair of every animal species, who live in an ark during the lengthy deluge. When the waters recede, almost a year after the rains first began, Noah sends out a raven and a dove so as to determine whether the land has dried sufficiently so that they can leave the ark to resettle the earth once again. Hashem promises that He will never again destroy all of Mankind by means of a flood, and He designates the rainbow as a sign for that eternal covenant.

Noah plants a vineyard, drinks from its produce, and becomes drunk. In his intoxicated state, he shamefully uncovers himself in his tent. While his son Cham dealt with his father inappropriately, Noah's other two sons, Shem and Yefet, cover their father in a respectful manner. Once sober, Noah responds by blessing Shem and Yefet, and by cursing Cham and his son Canaan. Generations pass and the world is repopulated. The people attempt to wage war against Hashem by building the Tower of Babel, and Hashem responds by mixing up their languages and dispersing them across the planet. The Torah portion concludes on an encouraging note with Abraham's birth and his marriage to Sarah.

∽ A Whole New World

by Yoel Spotts

"From everything that lives, two of each shall you bring into the ark"
(Genesis 6:19).

With this instruction, Noah is commanded to preserve every single species that roams the earth. While this certainly seems like the right thing to do, it also appears to be an impossible task. With the dimensions of the ark limited to relatively modest proportions, it seems highly unlikely that all the animals will find room aboard the ship. How, then, is Noah expected to fulfill such a command?

Fortunately, Noah has nothing to worry about. As the Ramban explains, although according to the normal laws of nature, the given measurements of the ark could in no way support every species on earth, Hashem in this case suspended those laws so as to preserve His creations. Through this miracle, every animal had ample room aboard the ark.

However, we are immediately presented with another difficulty: Since the necessity for a miracle seems unavoidable, why did Hashem give Noah such precise instructions regarding the measurements and other details of the ark? Why make Noah go through so much trouble? Why not allow Noah to build a simple little raft made out of a couple of 2x4's?

Once again, the Ramban provides the solution. Although a miracle is certainly necessary for the sake of all those animals waiting to board the ark, Hashem wishes to "minimize" that miracle in whatever way possible. Thus, he instructs Noah to build a large, solid ship that can at the very least support many of the animals. Only after the existing capacity of the ark has been filled, will Hashem suspend the laws of nature to create ample space for the remaining animals.

Clearly, this explanation provides an obvious lesson: As the Ramban states himself, Hashem does not want us to rely on miracles. Man cannot simply sit back, exert no effort, and expect Hashem to provide for his needs. Rather a person must work and struggle to achieve his goal. Only after a person can honestly say, "I have done all that I can," is he permitted to hope that Hashem will "bend the rules".

However, there appears to be a deeper message contained within the Ramban's explanation. Rabbeinu Bachya teaches, "Hashem created the world to operate according to the natural laws of the universe." When we look outside at the world, we see nothing special at first glance, just the same old plants and trees and other entities functioning in their normal manner. Without giving it a second thought, the world appears quite mundane and boring. The natural order of the universe arouses not a spark of excitement within us. It is only once we step back and examine the universe in greater detail that the world suddenly takes on a whole new meaning. The life cycle of Man, the workings of the cosmos, the interaction between animals and their environment – all exhibit the beauty, wonder, and magnificence of nature. Scientists continue to marvel at the preciseness and exactness with which the world operates. Suddenly, those laws which seemed so meaningless a moment ago now inspire a sense of awe for Hashem's creations. Thus, Hashem wishes to maintain the natural order of the world whenever possible. To suspend the laws of nature is to introduce an element of chaos into the spectacular and sensational harmony of the existing world.

Many people wonder why Hashem performs no miracles for us today. The answer lies not in some long-winded philosophical argument, but rather in simply opening our eyes to a whole new world, for miracles take place every second of every day right around us.

⌒ Conformity vs. Diversity
by Micah Gimpel

At the end of Parshat Noach, we are told about the infamous Tower of Babel, the story of society gathering to build a monumental tower with its peak high in the sky. Hashem, ostensibly upset, decides to foil their efforts by confusing their language so that they cannot understand each other, and by dispersing them across the world, hence leading to the formation of many different civilizations.

Traditionally, the Tower builders are understood to have been attempting to physically confront and challenge Hashem and His authority. However, Ibn Ezra cannot find reason to believe that the people of that time were stupid enough to think that their building a tall tower would enable them to encounter Hashem. Therefore, his understanding of the story is radically different. He explains that their intent was not to build a tower as a fortress, but rather as a headquarters. Their goal was to make a glorious name for themselves by establishing a center for all of civilization. This center was to be the heart of world society.

This philosophy appears to be noble and commendable. Unity is critically important for the development and success of any project. People naturally work together when there is a common goal or ultimate purpose, and having societal direction promotes a single solid social unit. If that is correct, there is one significant problem with Ibn Ezra's explanation: Why does the text imply that the generation of the Tower of Babel was punished for its actions? It would appear that they should have been rewarded for their concern for everyone and their goal of unifying the world's population. If their intention was not to challenge Hashem but to create a center for Mankind, why would Hashem mix up their language and scatter them across the world?

Though this ideology of unifying society can be productive, it can also be limiting. Without exposure to other groups with different histories and philosophies, one loses perspective and objectivity. The problem that existed in the generation of the Tower of Babel was that they were intentionally trying to limit society's growth and development. The Rashbam explains further that the reason Hashem reacted to that generation by disrupting their efforts was because they were not fulfilling nor pursuing Hashem's purpose for the world. The first commandment given to Mankind was "to be fruitful and multiply and fill the land" (Genesis 1:28). If Man limits civilization to one center, the conquest of the world is also limited. Hashem's reaction was not a punishment but rather a correction. Hashem spread everyone across the globe and confused their language to make complete unification virtually impossible, effectively conquering the world for Man and ensuring diversity.

From this interpretation of the episode of the Tower of Babel, we discover that Hashem desires the diversification of Man. To have every person a mirror image of his neighbor would be a tragic loss to society, as it might stifle people's creative genius. The fact that society has so many differences of opinion can be viewed as a positive expression of Man's uniqueness. There is much to be learned from people who are different from us, and all that is required is an open mind and a desire to "fill the land".

PARSHAT LECH LECHA

*P*arshat Lech Lecha (Genesis 12:1-17:27) begins with Hashem's call to Abraham* to leave his homeland and his father's house, his position of status and prosperity, to travel to the land that Hashem will show him. Upon arrival, with his wife Sarah* and nephew Lot, in the land of Israel, they discover it to be ravaged by a horrible famine, so they descend to Egypt for a temporary stay. The immoral Egyptians immediately capture Sarah, whom Abraham had identified as his sister, and take her to the Egyptian king. Hashem responds by afflicting the king and his household with a debilitating plague until he releases her, at which point they return to the land of Israel. When Abraham's and Lot's shepherds begin to quarrel, the two decide to part ways, with Lot choosing the fertile plains of Sodom as his portion.

The Torah then describes the infamous war between the four kings and the five kings, during which Lot is taken captive. Abraham responds by miraculously defeating the previously victorious four kings and saving his nephew, while refusing to take any of the honor or the spoils of war for himself. Hashem reassures Abraham that He is by his side, and promises that his descendants will be as many as the stars in the sky. Hashem then enters into the highly

---

Although their names are still Abram and Sarai throughout most of Parshat Lech Lecha, we (and many of the commentators) refer to them by their more familiar names, Abraham and Sarah, names Hashem gives them at the end of the portion.

symbolic Brit Bain HaB'tarim *(the Covenant Between the Parts) with Abraham, promising that his children will inherit the land of Israel, but not before being exiled into a lengthy servitude. Because she had no children, Sarah gives her maidservant Hagar to Abraham as a wife, and their son Yishmael is born. Years later, Hashem changes Abram's name to Abraham and Sarai's name to Sarah, and instructs him in the* mitzvah *of* brit milah *(circumcision). The portion concludes as Abraham, at the age of 99, circumcises himself and his son Yishmael, along with the other male members of his household.*

∽ A Perfect Thought
by Micah Gimpel

While Noah is characterized as already being "perfect – *tamim*" when we first encounter him (Genesis 6:9), the Torah implies that Abraham has not yet attained this level of perfection when Hashem charges Abraham: "Walk before Me and be perfect" (ibid. 17:1). Although the Torah qualifies the compliment to Noah, limiting his perfection to within his generation, Abraham, as an individual, seemingly lacks some trait whereby Hashem could not describe Abraham as "perfect" and therefore Hashem must direct him along a certain path. Why is Hashem advising Abraham to "be perfect" and in what way is Abraham deficient?

Abraham had a tricky and complicated mission in life. His independent revelation of the truth of monotheism placed him in uncharted territory where he would need to investigate avenues never before traversed. And, much like a path-maker in the wilderness, Abraham must pursue directions that could get him hopelessly lost or even lead him to life-threatening and mission-undermining destinations. Being an innovator, Abraham must take chances in order to develop, clarify, and understand this revolutionary concept of monotheism. In doing so, a real possibility emerges of his being led astray. This fact does not hint to a weakness in Abraham's faith, rather it bespeaks a truly complicated and intricate mission with many factors contributing to the final conclusion. Although today we understand the concept of a single G-d as almost intuitive, Abraham discovered and formulated the notion of monotheism from nothing (ex nihilo). Hashem, understanding all the potential pitfalls and detours that Abraham will likely face, advises Abraham to "walk before Him". However, while walking before Hashem, Abraham must "be perfect" in pursuit of his goal, in order to ensure the proper outcome.

Everyone has missions in life – personal, familial, and communal. In every mission potential threats abound and we run the risk of straying from the path of our desired destination. Even when we are charting our own paths, detours may cause us to lose our direction. As long as we strive for perfection, we can continue to pursue our mission with a degree of security. Of course, the threat still exists, but to a lesser degree. Abraham can and must traverse unknown territory to achieve his life's work, but with an orientation and mentality of sincerity and impeccability. We too must strive for perfection, reaching higher with sincere intentions.

∽ Trailblazer

by Michael Alterman

Our rabbis tell us that Hashem administered ten tests to Abraham throughout his life to give him the opportunity to prove his faith. From the command at the beginning of this week's portion to leave his family and homeland, to the *akeidah* at the end of next week's portion when he is asked to "sacrifice" his own son, we can easily comprehend why these are considered to be challenging ordeals. Most of us have never been faced with such circumstances and can hardly imagine that we would ever be able to pass such tests. How great must Abraham have been that he was able to stand up to such intense Divine scrutiny!

However, in Parshat Lech Lecha we read about Abraham's circumcision, his performance of the beloved *mitzvah* of *brit milah*, which is also counted by the commentators among the ten tests. The *mitzvah* of *brit milah* is one which truly distinguishes the Jewish people from the nations of the world, one which has been performed with great joy by Abraham's descendants, millions upon millions of times throughout history. It therefore seems difficult to understand why such an action would be considered a trial, especially for a great person like Abraham. Granted that it may have been physically challenging, but we are talking about somebody who had already shown that he was literally willing to give up his life for Hashem, as was clear from his successful completion of the earlier tests. How could the test of *brit milah* pose a challenge to someone of Abraham's stature?

Rabbi Moshe Feinstein explains that to understand why this was an appropriate test, we must first analyze Abraham's career and approach up until this point in his life. We know that he was a master at influencing other people to come closer to Hashem and to recognize the purpose of Creation. Abraham was an outgoing person who had totally dedicated his life to helping others, even at the expense of his own personal growth. He epitomized the attribute of *chesed*, loving kindness, and he used that trait in fulfilling his mission. However, his success was all made possible by his being somewhat similar to the people whom he was trying to influence.

The *mitzvah* of *brit milah* was a command to Abraham and his descendants to become totally different and separated from the rest of the world, something which would seemingly place a significant restraint on their ability to influence other people. Hashem was asking Abraham to redirect his efforts from a strategy which had been highly successful and embark on an unfamiliar path whereby he and his descendants would indirectly serve as a guiding light to the rest of the nations. In effect, Abraham was being asked to subjugate his own will and plan to that of Hashem's. *Brit milah*, therefore, was not merely a test of Abraham's physical dedication; it represented a struggle which shook the foundations of his perspective on life.

The classic commentators tell us a general principle that the actions of our forefathers are a sign for their children (*ma'ase avot siman l'banim*), meaning that everything which Abraham, Isaac, and Jacob did so many years ago served to instill their superior character traits into the lifeblood of the Jewish people. When Abraham followed Hashem's command, even though the request appeared to be illogical and counterproductive, he enabled every one of his descendants to make that same decision. When Abraham stood up against the ridicule of the world, which must have thought that he was out of his mind, he set a precedent which has been followed over countless generations in countless places all over the world. Let us aspire to fulfill the great potential which Abraham instilled within us.

☙ The Big Move
by Rabbi Norman Schloss

Parshat Lech Lecha begins with the first of ten tests or trials that Abraham was subjected to by Hashem. The portion opens, "*Lech lecha* – Go for yourself, from your land and from your birthplace and from your father's house to the land which I will show you" (Genesis 12:1). Hashem asks Abraham to put his trust in Him purely on faith and to follow Him to an unknown land. Lest there be any misunderstanding, Hashem clearly delineates for Abraham the parameters – he must leave his home and place of birth. The Torah tells us that Abraham does as Hashem wishes. However, the Torah then states, "Abraham took his wife Sarah and his nephew Lot, and all their wealth that they had amassed, and the souls that they created in Charan." If the Torah tells us that Abraham did all that Hashem commanded him, why repeat that fact again?

Rabbi Aharon Wolkin offers the following answer: There are many reasons why a person might choose to move from one place to another. Sometimes a person might leave because of familial reasons.

Many times a person will move for financial reasons or because the neighborhood is not safe or decent anymore. The Torah is telling us that these were not factors in Abraham's case. Familial reasons were not the issue here. If he was moving away, his wife and nephew would accompany him; they were his loved ones. He didn't go for financial reasons because Abraham took all of his wealth with him. As to Abraham leaving because of the possible bad influence of his neighbors, the Torah says that many people in the neighborhood joined him. In other words, the Torah is informing us of the greatness of Abraham – that he left purely to fulfill the wishes of Hashem.

There is one other place in the Torah where the special phrase introducing this test, *"lech lecha* – go for yourself"*, is also used. It is regarding the last trial that Abraham must undergo, the *akeidah* at the end of next week's Torah portion. Hashem commands, "Please take your son, your only one, whom you love – Isaac – and (*lech lecha*) go for yourself to the land of Moriah" (Genesis 22:2). Without any questions or hesitation, Abraham follows Hashem's bidding completely and faithfully, never demonstrating any change in attitude.

At first glance it seems that the first and last test are the same. Is there any difference between the *lech lecha* in this week's portion and the *lech lecha* of the *akeidah?* The Reisha Rav offers a fascinating explanation. In this week's portion we see how Abraham relates to the will and command of Hashem. In next week's portion we see how Abraham passed this lesson down to his son. Abraham's life has little meaning until he sees that the same devotion and dedication that he has for Hashem is also present in his son Isaac. That is why the first and last tests seem similar. Abraham has come full circle in his service of Hashem. This is the legacy and inheritance that is ours when we say that we are the "children of Abraham" – it is our steadfastness in keeping the *mitzvot* of Hashem, no matter the circumstances or where we may find ourselves. May we all merit to be called *Bnei Avraham*, children of Abraham.

PARSHAT VAYEIRA

arshat Vayeira (Genesis 18:1-21:24) begins with Abraham's incredible display of kindness, notwithstanding his extreme discomfort from his recent brit milah, *to those he perceives to be three men but who are really angels sent by Hashem. The angels deliver their message, declaring that Sarah will miraculously give birth to her first child within the year at the age of 90 (Abraham himself would be 100). After this they proceed to the city of Sodom. Hashem informs Abraham that the cities of Sodom and Amorah will be destroyed for their wickedness, and Abraham responds with a lengthy prayer and dialogue with Hashem on the cities' behalf. Unable to find even ten righteous citizens, Hashem proceeds to destroy the cities, but not before the angels save Abraham's nephew Lot and his family from the destruction. Thinking that the entire world had been destroyed, Lot's two daughters cause their father to become drunk so that they can each become pregnant by him, and they each give birth to a son. Sarah is abducted by Avimelech, the king of G'rar, who did not realize that she was married. Hashem responds by striking him with a plague which prevents him from touching her, and informs Avimelech that Sarah is in fact married, at which point she is released.*

Sarah conceives and gives birth to Isaac, and Abraham makes a huge celebration. Sarah sees Yishmael (Abraham's son from Hagar) as a menace to her own son's spiritual well-being.

Initially reluctant, Abraham follows Hashem's command to listen to his wife by expelling Yishmael and Hagar from his home. With Yishmael about to die of thirst in the desert, Hashem hears his cry and causes Hagar to find a well of water from which the youth is saved. Abraham signs a covenant with Avimelech in the city of B'ersheva, and they live in peace for many years. The Torah portion concludes with the akeidah, Abraham's tenth and final test, in which he shows his willingness to comply with Hashem's command to offer up his beloved son Isaac as a sacrifice.

෴ Speed
by Mendel Starkman

You are reclining in your easy-chair, relaxed and engrossed in a good book, sipping an ice cold glass of lemonade. Thoroughly enjoying this treasured relaxation, you are suddenly interrupted by the sound of your phone ringing. Hesitantly, you pick up the receiver to hear the voice of your friend, David. David is moving today and needs help carrying some boxes. Not wanting to disturb your time off with any sort of manual labor, you almost mechanically answer that no, you are busy now. Hanging up the phone, you return to the book's intriguing plot.

The Torah, at the beginning of this week's portion, describes in great detail how Abraham, when visited by three guests, demonstrated tremendous zeal in serving and taking care of them. Abraham "hastened to the tent to Sarah" so that she could prepare fresh bread, he "ran to the cattle" to prepare the greatest delicacies, and then "stood over them beneath the tree" while they ate in the shade, making sure that their every need was provided for (Genesis 18:6-8). Rabbeinu Bachya points out that even though Abraham was an elderly man and extremely weak from the circumcision he had undergone just three days prior, and despite the fact that he had many servants who could have attended to his guests, as a show of respect Abraham did everything himself, and with great zeal and enthusiasm.

At the end of the Torah portion there is another situation in which Abraham demonstrated this character trait of zeal. On the morning that Abraham arose to perform the *akeidah*, the Torah reports that he "arose early" to perform the *mitzvah* (ibid. 22:3). In this difficult situation, when Abraham was told to bring his beloved son, for whom he had anxiously waited so many years, as an offering, one would think that the last thing such a person would do is wake up early in the morning to embark on this mission! Yet we see that Abraham did. How can this be?

Once again we see an example of Abraham's personification of the character trait known as *zrizut* – being zealous, quick, and enthusiastic in performing Hashem's *mitzvot*. Abraham developed this trait to such a degree that even in this extremely difficult and trying situation, he was still able to overcome the natural desire to procrastinate, and he even woke up early to do Hashem's will. This teaches us an incredible lesson, that precisely at times when a situation is uncomfortable, we still have the ability to perform a *mitzvah* with zeal and enthusiasm, and especially when the *mitzvah* is not that difficult.

There is a well-known concept in human dynamics known as inertia – that a person's natural tendency is to try to remain as inactive as possible. This tendency is intensified when it comes to performing *mitzvot* because there is an added deterrent, the evil inclination, which will do anything in its power to prevent a person from doing an action that will entitle him to reward in the World to Come. With this in mind, we are left with a question: How does one go about acquiring the character trait of *zrizut*? How does one overcome his natural laziness to accomplish greatness?

There are two ways to do this: Rabbi Moshe Chaim Luzzatto explains that we can do this by focusing on all the things that Hashem does for us. For if we can recognize all the good that He constantly does for us, and the tremendous wonders that He performs from the time we are born until our last days, we will no doubt run to do whatever we can to reciprocate, to the best of our ability, by doing His *mitzvot* and exalting His name.

The second way, says the Chofetz Chaim, is to recognize the importance of each minute. We know that every word of Torah that a person studies is a *mitzvah* unto itself. If a person speaks at a normal pace, it would be about two hundred words per minute, so if a person talks about Torah for one minute, he gets two hundred *mitzvot* right there. Now consider, if a person learns for fifteen minutes, he gets three thousand *mitzvot*! If he learns for an hour he gets twelve thousand *mitzvot*! What if a person learned for a full day? What about a few days? All the *mitzvot* keep adding up, and the more *mitzvot* he does the more reward he gets. Within a short time, we have the ability to accomplish millions of *mitzvot*!

It is through this recognition that we can gain the desire to utilize each moment to its fullest, whether it be by learning Torah, helping others, or by doing any other *mitzvah*. But we need a special swiftness and zealousness to make sure we run to do them, while concurrently insuring that they are performed properly.

This idea of valuing each moment was explained in a parable by Rabbi Moshe Yitzchak HaDarshan. Imagine if everyone in a cemetery was given another half hour of life to acquire as much heavenly reward as they could. You would see people hurrying around, learning Torah, praying, visiting the sick, consoling the mourner, and giving charity, each person according to his or her ability. Now what if these people were given a few hours of life, or even a few days? Wouldn't they try to utilize their time to squeeze in as many *mitzvot* as possible? So what about us – do any of us know how much time <u>we</u> have left?

It is like the Chofetz Chaim once said: Life is like a postcard. When we start off, we write in big, scrawling print. But when we see that the postcard is running out of space and there is still so much more to say, we begin writing smaller and smaller, squeezing in words wherever there is room. It is the same with our *mitzvah* observance. We are not so careful about doing all that we can because we feel that there is so much time left. But as our life passes, we realize how little time there really is and we try to squeeze in as many *mitzvot* as we can. However, if we realize <u>now</u> the value of time, we can utilize ours to its fullest.

So when we are relaxing at home reading a book or doing anything that we would prefer not to interrupt, we should think back to these methods of achieving greater *mitzvah* observance. We must remember how kind Hashem is to us and how much we must do to reach even a minimal level of repayment to Him. We have to bear in mind the importance and value of every minute and every *mitzvah*. Lastly, we should consider that no matter how challenging it may be for us to do a *mitzvah*, is it any more challenging than it was for Abraham to take his son to the *akeidah*? Through this recognition, may we merit accomplishing more *mitzvot*, and thus increase our reward both in this world and the World to Come.

∽ What About Bob?

by Matthew Leader

If we had to take a poll to determine which book of the Torah is the most popular, there is no doubt that the book of Genesis would win hands down. As the connotative part of the "Greatest Story Ever Told", the first few portions seem to be giving us the background necessary to understand how we became a nation and where we are now. However, we know that the stories in Genesis are not merely entertaining narratives. Each one of our forefathers represents a specific attribute that we can strive to attain, and each event in their lives can teach us something pertinent even for today. This portion's theme is obviously the life of Abraham, and the Torah portion connects many of the major events of his life: his circumcision, the birth of Isaac, the exile of Hagar and Yishmael, and finally the ultimate test of the *akeidah*. However, in the middle of all these family events is something that seems somewhat out of place, the story of the destruction of the city of Sodom and Abraham's prayers on behalf of the city.

For what we can assume to be a cautionary tale, not many details are given in the text about what actually happened in Sodom for it to warrant the kind of spectacular Divine attention that the city received. The narrative describes how Sodom's inhabitants accosted visitors to their city. However, we understand that there must be more to their evil than that, and there is in fact a whole list of offenses that the *Midrash* and commentaries attribute to the Sodomites. One of the most infamous is that they were rabidly opposed to any form of hospitality; another is their staunch belief in the principle "even if I don't lose, I don't want you to gain". But what the Ramban tells us sealed their fate was their refusal to take care of their poor. Every other society of that time had some system in place for helping the less fortunate. But if their behavior was so bad, why did Hashem decide to destroy them at this specific time? Surely the Sodomite visitors and poor had been suffering for many years. And our second question is, what does this have to do with us today? Obviously we can always give more, but most of us support our fellowman in some way, whether it is through the local Jewish Federation, *Shabbat* hospitality, or spare change to the homeless.

Perhaps one question answers the other. The idea of hospitality or caring for the poor is not merely being "nice". It does, in fact, strike at the very reason for our existence. In short, humanity was put on earth to sanctify G-d's name, and the way we do this is by emulating as many of His Divine attributes as we can. When we help a fellow person, we are actually manifesting Hashem's attributes of *chesed* – loving kindness, and *rachamim* – mercy. Once a nation, group, or city refuses to carry out their basic responsibilities in this area, they have given up their reason for existence. This message had to be delivered within the story of Abraham, who himself personified the characteristics of *chesed* and *rachamim*. From his dealings with the angels visiting his tent and culminating with the *akeidah*, Abraham represented everything that the Sodomites rejected. Without the almost ironic picture of the righteous Abraham arguing with Hashem to save the sinners of Sodom, we would have missed out on a big part of the story.

These messages are not just grand philosophical ideas for us to think about. One of the ways that the Sodomites showed their lack of respect for humanity and Hashem was their subversion of the "rules of fair play", by stealing from each other in ways that were too small to be recoverable in court. Actually, most of us have probably witnessed the following scene: Strolling through the aisles of your local food emporium, you spy our protagonist Bob standing before a rack of especially delicious-looking grapes. They're big and they're juicy. Right now, Bob's thinking that he's not about to bring a whole bunch back to the family hacienda without first knowing that they are as good as they look, so he plucks off a couple for "testing". Sure there is a sign specifically asking patrons not to engage in this sort of gastronomic larceny, but, Bob thinks, "What are they gonna do – sue me for one grape?"

Well, no Bob, that's the point. We learn from Abraham how much we gain by thinking of <u>other's</u> needs and not taking everything for yourself. In stark contrast, Sodom teaches us that by creatively grabbing and withholding good from others, we only embark on the dismal road to destruction.

PARSHAT CHAYEI SARAH

*hayei Sarah (Genesis 23:1-25:18) begins with Sarah's death at the age of 127 and Abraham's search for a proper burial place which would be worthy of her greatness. Abraham refuses to accept the generous offer of Ephron (a member of the Chittite nation which lived in the land of Israel) to give him M'arat HaMachpelah in the city of Chevron at no charge, and Abraham ends up paying an extremely large sum of money for the plot, at which point he finally buries his beloved wife.*

Abraham sends his faithful servant Eliezer back to Abraham's homeland and family to find a suitable wife for Isaac. Upon his arrival in the town of Aram Naharaim, Eliezer devises a plan by which he will be able to select a modest, generous, and kind girl, fitting for his master's son. Eliezer prays to Hashem that He grant him success in his mission by causing his plan to work, and he decides to stand by the town's well, waiting for a girl to offer him and his camels water to drink. Such a person who would take the trouble to draw water for a stranger and his ten camels, acting above and beyond the call of duty, would certainly be of great character. Sure enough, Rebecca proves herself to be equal to the test, and after receiving gifts sent by Abraham, she brings Eliezer to her father's house. Eliezer recounts the day's events to her family and asks for Rebecca to return with him to marry Isaac. She accepts, and they are married. With Abraham's role as father of the Jewish people complete and the mantle of leadership passed on to the next generation, the portion concludes with a brief genealogy of Abraham's other chil-

dren from his wife Keturah (who many commentaries say is really Hagar) and his death at the age of 175.

∽ The Golden Oldies
by Rabbi Herbert J. Cohen, Ph.D.

I once asked a rabbi at our local Yeshiva High School if he had made any plans for retirement. He answered me succinctly, "I will retire when G-d retires me. Until then I have no plans to retire."

I thought of that conversation when studying this week's Torah portion. The Torah tells us that Abraham was old, advanced in age (Genesis 24:1). Literally, the Torah uses the term that Abraham was "coming in days". The commentators interpret this to mean that Abraham was able to make each day of his life count, even throughout his old age. Furthermore, he could remember what was achieved on each day of his life, for every day of his life was a day of accomplishment; and even when he grew old, his passion for good deeds did not diminish. He still summoned up new energy and wisdom to bring meaning to his daily existence.

Abraham's consistent achievements over his long life, in spite of the vicissitudes of time and the adversity which he faced, provide a model for all of us. As we grow older, we do not have to become less productive, or slow down spiritually or intellectually, nor do we have to reconcile ourselves to wasted days and unproductive activity. With Abraham as our inspiration, we can make our latter days the golden days of our lives.

∽ A Match Made in Heaven
by Daniel Lasar

In life, people often think that events happen because of sheer coincidence. We fail to realize that indeed it is the guiding hand of Hashem that causes things to happen at seemingly inauspicious moments. In this week's Torah portion, we find an excellent example of this phenomenon playing itself out. Eliezer, upon being instructed by Abraham to find a suitable wife for Isaac, prays to Hashem that He guide events so that the proper match will be found. No sooner had he formulated this supplication then Rebecca appeared and proceeded to display the requisite kindness in her beneficent treatment of Eliezer and his camels.

The Torah relates, "And it was when <u>he</u> had not yet finished speaking that suddenly Rebecca was coming out. . ." (Genesis 24:15). Rabbeinu Bachya points out that the Hebrew word for "he" used in the verse seems superfluous, and that instead of referring to Eliezer, "he" refers to Hashem. Thus, this verse relates how Hashem interceded to ensure that Eliezer would "chance" upon Rebecca at the opportune moment. Moreover, the commentaries explain that because of Rebecca's modesty, she rarely ventured to the well, but Hashem caused her to go, specifically on that day.

Were a similar scene to play itself out today, one would perhaps fail to take note of the providential direction of the event. Observers may see a meeting between two people as mere happenstance – a casual incidence of "boy meets girl". It is important to realize, however, that in the larger scheme of things, such an incident cannot be viewed as being so simple; Isaac's and Rebecca's *shidduch* (match) is an excellent example of Hashem working behind the scenes and directing world events. Perhaps this Torah narrative most effectively represents the Jewish term "*basheirt*", commonly used in reference to one's future spouse who will be met at the "properly ordained" time, and more broadly referring to the concept that everything flows from Hashem's will.

Thus, the description of the amazing rendezvous between two of the essential progenitors of the Jewish people should sensitize us to realize that at every turn in life, at every crossroad of uncertainty, and at every moment of interaction, there are events which are not merely accidental, but rather examples of Hashem's active participation in our daily lives. Things do happen for a reason; it is just that with our limited spiritual sensitivity, we are not always cognizant of their purpose.

∽ Falling in Love?

by Benyamin Cohen

"He married Rebecca, she became his wife, and he loved her"
(Genesis 24:67).

What is love? In this week's Torah portion, we are told that Isaac married Rebecca and <u>then</u> he loved her. It seems out of sequence from what we are used to. Wouldn't it be more logical for Isaac to love Rebecca first and <u>then</u> marry her?

Perhaps we can learn a lesson about love from Isaac's actions. In today's society, we say the word "love" so casually. We use the word indiscriminately, thereby rendering it a meaningless term. Count the number of times you say the word "love" during the course of the day and you will be quite surprised. Phrases like "I just love that out-fit" or "I love Chocolate Fudge Twirl ice cream" are heard constantly. But can you really, truly love an inanimate object? Even when we say that we love a person, another human being, do we really love them for the right reasons? Or do we contrive our own definition of love by thinking that I love her because she's beautiful or I love him for his money?

Isaac is reminding us of the true meaning of love. Many times, people fall in love, get married, and the relationship starts to go sour from there. Isaac is teaching us that instead of <u>falling</u> in love, we should be <u>rising</u> in love. A relationship between husband and wife should be a dynamic one. We shouldn't "fall" into our love and then watch it fall with us. The verse is telling us that when Isaac got married, his love was just beginning. His love for Rebecca grew everyday, knowing no bounds or limitations. His love was real; it was not static, nor did it become stale depending on what Rebecca was wearing or by the situation they were in. It was an everlasting love, one that we should try to emulate.

PARSHAT TOLDOT

oldot *(Genesis 25:19-28:9) begins with Isaac and Rebecca praying to Hashem for a child. Rebecca finally conceives, and after a difficult pregnancy she gives birth to twins – Esau and Jacob. Their personality differences soon grow apparent, as Esau turns to hunting while Jacob is pure and wholesome, spending his time studying Torah. Returning from a hunting expedition, exhausted and starving, Esau finds Jacob cooking a pot of lentil soup. Jacob agrees to give his older brother a portion from the pot of soup in exchange for the spiritual birthright, and the deal is completed.*

Faced with a horrible famine, Hashem tells Isaac to remain in the land of Israel rather than descend to Egypt as his father Abraham had done years before, so Isaac and his family settle in G'rar (the land of the Philistines which is within Israel's borders). Hashem reassures Isaac that his descendants will become a great nation, as many as the stars in the heavens. After experiencing incredible financial success, Isaac comes into continual conflict with King Avimelech over the wells which Isaac dug anew. However, they finally make peace, and the treaty which was signed between Avimelech and Abraham (see last week's portion) is reconfirmed. Many years later, Isaac decides to bless Esau as the firstborn. At Rebecca's behest, Jacob disguises himself as his older brother and receives the blessings of the firstborn (which rightfully belonged to him). The portion concludes with Jacob fleeing from Esau's wrath for "stealing" his blessing and escaping to Charan to stay with his mother's brother, Laban, where he is to find a wife.

∞ Well of Strength
by Rabbi Lee Jay Lowenstein

There is, perhaps, no more enigmatic figure in all of the Torah than our forefather Isaac. Aside from this week's portion, we are told virtually nothing about the man, his times, and his life accomplishments. Instead, we are left to believe that after his climactic feat of stretching out his neck to receive his father's blade, this towering persona retires to a quiet life of digging wells. Equally frustrating is the seemingly minor, passive role he plays in the episodes in which he does appear. He is <u>taken</u> by his father to be slaughtered to Hashem; Abraham's servant Eliezer is sent to <u>find a wife for him</u>; his wife <u>pressures</u> him into sending away Jacob to search for a wife; his son Jacob <u>manipulates</u> him into giving him the blessings. Why does Isaac seem to be buffeted about like a puppet, mere clay in the hands of those around him? What lessons are we to learn from the apparently unusual behavior of the second, great Patriarch of the Jewish people?

Our sages teach us that the Patriarchs were far more than biological progenitors of the Jewish nation. Each one functioned as a "gatekeeper" who unlocked heavenly portals allowing us to establish a relationship with Hashem in uniquely different ways. Through their embodiment of the very same attributes with which Hashem interacts with us, by mirroring His ways, they were able to alter their spiritual genetic makeup, bequeathing to their descendants the Divine qualities which were their lifelong accomplishments.

Abraham embodies Hashem's quality of loving kindness, *chesed*. Every action, every thought, every word he spoke was filled with expressions of love and concern for humanity. Isaac is the personification of the Divine attribute of strength, *gevurah*. In *Pirkei Avot* (4:1) our rabbis teach us: "Who is strong? One who conquers his passions." Strength is not measured by what you do, but in what you do not. Self-control, discipline, regimentation are the tools of the mighty, the one who cannot be swayed by fleeting emotions and the whims of spontaneity. Logic would dictate that this quality should be present in all of Isaac's relationships and interactions. Surely no one would question that it took immeasurable fortitude to calmly offer himself on the altar, but what of the rest of his life? Where do we see this attitude shining forth?

Creation is a manifestation of Hashem's kindness. He had no personal <u>need</u> in bringing us to life. Hashem is the essence of perfection, the very antithesis of the concept of "need". His intentions were solely that He may shower His blessings and benevolence upon us. Hashem wishes to give us the greatest prize of all, the gift of eternity which comes only from bonding to Him via His commandments. However, there is one slight problem, so to speak, with His overflowing love.

The desire to give is so strong that if it were to go unchecked, Hashem would pour out His Divine light in such quantities that the very purpose of creation would be abrogated. Instead of giving human beings the opportunity to earn perfection, to battle and learn to struggle on their own, He would have given us the prize without our having to lift a finger. While it may seem enticing to live a life of tranquillity, one with no challenges or obstacles to overcome, we know deep down that this would not be truly satisfying. We would feel robbed of our dignity, denied the chance to achieve something of our own. It was therefore necessary for Hashem to constrain Himself, as it were, to hold back His abundant love, thereby providing us a chance to "earn it the hard way". This by no means diminishes the love; on the contrary, it enhances it, making it more real. This is similar to the way we parents feel watching our children struggle with adversity. How we wish we could take the blows for them, to cushion them from the humiliation or pain of defeat. Yet we know that to do so would destroy their sense of self, their feelings of competence and inner security.

This is the application of Hashem's attributes of *chesed* (loving kindness) and *gevurah* (strength). His kindness wishes to bestow upon us the greatest good imaginable. The attribute of *gevurah*, of restraint, prevents His kindness from overpowering us, from smothering us. It may well be said then that it is the quality of *gevurah* which enables the quality of kindness to become meaningful and effective, giving us the space necessary to create our own eternity.

Isaac embodies *gevurah*. It is his mission to facilitate the kindness of Abraham. How does he accomplish this? He "steps out" of the picture; he restrains himself and allows the memory of his father, the legacy of his father to be perpetuated. He could have created followers of his own, had a party platform which conformed to his liking, yet he chose to negate his identity in order that the world should get an extra dose of the kindness of Abraham. Our sages tell us that Isaac was an exact double of his father. It is no coincidence. It was his job to <u>be</u> his father.

What is the difference between a well (*b'er*) and a spring (*ma'ayan*)? A well draws from a particular source and contains a finite quantity of water. A spring, on the other hand, is alive with a vitality of its own. Isaac digs wells, but not just any wells, he digs the wells which his father had dug and names them the same names his father gave them. He is not alive in his own right, he is connected to his father's source.

In every interaction in which he partakes, Isaac plays the passive role. He is not incompetent or a fool. On the contrary! He has mastered the ability to cloak himself in the background, to make believe that he is not there. Yet he remains, subtly bringing out the best in those around him by letting them feel important, by letting them sense accomplishment as they perform actions for him. This is true *gevurah* indeed!

We as parents must take the lesson from the father whom our sages say is the "true father" by learning to let go of our children, to not dominate their every decision. Like a shadow we must hover cautiously, touching and not touching, so that they may come to discover their identity all on their own. This is true kindness, one that mimics the Divine.

ᕫ **A Pot of Beans**

by Rabbi Shlomo Freundlich

In this week's Torah portion, we read about the birth of Jacob and Esau, and the different natures and interests characterizing each of these boys. Jacob is the diligent student of Torah, while Esau is infatuated with the outdoors, demonstrating great skill in hunting and trapping animals. However, as the boys mature, Esau veers completely from a moral course and exercises no restraint in the quest to satisfy his desires.

The *Midrash* tells us that on the very day that Abraham died, Esau committed some of the most heinous crimes, including the cardinal sins of murder and rape, returning home that evening completely exhausted and on the verge of collapse. This is what the Torah means when it tells us that Esau came home from the field tired (Genesis 25:29). The famished Esau takes note of his brother Jacob cooking a delicious lentil stew (which was to be eaten by Isaac during the *seudat havra'ah*, the first meal served to mourners upon returning from the cemetery). In his typically boorish manner, Esau implores Jacob to give him a portion of the tasty stew. Jacob, sensing an advantage over Esau, offers him the food in exchange for the *bechorah*, the spiritual birthright reserved for the firstborn. Esau contemplates the offer and cynically responds, "Behold I'm going to die one day, so what do I need the birthright for anyway?" (ibid. 25:32). Amazingly, Esau barters away eternity and spiritual distinction for a pot of beans. A pot of beans!! Is he crazy?!

Rather than deal with Esau and his warped value system, let us look inwardly and analyze if we too squander away opportunities to achieve eternity for our own version of a "pot of beans". Our rabbis tell us about the awesome merit one accrues for responding with the phrase "*Y'hei sh'mei rabba m'vorach* – May His great name be blessed" during the recital of the *kaddish* prayer. Such a response has the power to annul a lifetime of harsh decrees ordained against us. But how many of us find ourselves talking nonsense with our friends rather than seizing this powerful spiritual moment? When confronted with the choice of going to synagogue or watching a favorite TV show, do we opt for eternity or the idiot box?

When the rabbi studies a short *halachah* between *Minchah* and *Ma'ariv* services, do we run to hear the lesson, or do we step outside to hear the gossip? Don't we also squander opportunities for eternity in exchange for our "pot of beans"? Esau may have been crazy, but can't we also find a little bit of Esau inside ourselves which we must strive to eliminate? May Hashem grant us the wisdom to serve Him faithfully.

PARSHAT VAYEITZEI

ayeitzei (Genesis 28:10-32:3) begins with Jacob escaping from Esau and leaving his parents' home to travel to Charan, where he will stay with his uncle Laban. While spending the night at the future site of the Beit HaMikdash, *Hashem appears to Jacob in the dream of a ladder extending from heaven to earth on which angels are ascending and descending. From atop the ladder, Hashem promises Jacob that his descendants will inherit the land of Israel. Upon arriving in Charan, and after rolling a huge stone off of the mouth of the town's well so that the local shepherds could water their flocks, Jacob meets Laban's daughter Rachel and agrees to work for Laban for seven years for her hand in marriage. When the wedding night finally arrives, Laban deceives Jacob by substituting his older daughter Leah in Rachel's place. After waiting a week, Jacob marries Rachel also, but not without being forced to commit to another seven years of labor.*

Over the next few years Rachel remains barren, while Leah gives birth to six sons and a daughter, and Bilhah and Zilpah (the maidservants of Rachel and Leah respectively) each have two sons with Jacob. Finally Rachel also has a son, Joseph. Jacob becomes very wealthy during his stay with Laban, amassing a huge flock even while Laban continually tries to swindle him throughout his twenty-year stay. After seeking counsel with his wives, Jacob and his family flee from Laban, who pursues and confronts him, upset that he left without saying goodbye and arrogantly claiming that Jacob stole his idols. After Laban searches through their possessions and does not find the idols (which Rachel took, unbeknownst to Jacob, to prevent her father from worshipping them), Jacob and Laban have a heated argument. Eventually they sign a treaty, promising to remain peaceful, and the portion concludes as they part ways.

CO **Carbon Copy**
by Rabbi Shlomo Freundlich

Sadly, there are those who will read the Biblical narrative of Jacob's years in the house of Laban and thrill to what they consider the type of stuff that produces best-selling novels or blockbuster movies. A magnificent plot filled with intrigue, drama, romance, and suspense is unfortunately what many consider to be the Torah's intent in describing the events surrounding the building of the family from whom the Jewish people descends. However, those who study the story of our Patriarchs and Matriarchs through the lenses of our sages and classical Torah commentaries gain profound insights into the human condition, learn fundamental principles of Torah thought, and are presented with lofty goals to which to aspire. One such lesson is pointed out by Rashi, a comment that without careful analysis goes almost unnoticed.

The Torah relates how Jacob discovers he has been tricked by Laban into marrying Leah rather than Rachel for whom he has toiled so diligently for seven years. Jacob's strong protest to Laban falls on deaf ears and the cunning Laban has the chutzpah to offer Rachel to Jacob in exchange for another seven years of hired labor. Jacob has no recourse but to accede to the conditions of Laban (Genesis 29:25-28).

One can only imagine the utter frustration Jacob must have felt. Moreover, the *Midrash*, in relating the awesome spirituality of Jacob, informs us that his image is engraved on Hashem's heavenly throne.

His personality was a perfect balance of the qualities of his grandfather and father, Abraham and Isaac. Jacob surely lived on a spiritual plane unfathomable to us. The distraction of having to work as a shepherd for seemingly no justifiable reason, was to rob the world of the spirituality Jacob might otherwise invest it with had he been allowed to serve Hashem unfettered by the stresses and responsibilities involved in the faithful safeguarding of Laban's flock. And Jacob surely knew this.

Yet when describing Jacob's agreement to Laban's terms, the Torah states, "And he worked for him <u>another</u> (*acheirot*) seven years." Rashi notes that the word *acheirot* seems to be redundant. The text could have simply said, "And he worked for him seven years," and it would have meant the same. In explanation, Rashi records a remarkable *Midrash*, that Jacob served Laban during the second stint of seven years with the same zeal and devotion he displayed during the first seven years. They were in fact <u>another</u> set of seven years, a duplication of his first seven-year contract with Laban. No grudge, no ill will, no short-changing Laban was evident. The same extraordinary commitment to the task that marked his first seven years, when he thought he was laboring for Rachel, was the hallmark of the second period of seven years which Laban deceitfully imposed upon him for the right to finally marry Rachel.

Jacob's bedrock belief that whatever Hashem presents one in life is totally for the best, neutralized any negative responses toward Laban. After all, how can one bemoan or complain about the good that one has received!

This alone would be an important lesson for us. But Rabbi Yosef Salant makes another astonishing observation. The *Midrash* on *Eichah* (Lamentations) relates that at the time of the destruction of the first Temple, the Patriarchs and even Moses begged Hashem to grant mercy and end the exile speedily. However, these prayers went unheeded. Rachel then approached the Divine throne and put forth an emotional plea. She challenged G-d's stern judgment by recalling how she, a mere mortal of flesh and blood, remained silent when her sister Leah went to the *chupah* (marriage canopy) in her place. Rachel absorbed the pain of having to share Jacob with another woman rather than cause her sister humiliation. Why then, she demands, can Hashem not somehow tolerate the wayward behavior of the Jews as they turned to other gods. The *Midrash* continues that it was in fact Rachel's plea that evoked the Divine mercy that allowed the Jews to return to the land of Israel and build the second Temple.

Working an extra seven years for Rachel may have appeared to a lesser person as a "rip off". But it was this "rip off" that set the stage for the events that would bring about the salvation of the Jewish people years later. May we merit to see speedily in our days how all the seemingly difficult and dark chapters in our history form the tapestry of events that bring about our ultimate redemption.

☞ This Is Your Life

by Rabbi Yossi New

On his way from his parents' home in B'ersheva to Laban's house in Charan, Jacob camps overnight at a place he will later name Beit El. The Torah states that he took some stones, placed them around his head, and went to sleep (Genesis 28:11). Rashi notes that the stones served to protect Jacob from wild animals. This explanation begs the question – why didn't Jacob camouflage his entire body with stones? Why surround only his head?

Jacob's journey from B'ersheva to Charan can be understood as a model for the journey of life. Hopefully we all begin life in B'ersheva, a warm and caring home, and most importantly an oasis for moral and spiritual growth. The time comes, however, when the umbilical cord is cut and we must confront the "real" world with all its challenges and obstacles. The word Charan is associated with the Hebrew word "*charon*" which means "anger". It is a metaphor for the world at large where materialism contests with spirituality and "angers" G-d.

Jacob knew he would get involved in material and mundane matters. He and we have no choice but to do so. However, he resolved to protect himself from becoming overly enamored and obsessed with these matters, for it leads to immoral and decadent behavior. Jacob was willing to expose his hands and feet to Charan, but not his head. Yes, he would physically do what it takes to function and even succeed in the secular world, filled with wild animals of all sizes and forms, but his passion and love for Torah and spiritual development would always be preserved and nurtured.

PARSHAT VAYISHLACH

arshat Vayishlach (Genesis 32:4-36:43) begins with Jacob and his family returning from the house of Laban to the land of Israel, only to find Esau heading towards them with 400 men, apparently ready for battle. After preparing his family for war and praying to Hashem for help, Jacob attempts to appease his brother by sending him a lavish gift of many animals. After his family crosses the river to await their meeting with Esau, Jacob is left alone for an all-night "confrontation" with an angel disguised as a man, and although Jacob is victorious, he is left limping from a hip dislocation. Rejoining his family, Jacob encounters Esau, who accepts him with a new-found brotherly love and insists on escorting Jacob to his destination. Jacob states that he does not want to inconvenience Esau, and they part ways. Yet another crisis arises as Jacob's daughter Dinah is abducted and raped by Shechem, the prince of a town of the same name. Jacob's sons, outraged at the humiliation caused to their sister, trick the town's residents into circumcising themselves under the preconception that they would then be allowed to intermarry with Jacob's family. Simeon and Levi (two of the brothers) then decimate the entire city and save Dinah.

Jacob returns to Beit El where Hashem originally appeared to him in the dream of the ladder (mentioned in last week's portion), and he builds an altar there. Hashem blesses Jacob and gives him the additional name, Israel. Soon after, Rachel dies while giving birth to Benjamin, Jacob's twelfth and Rachel's *second son, and Jacob buries her in Beit Lechem. Finally, Jacob returns home and is reunited with his father Isaac. The Torah relates that Isaac died at the age of 180, and the portion concludes with a lengthy genealogy of Esau's family.*

The Good Sons
by Rabbi Elie Cohen

When Simeon and Levi attack the city of Shechem and vanquish its inhabitants to save their sister Dinah, the Torah goes out of its way to describe them as being "the two sons of Jacob" (Genesis 34:25). By now we should certainly be well aware of their genealogy. Rashi comments that by repeating the obvious, the Torah is highlighting the fact that although they were biologically Jacob's sons, they were not <u>acting</u> as his sons, for they did not seek his advice in this matter.

If we were asked what quality would be essential for someone to be considered "acting as a son", our first thoughts would probably be honoring one's parent or looking after his needs. But Rashi is apparently revealing something different to us. The most basic ingredient to be considered "as a son" is that he seeks his parent's advice.

Indeed, if we examine the etymology of the Hebrew word for son, "*ben*", we get the same impression. When Noah is born, the Torah states in reference to his father Lemech, "And he bore a son (*ben*)" (ibid. 5:28). Rashi comments there that the word "*ben*" is related to the root form "*banah*" meaning to build, and that from Noah ultimately the world was rebuilt. In the Friday night and *Shabbat* morning services we refer to students of Hashem and His Torah as "sons" and "builders". We therefore understand that the role of a son is to build upon the principles of the father – to actualize his ideas. Thus, the Torah subtly rebukes Simeon and Levi for acting without the advice and consent of their father. Their relationship was merely a biological one because they were not acting in congruence with his will.

The Torah calls the Children of Israel "sons of Hashem" (Deuteronomy 14:1). As sons of Hashem, we should be inspired to perform our every action by consulting our Father, through His Torah, to truly build upon His principles in this world.

◎ **Oh Brother!**
by Avi Lowenstein

After fleeing the land of Israel and his bloodthirsty brother Esau, Jacob struggles to raise his family amid the fraudulent activities of Laban. Now, on his way back to the land of Israel, Jacob must once again meet his sinister brother. Preparing for the confrontation, Jacob prays to Hashem, "Rescue me, please, from the hand of my brother, from the hand of Esau, for I fear him" (Genesis 32:12). What is the meaning of this prayer? Jacob had only one brother; would it not suffice to ask for salvation from either "my brother" or "Esau"? Why was Jacob so specific?

The Beis HaLevi explains that Jacob anticipated two possible dangers in confronting Esau. Of course, there was the fear that Esau was still seeking revenge, and that he was planning an all out military attack with the army he had brought along. For this eventuality, Jacob asked Hashem to save him "from the hand of Esau". Nevertheless, Jacob was more worried about the other possibility. There was a chance that after all these years, Esau had decided to live peacefully with his brother and was now coming to greet him with a large welcoming committee. Although on the surface this would seem to be anything but a threat, Jacob realized the extreme danger that lay in such a possibility. By acting in a brotherly way and maintaining continued contact, Esau could subtly intertwine his "values" with those of Jacob who had so carefully implanted proper Torah morals and values in himself and his family. In response to this threat, Jacob also prayed "save me from the hand of my brother".

The values of Esau and the other nations of the world are diametrically opposed to those of Jacob and the Jewish people. Esau directs his efforts towards worldly pursuits, while Jacob believes that "This world is like a hallway to the World to Come" (*Pirkei Avot* 4:21). When Esau and Jacob become too brotherly, Jacob's values become diluted and distorted by the tempting values of Esau.

The result is all too clear to us in our time when we find the Jewish people experiencing a severe identity crisis and suffering from the scourge of rampant intermarriage. In the Holocaust, we felt the brute force of Esau's violent "hand"; now we appear to be falling victim to his "brotherly" one.

At this point, we must ask ourselves what we can do about the situation. To answer this question, we once again look at Jacob's actions as described in this week's Torah portion. After the confrontation had ended, Esau returned home to the land of Seir and Jacob went to a place called Sukkot. The Torah relates that Jacob "built a house for himself, and for his livestock he made booths; he therefore called the name of the place Sukkot (booths)" (Genesis 33:17). The question is asked: Why did Jacob name the place after the temporary booths he made for his livestock – would it not have been more appropriate to name it after the more substantial dwelling which he made for his family?

The answer is simple. After meeting with Esau, someone who believed that the goal of life is to amass great material wealth, Jacob wanted to create a reminder that life is transitory and that the acquisition of material wealth is not the purpose of life. Therefore, he named the place after the <u>temporary</u> booths that he made for his cattle. The lesson for us to learn from Jacob's actions is that in our time, when we are so exposed to the values of Esau, we must make sure to remember what our values are. The only way to achieve this is by strengthening our knowledge and commitment, something which can be accomplished only through the study of the Torah.

PARSHAT VAYEISHEV

arshat Vayeishev (Genesis 37:1-40:23) begins by describing Jacob's great love for his son Joseph which incites the other brothers' hatred. Their jealousy increases when Joseph tells them about his two dreams which indicate that they will one day be subservient to him. Jacob sends Joseph to check up on his brothers who are tending the flock away from home, and upon seeing him approaching they plot to kill him. Reuben convinces the brothers not to kill Joseph, but is unable to totally save him as the brothers sell Joseph into slavery in Egypt. After dipping Joseph's coat in blood, they return to their father who assumes that his beloved son was torn apart by a savage beast. The Torah digresses to relate the story of Judah and his daughter-in-law Tamar.

The narrative then returns to Joseph in Egypt, where he becomes an extremely successful slave and is placed in charge of his master Potiphar's household. Potiphar's wife repeatedly tries to seduce Joseph, and when he refuses her advances, she screams and claims that he tried to rape her. Joseph is thrown into prison where he is once again placed in a position of leadership, this time being put in charge of the prisoners. Ten years later, Pharaoh's chief butler and baker are thrown into the same prison. One night they each have a perplexing dream which Joseph accurately interprets, and the portion concludes as the butler is returned to his former post and the baker is executed, just as Joseph had predicted.

∞ Impulse Buying

by Joshua S. Feingold

"The brothers saw Joseph from afar; and when he had not yet approached them they conspired against him to kill him" (Genesis 37:18).

From the Torah's description of the brothers' decision-making process, their resolution to kill Joseph appears quite rash. Murdering their brother does not seem to be a premeditated act. Only when they saw Joseph coming did they begin scheming against him, and after a rushed meeting, they quickly decided to kill him. Reuben stepped in and advised the brothers not to kill Joseph with their own hands, but instead to throw him into a nearby pit. Secretly, Reuben hoped to rescue Joseph from the hands of the brothers and return him to their father (ibid. 37:22).

Without getting into a discussion of what the brothers' rationale was in their decision to kill Joseph, perhaps we can focus on the steps which Reuben took to <u>prevent</u> the murder, and by examining his response to the brothers' plans we can derive a valuable life lesson. Reuben had the foresight to recognize that if the brothers killed Joseph <u>now</u>, they would probably regret their actions <u>later</u>. Reuben figured that if he could delay his brothers and give them some time to think about the repercussions of their actions, they would change their minds. In fact, by convincing the brothers to wait, he saved Joseph from certain death. The Torah relates that after the brothers considered their actions more carefully, they decided to sell him as a slave, saying, "Let our hand not be upon him, for he is our brother, our own flesh" (ibid. 37:27). The truth is that this was also a rash decision, one which they would later come to regret.

We often make quick decisions and do not give our actions enough serious thought. In some life situations, our actions are not necessarily final. When it comes to making a purchase, most stores have good return policies. Store owners know that many of us will see something we want and because of our mood will buy it on the spot, only to discover when we arrive home that the impulse has vanished. We regret purchasing the item and return it to the store. As a friend of mine once advised me, "Never go grocery shopping on a fast day, or else you will end up with all kinds of food you will never eat." On a fast day, everything looks great, even that fat-free, no sugar, hunk of tofu appears quite appetizing. Only after we have food in our stomach do we realize the stupidity of our actions.

Unfortunately, there isn't always a simple method by which to undo our actions. King Solomon said in Ecclesiastes, "A wise man's eyes are in his head" (2:14). Rashi explains that the wise person is the one who acts only after thinking through the consequences. The person who makes quick, rash decisions is being foolish.

We must learn from Reuben's strategy and take heed of the advice of our forebears. When we take action, we should try to think of all the possible outcomes that might happen as a result of what we do. Even trivial things such as purchases should be given some thought. Try the following experiment. Next time you consider making a large purchase, wait a few days and see if you still want the item. You might just save yourself a few dollars, and a shlep back to the store.

The Little Things in Life
by Rabbi Reuven Stein

In this week's Torah portion we read about the horrible adversity which Joseph faced. First his brothers wanted to kill him, and then he was sold into slavery. Just when his situation started to look better, he was thrown into prison where he remained for twelve long years. What gave Joseph the patience to persevere and overcome the tremendous obstacles which he faced throughout his life?

Perhaps his strength to endure so many hardships came from his mother Rachel's outlook on life, as is evidenced by the remark she made when he was born: "Hashem has taken away my disgrace" (Genesis 30:23). Rashi explains that one aspect of her disgrace was that, being childless, people would assume that she was at fault for anything that went wrong in the house. Once a child is born, accidents can usually be attributed to the child.

At first glance, this would appear to be an extremely strange concern for Rachel to have. Rabbi Chaim Shmulevitz explains that Rachel recognized the importance of every minor blessing in her life, and she was therefore able to thank Hashem for everything that happened to her. Rachel was so grateful when she finally had a child that she was able to appreciate every one of the benefits, even the trivial detail that with a child in the house she would not receive all of the blame for accidents which occurred. Rachel passed this attribute on to Joseph, giving him the special ability of seeing and appreciating even the little things. By focusing on the minor blessings in his life, Joseph was able to manage and overcome adversity.

We find the first example of an incidental blessing amidst his misery when Joseph is sold as a slave. Rashi points out that while most caravans at the time carried foul-smelling cargo, Hashem sent a small reminder to Joseph that He was with him by arranging for Joseph's caravan to be carrying fragrant spices and perfumes (ibid. 37:25), making his horrible experience a little more bearable. Another example occurs when Joseph is accused of raping Potiphar's wife, causing his reputation to become besmirched and making him the subject of slanderous conversation throughout Egypt. Hashem arranged for another scandal to hit the press, the ousting of two of Pharaoh's officials, the chief butler and baker, to shift the subject of discussion away from Joseph. This sign gave Joseph the courage to endure his lengthy prison ordeal. We also find that throughout his slavery and prison time, as bad as it was, Hashem always remained with him, helping him find a degree of favor in other people's eyes which enabled him to rise to positions of prominence.

So too in our lives, even amidst very adverse situations, we can use the lesson of Joseph to find the silver lining in everything that happens.

In this way, we will develop a greater recognition that Hashem is with us and we will be better equipped to overcome life's difficult situations.

◌ Joseph as Pronoun
by Avi Wagner

The catalyst triggering most of the latter events in this week's Torah portion is the contempt the brothers felt towards Joseph because of the favoritism Jacob showed to him. The sages of the Talmud (Tractate Shabbat 10b) derive from this incident that one should never single out one child for special treatment. Even though Jacob gave only two more coins worth of silk (the special coat) to Joseph than he did to his other children, Joseph's brothers became jealous and sold him into slavery. The ultimate consequence of this action, point out the sages, is that our forefathers were exiled into Egypt.

The Torah describes Joseph as being a "*ben zikkunim*" to Jacob, literally meaning a child born in his father's old age. However Onkelos interprets the term to mean "wise son", while Rashi adds that Joseph was Jacob's prized student and that the great sage taught his son all that he had learned. Rabbi Samson Raphael Hirsch explains, in the same vein, that the coat was representative of the transmission of wisdom from father to son and that was what made Joseph special.

Jacob viewed Joseph as a continuation in the line of the Patriarchs that began with Abraham. One essential problem existed in singling out Joseph. His brothers did not scorn their father's wisdom, as did Esau to Isaac and Yishmael to Abraham. The brothers wanted nothing more than to be a part of the chain of tradition and reap the bounties of their father's wisdom. Seeing that Jacob had not conveyed to them the attention they felt they deserved, they hated Joseph. The brothers felt that Joseph and his coat were both indications of their inferiority.

Their jealousy prevented them from communicating with Joseph. When they threw Joseph into the pit, they refer to their brother by the pronoun "him" numerous times, not once calling Joseph by name. So much did they covet the love of their father that they saw Joseph merely as a "him", available for disposal if necessary. It is only Judah who stands up and calls Joseph "*acheinu* – our brother" (Genesis 37:26-27). Only through the recognition of the familial relationship, which implicitly includes responsibility and a form of possession (<u>our</u> brother), do the brothers behave more civilly towards Joseph.

Clearly, the Torah shows that the consequences of parental favoritism may be disastrous and that it is important for parents to recognize and acknowledge the good qualities in <u>all</u> of their children, even if one child is particularly exemplary. Likewise, only when we remember that others are "our brothers" will we behave in a manner that overrides jealousy and anger.

PARSHAT MIKEITZ

ikeitz *(Genesis 41:1-44:17) begins with Pharaoh's famous two-part dream about seven scrawny cows devouring seven robust cows, followed by seven thin ears of grain swallowing seven healthy, good ones. When his advisors and necromancers are unable to adequately solve the perplexing riddle, Pharaoh summons Joseph, who had been in prison for a total of twelve years, to interpret his dreams. Ascribing his power of interpretation solely to Hashem, Joseph tells Pharaoh that after first experiencing seven years of extraordinary and abundant crops, Egypt will be ravaged by seven years of a devastating famine. Joseph therefore advises Pharaoh to seek a wise man to oversee the collection and storage of the abundant food during the years of plenty. Impressed with the brilliant interpretation, Pharaoh appoints Joseph to be the viceroy of Egypt, making him the second most powerful man in the land. Joseph's wife Asnat gives birth to two sons, Menashe and Ephraim, and the years of plenty and famine unfold just as Joseph had predicted.*

With the famine also devastating the land of Canaan, Joseph's brothers descend to Egypt to purchase food. When they do not recognize their royal brother, Joseph sets in motion a plan to determine if the brothers have fully repented for their sin of selling him almost twenty-two years before. Joseph acts detached and accuses them of being spies, holding Simeon as hostage while the rest of the brothers return with the food to Canaan. Joseph, still unrecognized, tells them that Simeon

*will be released only when they return to Egypt with their young-
est brother. Initially reluctant, but faced with the heightening
famine, Jacob finally agrees to allow the brothers to take
Benjamin with them. Upon their arrival in Egypt, Joseph tests
the brothers further by treating them all well, but showing blatant
favoritism to Benjamin. When the brothers are finally sent back
home with their sacks full of grain, Joseph conceals his goblet
in Benjamin's bag and he is accused of stealing the precious
object. The portion concludes with the looming threat that
Benjamin will be made a slave to the Egyptian ruler.*

☞ United We Stand

by Yoel Spotts

When describing the healthy stalks in Pharaoh's "dream of wheat", the Torah says, "And behold, there were seven healthy, good ears of grain growing on a <u>single stalk</u>" (Genesis 41:5). It is interesting to note that concerning the thin ears of grain, the Torah does not mention that they grew on a single stalk. It does not seem likely that this difference should be inconsequential, as we know that every detail mentioned by the Torah is important and should not be overlooked. Thus, the question must be asked: Why does the Torah describe the good ears as growing on one stalk while omitting this detail concerning the unhealthy stalks?

The Otzar Chaim proposes an ingenious solution to this discrepancy. He explains that we can, in fact, learn an important lesson from this difference in description: That which is good and purposeful tends to merge and unite. However, that which is evil and meaningless cannot tolerate harmony and accord. For this reason, the good and healthy ears grew on one stalk. Because of the pure and good disposition of the ears, it was only natural that they should unite to grow on one single stalk. On the other hand, the thin and unhealthy ears, naturally seeking disharmony, "chose" to grow on separate stalks, because in truth, any union of evil is only for the advancement of each individual's own selfish needs and desires.

Interestingly enough, when one surveys the past few thousand years of Jewish history, one notices this message to be especially true. The Jewish people have never represented more than a tiny fraction of the world's population. Nonetheless, as Mark Twain once noted, the Jewish people have remained, have survived, and have continued to be heard of in the world. How can this be possible? Logic would dictate that the Jewish people, with all their trials and tribulations throughout the years, should be long gone. More specifically, we find throughout Jewish history cases of small numbers of Jews battling enemies much larger and stronger. Yet, somehow, the Jewish people emerge victorious. Most recently, we have seen examples of this in the wars fought by the nation of Israel against the surrounding Arab countries, including the War for Independence and the Six-Day War.

However, the classic example of a small Jewish faction defeating a larger enemy can be found in the story of *Chanukah*. A small number of Jewish soldiers rose up in rebellion against the powerful Greek army and succeeded in driving the Greeks out of Judea. This miraculous feat, probably more than any other event, serves as a microcosm of Jewish history. What, then, is the secret of our success?

It would appear that the answer lies in the concept mentioned above. When a number of individuals set out for the common purpose of doing good, they will naturally unite to form a cohesive group. In the story of *Chanukah*, the mission of restoring order and peace to the holy Temple and the land of Judea led to the formation of a united group. And as the old adage teaches, five sticks held together are more powerful than ten separate sticks. The Maccabees, banded together for the purpose of good, were able to defeat the Greek army which was made up simply of individuals, each one only seeking to further his own desires. It is the same thing with the Jewish nation as a whole. When we set off on a holy mission, we instinctively form an unbreakable and invincible force that enables us to overcome our adversaries. This is the secret of our success.

It is not my intention to diminish the miraculous nature of the Maccabees' victory. There is no question that the defeat of the Greeks could not have taken place without Divine intervention. I am only proposing the medium through which the miracle took place. Therefore, among the other lessons of *Chanukah*, we can also derive this important teaching from the Holiday of Lights. And as we light the *menorah* and see all the candles lit – and notice that although each individual candle only emits a small glow, all the candles together form a spectacular display of fire and light – we can remember *Chanukah's* message of the survival of the Jewish people.

∽ The Importance of Storage
by Benyamin Cohen

Upon informing Pharaoh of the impending problem of seven years of famine in Egypt, Joseph suggests a brilliant solution. He tells the king to stock up warehouses of food during the preceding seven years of plenty in order to ensure survival during the seven years of famine. Joseph's advice was not only pertinent to the situation in Egypt, but it is also relevant to us today.

The concept of taking moments of abundance and storing them so that they can later be used during moments of famine can be applied to our daily lives. Oftentimes, we are confronted with instances of "famine" when our spiritual strength is weak. The way we utilize the moments of "abundance" will determine how successfully we will cope with those difficult times.

Joseph told Pharaoh to build a base upon which they could rely during the years of famine. In a sense, it is this kind of foundation which is necessary for us to survive through bad times. If, during the years of plenty, we acquire the proper tools necessary to succeed in life, then we will have the ability to survive during the years of famine.

PARSHAT VAYIGASH

*P*arshat Vayigash (Genesis 44:18-47:27) begins with Judah's impassioned plea to the powerful Egyptian ruler (Joseph still in disguise) for Benjamin's life, claiming that Jacob would surely die from sorrow if he lost Benjamin. Judah offers to remain in Egypt as a slave in his younger brother's stead. Joseph, unable to restrain himself any longer, reveals his identity to his stunned brothers and forgives them for selling him into slavery so many years before, stating that sending him to Egypt was a part of the Divine plan to prepare for their survival from the famine. Joseph then sends them back to the land of Israel, laden with gifts, to bring Jacob and their families down to Egypt where they will live in the province of Goshen. Before Jacob leaves home, Hashem appears to him in a "vision of the night", reassuring him that He will be with them and that they will eventually return to the land of Israel as a great nation. After twenty-two years of separation, Jacob is finally reunited with his beloved son Joseph, and they are brought to meet Pharaoh. The portion concludes by describing how Joseph uses his vast power to amass nearly all of the wealth of Egypt for Pharaoh's treasury.

⌒ Aristotle's Hypocrisy
by Rabbi Yossi Lew

The story is told that Aristotle was once caught by some of his students "red-handed", committing a degrading act that was unbecoming to him. The students were dumbfounded. After all, they reasoned, we are dealing with one of the greatest thinkers of all time, and consequently he should personify the ultimate person. How could he stoop to such a level? Sensing the need for damage control, Aristotle declared, "What's the problem? Aristotle hasn't changed. Tomorrow's lecture will still take place at nine o'clock. But right now I'm behaving like an average human being, just like all of you would behave!"

The reaction to the above story is predictable. What hypocrisy!? How can a person with such depths in understanding stoop to such a level of degradation? History does not record the reaction of Aristotle's students to his declaration; however, one can well imagine that those students who witnessed this behavior were probably unable to participate in the next day's lecture.

This separation between thought and deed is rather common. We all study and are cognizant of various moral and virtuous modes of behavior, yet when it comes to implementing these wonderful philosophies, there seems to be an impediment. What's missing? How can we infuse our actions with the values which we so easily understand?

The ability to connect the logical conclusions of the mind with its execution into action is a mental faculty known in Hebrew as "*daat*". The word *daat* literally means knowledge. However, the Torah also uses this word in reference to the bond between husband and wife, indicating that *daat* implies a degree of knowledge which connects and attaches. This means that it is insufficient to simply arrive at lofty conclusions; one must also bind himself to that conclusion, unifying the mind and the heart (which controls the actions), thus obligating oneself to carry out that which was so clearly understood.

This explains an unusual expression which the Torah uses in this week's portion. After the dramatic description of Joseph's revelation to his brothers, the Torah relates that Joseph "fell on Benjamin's neck and he cried, and Benjamin cried on his neck" (Genesis 45:14). Our sages explain that Benjamin cried because he perceived the ultimate destruction of the *Mishkan*, the Tabernacle which would eventually be in Joseph's portion of Israel, and Joseph cried because he perceived the destruction of the *Beit HaMikdash*, the holy Temple which would be in Benjamin's portion of land. Leaving aside the question as to why they were crying over the future destruction at this time, it still needs to be clarified why they were crying specifically on each other's necks. Wouldn't it make more sense for the encounter to take place on or near the head, the loftiest place of the body?

Indeed, the function of the neck is unique, for in a healthy situation it acts as a conduit between the head and the heart (and therefore the rest of the body). Since the intellect is physically situated in the head, our thoughts can be said to also be channeled through the neck. A blockage in the neck, obstructing clear passage for the flow of thoughts, is obviously an unhealthy condition. The function of the neck is therefore analogous to the function of *daat*: They both exist in order to forge the connection between the thoughts of the mind which are translated into the actions controlled by the heart.

This is why the brothers cried on each other's necks. The Temples were destroyed as a result of the sins of the Jewish people. In other words, the Jewish people did not translate into action what they knew in their minds. A blockage existed. When mourning the destruction, therefore, the brothers cried specifically on the neck, teaching us that intellectual understanding alone is insufficient. Action and deeds are the paramount and preeminent goal.

∞ Vision of the Night
by Matthew Leader

This week's portion is surely one of the most exciting in the Torah. Upon first reading it we find all of the makings of a great soap opera: Tension-filled meetings between a disguised Joseph and his estranged brothers, Joseph's dramatic revelation of his true identity, and finally the moving and joyous scene when the bereft father is reunited with his long-lost favorite son.

However, Rabbi Meir Simcha HaKohen of Dvinsk notes an interesting point about Jacob's behavior just before his reunion with Joseph.

When Jacob learns of his son's survival and good fortune, he immediately makes preparations to reunite his family in Egypt, and as he begins the journey he brings *korbanot* to Hashem. One would expect that the offerings would be brought purely out of gratitude to Hashem that Joseph was still alive and had become so successful, but in fact we find that they were also an indication of Jacob's immense trepidation at the thought of leaving the land of Israel. Hashem therefore appears to Jacob in a "vision of the night" and assures him that He will accompany the Jewish people into Egypt, and will make Israel into a great nation (Genesis 46:1-4). At first, this incident does not seem to be in keeping with the rest of the story. Why would Jacob be afraid at the time of his greatest joy? Although he was entering an unknown land, didn't Joseph's lofty position as viceroy of Egypt all but guarantee that his family would be well taken care of?

Jacob was the only one of the forefathers to whom Hashem appeared in a "vision of the night". We can understand the significance of this distinction if we look at the events of this week's portion in their general context. Each forefather personifies a different aspect of Judaism and our history. While Abraham is the "conqueror" of the land of Israel and Isaac characterizes the Jewish people living in the land of Israel, Jacob represents the Jewish people in *galut*. Knowing through Divine inspiration that this was to be the beginning of the lengthy exile in Egypt, Jacob was hesitant to leave. Thus, Hashem spoke to Jacob in a "vision of the night", reassuring him that his descendants would make it through the long night of exile which was about to befall the Jewish people, because Hashem Himself would be with them. If the Jewish people will follow Hashem's *mitzvot* while in exile, Hashem promises to remain with them and to lead them through the darkness. With Hashem's reassurance, Jacob was able to continue his journey down to Egypt, satisfied that he was following the Divine plan.

It is for this reason that the institution of the evening *Ma'ariv* prayer service is attributed to Jacob, for he is the "father" of the *galut*, symbolized by the night, and Jacob knew that we would need the strength of Hashem's help in the darkness. May we merit seeing this darkness end and our long night of exile come to a conclusion.

PARSHAT VAYECHI

arshat Vayechi (Genesis 47:28-50:26), the final portion of the first book of the Torah, describes Jacob's actions immediately preceding his death in Egypt, beginning with his making Joseph swear to bury him in the land of Israel. Jacob then gives Joseph's two sons, Menashe and Ephraim, a special blessing which confers upon them the elevated status of being two separate tribes amongst the Children of Israel. Notwithstanding Joseph's protest, Jacob insists on giving the younger Ephraim the right-hand position of primacy during the blessing, stating that Ephraim would be greater. Jacob then proceeds to give each of his other sons their individual blessing, in accordance with their own unique character traits and missions. Jacob passes away at the age of 147 and is brought by his sons, accompanied by a great procession of Egyptian royalty, to the land of Israel where he is buried in the M'arat HaMachpelah, alongside his wife Leah, parents Isaac and Rebecca, and grandparents Abraham and Sarah. Upon their return to Egypt, Joseph's brothers fear that he will finally take revenge now that their father was dead. Joseph reassures them that he bears no hard feelings, stating that his being sold into slavery was all part of the Divine plan. The portion concludes with Joseph's death and the Jewish people's promise to carry his bones with them to Israel when they are finally redeemed.

The Lion King

by Rabbi Chaim Goldberger

When Jacob blesses each of his sons in this week's Torah portion, he refers to Judah as a lion. In what way is Judah like a lion? We would assume that just like a lion is king of the beasts, so too is Judah to be the king of the Jewish people. In fact, King David eventually descends from the tribe of Judah, as does the *Mashiach*, who will also be king of the people.

But is this the only meaning of the metaphor of the lion? Not all kings are called lions. In fact, Reuben, Judah's eldest brother, was to have been king himself until he lost the privilege after a bad judgment error in Parshat Vayishlach (Genesis 35). His kingship was described with the term "*az* - bold" which *Pirkei Avot* (5:23) says is the quality of the leopard, not the lion. So in what way is Judah like a lion?

My mentor, Rabbi Yochanan Zweig, likes to explain this by referring to a passage in the Talmud at the end of Tractate Kiddushin: *Rabbi Shimon ben Elazar said: My whole life I have never seen a deer working as a farmer, nor a fox working as a storekeeper, nor a lion working as a porter, yet they receive their livelihood without difficulty, and they were only created to serve me! I (Man), who was created to serve the Almighty, should all the more so receive my livelihood painlessly, except that I compromised myself by sinning (i.e. Adam, by sinning in the Garden of Eden, made earning a living a matter of struggle and toil).*

Of the three occupations that appear in this passage, all but one seems to make sense. The job of storekeeper is one that would seem to call primarily for brains, the job of porter for brawn, and the job of farmer for a combination of the two. So if a fox were to take a job, suggests the Talmud, it would be running a store, as the fox is known for his cunning. And if the deer were to work, it would make sense for him to be a farmer, as the deer has the body strength to work the field and the intellect to effectively manage his estate. But why would the lion be a porter? The roaring, majestic king of beasts should be relegated to simple, blue-collar, back-breaking labor if he had to work for his living? How can we understand this?

Rabbi Zweig points out that the lion would not be a porter to other animals – he would remain their king. Rather, he would be a porter to Man. What is so noble about being a "shlepper" for Man? Because a porter's job is to be of total and absolute service to his customer. The sales of the storekeeper and the pricing structures of the wholesale farmer are just as self-serving as they are for the benefit of the consumer. But not so with the porter. His job is simply to please the customer. The king of beasts is the one who realizes that his greatest and most noble function is to allow himself to be totally used by Man, his superior.

This is Judah. Judah, the man who would be king, is the one who admits his absolute inferiority to the King of all kings, and thus his kingship would be one of vigorous and mighty rulership of the people, while at the same time one of humble and devoted service to the Almighty. This was King David, at once a mighty and powerful sovereign and also a humble, pious servant and sweet singer to Hashem. This will also be the quality of the *Mashiach* – both a majestic king over Man and a humble servant of Hashem. May he come soon in our lifetime.

⌘ Bad Habit

by Benyamin Cohen

Man often views life through the eyes of habit. Most of our transgressions stem not from a conscious desire to stumble, but rather from an internal lack of appreciation for a particular action. Rabbi Chaim Shmulevitz describes this spiritual monotony as "*tardeimat hahergel*". This inability within Man to shift his perspective can have tragic consequences, as is evidenced from the *Midrash* in this week's Torah portion which describes the story of Jacob's burial in detail.

Upon arriving at the *M'arat HaMachpelah*, Esau accosted Jacob's children and claimed the right to the grave that was to be used for Jacob. A debate ensued and the brothers sent Naphtali, who was known for his speed, to run to Egypt for the appropriate documents.

Amidst the ruckus, Dan's deaf son Chushim exclaimed, "Are we going to wait until Naphtali returns while my grandfather is lying in a state of disgrace?!" Immediately, Chushim took a sword and chopped off the head of Esau.

Rabbi Shmulewitz wonders why the other descendants of Jacob, his own sons, weren't as troubled by the events as was Chushim. He explains that the sons of Jacob were so mesmerized by the verbal debate with Esau that in the interim they ignored the disgrace of Jacob's unburied remains. The sons of Jacob were plagued with spiritual boredom, "*tardeimat hahergel*", which desensitized them to the most urgent issue at hand – their father's burial. Only Chushim, whose inability to hear prevented him from participating in the argument, achieved a clarity of mind and a fresh perspective which precipitated his response.

The ability to shift our perspective can remedy much of our spiritual malaise. The yoke of *mitzvot* can be viewed either as a burden, a bag of stones to be lugged through life, or as a sack of diamonds, which when carried to its destination brings much reward. A well-known contemporary motivationalist comments that an alarm clock is, in essence, an opportunity clock alerting us to the many potentially constructive hours of the day. Likewise, praying to Hashem is not a daily chore, but a chance to communicate with the Divine.

In the portion of Nitzavim, the Torah writes that repentance is not far away, but is within each person's grasp. The Hebrew word for repentance is *teshuvah*, and the root of that word is "*shuv*" – to return. For most of us, the crucial element in repenting is a shift in our perspective.

A great rabbi once asked his students the difference between east and west, or in other words, the difference between right and wrong. The rabbi answered by facing his body to the east and then turning 180 degrees to the west, enforcing the point that to do proper *teshuvah* one must shift directions, essentially turning onto the right path. "Bring us back to you Hashem, and we shall <u>return</u>, renew our days as of old" (Lamentations 5:21).

CB Sealed Shut

by Michael Alterman

Aside from being the final portion in the book of Genesis, Parshat Vayechi is unique for its peculiar appearance in the Torah scroll. Unlike every other Torah portion which is clearly separated from its neighbor either by beginning on a new line in the Torah scroll or by skipping a significant number of spaces, Parshat Vayechi is *stumah* or closed off, following directly on the heels of the previous portion without the normal division. Rashi states that by "closing" off the normal separation, the Torah is signifying that with Jacob's death, the eyes and hearts of the Jewish people were closed and clouded by their bitter servitude to the Egyptians, which began at the time of his death.

There is only one problem with Rashi's explanation: The physical enslavement did not actually begin for at least another fifty years, after the deaths of Joseph and the rest of the brothers. What could Rashi be talking about?

The Sfas Emes answers that Rashi is not referring at all to the physical slavery which the Jewish people would later undergo; rather he is referring to the spiritual malaise which overtook the Children of Israel when Jacob died. While the great Patriarch was alive, his children and grandchildren were able to fend off the terrible influences which pervaded the immoral Egyptian society, remaining separate in their province of Goshen. However with Jacob gone, it was only natural for the Jewish people to begin to feel more comfortable in their foreign residence, letting down their guard and allowing aspects of the contemptible Egyptian atmosphere to slowly seep into their national psyche. Already at the time of Jacob's death, their eyes and hearts began to become clouded with the impurity of their environment.

By referring to a spiritual servitude with the same term usually applied to a physical enslavement, Rashi is sending us a powerful message about the gravity of falling prey to the influences of a foreign nation: Just because we are not physically enslaved does not mean that we are safe from becoming subjugated to the society around us.

EXODUS

PARSHAT SHMOT

arshat Shmot (Exodus 1:1-6:1) begins by describing the gradually increasing enslavement of the Jewish people in Egypt. It is Pharaoh's plan that the backbreaking servitude will stunt their rapid physical growth. Pharaoh decrees that every Jewish newborn male child should be killed, but the righteous Jewish midwives risk their own lives and refuse to comply. Moses is born, and when his mother is unable to keep him hidden from the Egyptian authorities any longer, she places him in a basket and sends him down the Nile River. He is found by Pharaoh's daughter and raised in the royal palace. Already a grown man, Moses kills an Egyptian who he witnessed beating a Jew, and when the word gets out, Moses is forced to flee to the land of Midian. There he marries Tziporah, the daughter of Yitro, and they have two sons.

While Moses is shepherding his father-in-law's flock, Hashem appears to him in the miraculous burning bush and instructs him to serve as His agent in redeeming the Jewish people from Egypt. Moses is initially reluctant to take on the responsibility, insisting that he is unworthy of the position and incapable of speaking to Pharaoh. When Moses doubts that the Jewish people will believe that he was sent by G-d, Hashem shows him three miracles to perform before the people which will demonstrate his Divine appointment. The miracles also include a stern message to Moses, reprimanding him for doubting the people's faith and for seemingly contradicting Hashem. Finally, after an extended discussion, Moses acquiesces to Hashem's command and journeys to Egypt. Along the way, he meets up with his brother Aaron whom Hashem had sent to assist him. After first speaking with the Jewish people, Moses and Aaron encounter Pharaoh, who not only refuses to grant their request for a three-day respite to worship Hashem, but even increases the slaves' heavy workload. The portion concludes with the people complaining to Moses and Aaron for worsening their plight, and Hashem's promise to Moses that He would indeed free the slaves from Egypt.

⊙ Saddle Your Donkey

by Benyamin Cohen

Upon his return from Midian, the Torah states: "And Moses took his wife and sons, and he placed them on the donkey and returned to the land of Egypt" (Exodus 4:20). Why does the Torah bother to tell us his means of transportation? Furthermore, what does "the donkey" indicate? Rashi answers that this donkey was special – it was the same donkey which Abraham rode on his way to sacrifice his son Isaac.

The first thought which comes to mind when one hears this is that it must have been a very old donkey. Why did Hashem keep this donkey alive just so Moses could ride it into Egypt? Additionally, Rashi says that this will be the same donkey that *Mashiach* will ride. Why is this donkey so important?

As mentioned above, there are three episodes in which this donkey appears – Abraham going to sacrifice Isaac, Moses returning to Egypt, and the eventual arrival of *Mashiach*. Let's examine these three incidents.

Abraham's willingness to give up his only son, the progenitor of the Jewish nation, serves as the supreme example of personal sacrifice. There were no questions asked, no second thoughts. Hashem's request seemed "illogical", but, nevertheless, Abraham still continued forward. Moses is told to go to Egypt and take out the Jewish people. In a way, he is being sent into the lion's den. This mission also seems unreasonable. So too, *Mashiach's* impending arrival to take us out of exile appears illogical, at times even impossible. Rashi is telling us that that they all went (and will come) to their missions on this donkey, not only in the physical sense, but also metaphorically. They all brought the same attitude, the same zeal and enthusiasm to their tasks.

Now, another question must be asked: Why a donkey? What is its significance? The answer dates back to the beginning of time. Man was created from two elements – the dust of the earth and the *ruach Elokim*, spirit of G-d. Every human being is a combination of the mortal and the immortal, the physical and the spiritual. Each person has within himself a segment of heaven and a segment of earth.

This dichotomy results in a constant battle for supremacy within us. Our physical side drives us towards our immediate, material desires – for example, food and material wealth. On the other hand, our spiritual being, our soul, strives to achieve greater authority and influence. At times, our spiritual essence can even control our physical being, like on *Yom Kippur* when we cease from eating. This constant struggle within each of us is the battle of life.

In the field of psychology, Freud developed the idea of a tripartite subconscious consisting of the id, ego, and superego. The id represents our animalistic nature, our physical desires. Our ego attempts to override the id, and the superego tries to override the ego. The word *chamor* (Hebrew for donkey) shares the same root as the word *chomer*, which represents our physical aspects, our body. Our soul has to subjugate our physical desires. It has to saddle our donkey and subdue our animalistic instincts.

At the binding of Isaac, "Abraham saddled his donkey" (Genesis 22:3). He controlled his physical desires. In order to go through with the "sacrifice" of his son, he had to override his *chomer*. Similarly, in this week's Torah portion, Moses and his family overcome the <u>same</u> donkey, the same physical desires. The trip seemed illogical and impossible, but Moses curbed his physical reasoning. And when *Mashiach* comes riding on that same donkey, he will have the self-same ability to overcome the physical and defy the normal course of circumstances.

That donkey is still walking around somewhere today. We need to find him and saddle him up.

Based upon a class given by Rabbi Benjamin Blech.

The Egyptian Exile
by Rabbi Danny Gimpel

In this week's Torah portion we encounter the Jewish people as a nation for the first time. No longer are they individuals who descended into Egypt with Jacob; they have grown and multiplied into a vast and powerful nation. Strangely enough, this blossoming occurred in the context of the first Jewish exile. Hashem told Abraham many years before that his descendants would be strangers in a strange land, experiencing slavery and affliction (Genesis 15:13). However, Hashem never told Abraham anything about the inhumane torture and murder which would become a major part of their experience in Egypt. Why was this exile so harsh and cruel?

Interestingly, our rabbis seem to offer another reason for the exile. The Talmud teaches that a parent should never favor any one of his children over the others, as the consequences of such behavior can be disastrous. Because Jacob favored Joseph by giving him a special coat, engendering hatred and jealousy (albeit unintentionally) in the brothers, the Jewish people eventually were exiled to Egypt. From this passage, it seems that the Talmud attributes the exile to Jacob's favoritism and the brother's jealousy. But how can that be the cause if Abraham had already been told that his children would experience the exile many years <u>before</u> Jacob was even born?

The commentaries answer this apparent contradiction by explaining that the Talmud does not intend to tell us why the Jewish people ended up in Egypt, but rather why their affliction was so harsh. While the exile was decreed in the time of Abraham, as the Torah describes, it would not have been as harsh if Jacob had not favored Joseph, causing the brothers to become jealous.

In this week's portion we find that Moses also did not initially understand why the Jewish people deserved such harsh treatment in slavery. However, when he encountered an Egyptian beating a helpless Jew, the Torah tells us that "[Moses] turned this way and that, and saw that there was no man" (Exodus 2:12), which the *Midrash* explains to mean that Moses saw that there was no Jew around to save the beaten man from the Egyptian. They were so concerned with their own problems that when a fellow Jew needed help they would look the other way. After Moses took matters into his own hands, killing the Egyptian and hiding the body in the sand, he later proclaims, "Indeed, the matter is known" (ibid. 2:14). Rashi explains that Moses was saying that he now understood why the Jewish people were suffering so greatly. As a matter of fact, two Jewish witnesses, Datan and Aviram, informed Pharaoh that Moses had killed an Egyptian. Moses realized that a baseless hatred existed among the Jewish people which was deserving of harsh torturous slavery.

This type of behavior towards one another can perhaps be directly linked to the favoritism which Jacob showed to Joseph and the jealousy and hatred which it engendered amongst the brothers. This same animosity resulted in the affliction of the Jewish people being much greater than was originally decreed by Hashem.

How careful must we be to always consider what the consequences of our actions will be! Often we do things that are genuinely not intended to be harmful. Even so, the lasting effect of our actions towards others should not be rationalized after the fact, for the damage may have already been done. Therefore, great care must always be exercised to act properly in the first place.

∽ Nile Surfing

by Stuart Werbin

*"It happened in those days that Moses grew up and went out to his breth-
ren and observed their suffering" (Exodus 2:11).*

Imagine how great life must have been for Moses in the king's palace.
He was at the prime of his youth, living as a prince in the Egyptian
empire, the strongest and most advanced nation of the time. He had
the world in the palm of his hand. Yet, Moses spends his free time
neither Nile surfing nor pyramid-climbing, but instead going out
amongst the Jewish slaves in an attempt to understand their plight
and to help them. Moses even kills an Egyptian who was beating a
Jew, an event which eventually costs him his princehood and exiles
him from Egypt.

We see here one of the reasons why Moses was able to develop
into the great leader that he was. A Jewish leader must work totally
and selflessly for his nation, and be completely uninterested in the
fulfillment of his own desires or the promotion of his own glory.
A leader must struggle for the needs of his people and for the sake of
Hashem. May we merit to come to this level of truth within ourselves,
and do what we know is right and what Hashem wants from us. We
must endeavor to not only be concerned with ourselves, but to seek
the welfare of all our fellow Jews through acts of loving kindness.

PARSHAT VAEIRA

aeira *(Exodus 6:2-9:35)* opens with Hashem reassuring Moses that He will indeed redeem the Jewish people from servitude and bring them into the land of Israel. After the Torah interjects a detailed genealogy of the tribe of Levi (Moses' family), Hashem reminds Moses that Pharaoh will initially refuse to set the Jewish people free, and Hashem gives Moses more detailed instructions for the upcoming encounter with the king of Egypt. Moses and Aaron go before Pharaoh again to request a three-day hiatus from work so that the Jewish people can worship Hashem in the desert, and Moses' staff is miraculously turned into a serpent as a sign of their Divine mission. When the Egyptian sorcerers counter by transforming their staffs into snakes as well, Moses' staff swallows up theirs. Even so, Pharaoh adamantly refuses to free the Jewish people, and the series of ten gruesome and torturous plagues begin. The first seven plagues are described in this week's portion: Blood, frogs, lice, a swarm of wild beasts, pestilence, boils, and hail. Despite the plagues, Pharaoh continues to refuse to free the Jewish people, as his heart is hardened. The portion comes to a close in the middle of these momentous events.

∽ The Power of Speech
by Yoel Spotts

At the beginning of this week's Torah portion, Hashem instructs Moses to make a second visit to Pharaoh on behalf of the Jewish people.

In order to properly equip Moses for the confrontation, Hashem provides him with a sign to present to Pharaoh in the hope that it will convince him to allow the Jewish people to leave Egypt. Moses is instructed by Hashem to take his staff and to throw it on the ground, whereupon it will be transformed into a snake.

Regarding this sign, Rabbeinu Bachya wonders why Hashem chose to turn the staff into a snake. Why not some big and frightening animal like a lion or a rhinoceros? Wouldn't that have made a bigger impact on Pharaoh? Rabbeinu Bachya responds that Hashem wished to send Pharaoh a message: Just as the sin of the original snake in the Garden of Eden was committed through speech, so too was Pharaoh's main transgressions through speech when, during the first encounter, he uttered the words, "Who is Hashem that I should listen to His voice?" (Exodus 5:2). The sin of the snake is well documented – in order to tempt Eve into eating from the forbidden tree, the snake taunts her that if she partakes of the fruit "you will be like G-d" (Genesis 3:4). Rashi explains that the snake was insinuating that just as Hashem derived all of His power to create the world by eating from the tree, so too Eve would be able to create worlds by consuming the forbidden fruit. Thus, Pharaoh, by denying Hashem's existence, had followed in the footsteps of the original abuser of speech – the snake who had ridiculed and belittled Hashem's strength.

However, in the case of Pharaoh's infamous declaration of denial mentioned above, perhaps there is more to the story, for there seems to be an interesting nuance in the language used by Pharaoh: "Who is Hashem that I should listen to His <u>voice</u>?" Pharaoh was not asking – Why should I believe that Hashem exists, but rather why should I listen to His <u>voice</u>. "Just because He said that the Jews should be allowed to leave, I should listen to Him?" demanded Pharaoh. "Where are the buildings He has built, the wars He has won, the fortunes He has amassed? Show me a concrete display of His power and then we'll get down to business. But you want me to listen to His voice?! Why? Speech means nothing; anyone can say whatever they want whenever they want."

Pharaoh had underestimated the importance of speech. He needed to be reminded of the incredible potency of the spoken word. "You think speech means nothing," responded Hashem, "remember the snake! Remember the snake's sin and its consequences. Recall that the entire future of Mankind was forever changed as a result of the snake's slanderous speech and Eve's acceptance of his malicious lies. Instead of a long life of comfort in the Garden of Eden, Man was doomed to roam the land and work the earth for his daily sustenance. You may think that talk is cheap, but it certainly was expensive for the Garden of Eden trio. Remember the power of speech before you mock the potency of My voice. Consider the strength of your words before you thoughtlessly speak without any concern for what you say." Pharaoh, however, failed to recognize the sign and refused Moses' demands. As a result, Hashem had to demonstrate His power in a form which even Pharaoh could understand by sending the Ten Plagues.

In today's day and age, it can be very difficult to appreciate the true significance of the spoken word. People have devalued the importance of speech to such an extent that we are neither disturbed nor concerned about what happens to come out of our mouths. However, the Torah has expressed to us in several places the true power of speech. A quick perusal of the first chapter of Genesis reveals that the words, "And Hashem said, let there be. . ." precede almost every act of creation to indicate that Hashem's speech in effect created the world. The Torah wishes to teach us that because we are created in the image of G-d, we too have the power to "create worlds" with the words we speak. Pharaoh failed to realize this message and felt that he could let his tongue run free, but it is important for us to remember to think – <u>before</u> we speak.

⊂⊃ Double Trouble
by Rabbi Shlomo Freundlich

In this week's Torah portion, we find Hashem instructing Moses to tell the Children of Israel that the time has arrived for their redemption.

Curiously, though, when referring to Hashem's promise to save the Jews from their exile in Egypt, the Torah spells *sivlot Mitzrayim*, the bondage of Egypt, <u>without</u> the letter *vav* – in its *chaser*, deficient, form (Exodus 6:6). Yet, in the very next verse, we find the word *sivlot* spelled <u>with</u> the letter *vav* – in its *malei*, complete, form. This is a reference to the awareness the Jews will have – after having been chosen as Hashem's people – that it was Hashem who saved them from the bondage of Egypt.

Rabbi Yosef Salant notes this discrepancy and suggests an approach which, in essence, defines the nature of the Egyptian exile. This exile was two-fold in nature. First, there was *inui haguf*, the physical subjugation and persecution of the Jewish people. The Children of Israel were beaten, brutalized, and required to perform backbreaking labor. However, there was a second and more insidious aspect of this exile, one which posed a greater threat to our people than *inui haguf*. This was *inui hanefesh*, the persecution of the soul. We became desensitized to the spiritual side of life. Being so enveloped in slave labor, we assumed a slave mindset to the point that we began to lose sight of our spiritual legacy inherited from Abraham, Isaac, and Jacob. So stripped were we of these sensitivities to spirituality that we began to view redemption solely as an emancipation from the oppressive physical conditions of bondage, not sensing the devastating toll the exile of Egypt had taken on our spiritual sensibilities as well.

In this vein, we can understand what is meant when Hashem says, "I see the pain of my people Israel in Egypt and hear their cries as a result of their oppression." In the Hebrew text, the two-fold term "*ra'oh ra'iti*" is used to mean "see" (Exodus 3:7). The Jews cried out to Hashem because of physical oppression, but Hashem saw <u>both</u> their physical pain and spiritual malaise. Moses therefore tells the Jews that Hashem will take them out of *sivlot Mitzrayim*, the bondage of Egypt, written in its deficient form because the Jewish people were lacking full appreciation of the toll the exile had taken on them. It is only after they will renew their relationship with Hashem at Mt. Sinai and experience the ecstasy of Hashem's closeness, feelings they had lacked during their bondage in Egypt, that they will <u>fully</u> perceive the *sivlot Mitzrayim* (written in a complete form with the letter *vav*) to which they had been subjected, both in the physical and spiritual sense.

Many of us are complacent and satisfied with the present level of our spiritual standing. We do not feel the need to make time to find an extra hour to either attend a class or learn a bit of Torah on our own. We can't imagine what that added learning lends to the quality of our Jewish lives until we experience it. Only then will we wonder how we could have gone without it.

CO Fragile: Handle with Prayer
by Rabbi Elie Cohen

Rabbi Moshe Chaim Luzzatto interprets a verse in the book of Jeremiah (23:29) which compares the words of the Torah to fire. He explains that each word of the Torah is like a hot coal. When one looks upon it, he is unimpressed. If, however, he lifts the coal and blows it, a flame emerges. So it is with the Torah – if one reads its words carefully, involving oneself in its study, the radiant light of the Torah emerges.

A case in point seems to be in this week's Torah portion discussing the plague of *arov*, or wild animals. Pharaoh begs Moses to pray to Hashem that the plague should cease. Moses indeed beseeches Hashem and the plague comes to a halt. The root form employed here by the Torah for the word "pray" is "*atar*" (Exodus 8:24-26). Just like in English – where, for example, the words eat, eaten, and feed are active, passive, and causative respectively – so too in Hebrew, verbs can be conjugated in many different ways, determining both their form and their meaning.

When the Torah writes that Pharaoh pleaded with Moses to pray on his behalf, Pharaoh uses the causative form of the root "*atar*" (Exodus 8:24). When Moses actually prays, the Torah employs the active form (ibid. 8:26). Why the difference? Rashi explains that the causative form which Pharaoh uses means to increase one's prayer and to make the prayer lengthier. On the other hand, the active form which Moses uses means to increase and intensify the act of praying itself.

This reveals to us a fascinating secret about the concept of prayer. Pharaoh viewed prayer merely as the uttering of certain holy charms, and the only way to make them more effective would be to quantitatively say more of them. The Torah's view of prayer, however, is entirely different. The main thing is not the text or length of the prayer, but the act of prayer. This is so because prayer is not a method of informing Hashem of our needs, for He already knows them. Rather, prayer is a way of improving ourselves, making ourselves more worthy of His gifts.

Prayer is an opportunity to grow. It is an opportunity to understand better and to draw closer to our Creator. May we merit to utilize the occasions of prayer to their maximum.

PARSHAT BO

o *(Exodus 10:1-13:16) begins with the eighth plague that Hashem brings upon the Egyptians as the land is covered by swarms of locusts, destroying all of the remaining crops. After the* plague is removed at Pharaoh's behest, he once again refuses to set free the Jewish people, and the ninth plague of darkness encompasses the land. When that plague ceases, Pharaoh becomes even more defiant about not freeing the slaves, at which point Moses warns Pharaoh about the upcoming tenth plague, the death of the firstborns. The Torah interrupts the narrative here with the first mitzvah given to the Jewish people as a nation – the sanctification of Rosh Chodesh, the new month, beginning with the month of Nissan. Hashem teaches Moses about the korban Pesach and the rest of the laws of the Passover holiday, which Moses transmits to the Jewish people. At midnight of the appointed night, the plague strikes, with every non-Jewish first-born dying, including Pharaoh's own son, and the Egyptian king speedily sends the Jewish people from his country. The Children of Israel travel forth in a hurry with the great wealth they have just been given by the Egyptians. The Torah portion concludes with various mitzvot relating to the Exodus.*

Plagued
by Rabbi Yonason Goldson

"With ten utterances the world was created. What does this teach us? Indeed, could it not have been created with only one utterance? This was to exact

punishment from the wicked who destroy the world which was created with ten utterances, and to bestow goodly reward upon the righteous who sustain the world which was created by ten utterances" (Pirkei Avot 5:1).

When Hashem contemplated the creation of the world, He envisioned a simple plan: Good and evil would coexist, but would remain wholly separate and distinct, rigidly defined and removed from each other. Looking into the future, however, Hashem foresaw that Adam would abuse his free will, and that as a result of his transgression he would cause good and evil to become mixed within himself in an intolerable way. When this would come to pass, the universe would simply self-destruct.

Hashem therefore anticipated the future and created the world not along a single spiritual axis; rather He designed it to be multi-axial, to accommodate a variety of possibilities that could arise through the intermingling of good and evil.

The *Mishnah* quoted above describes this plan in terms of the Ten Utterances, the systematic process of Creation which would allow the world to continue to exist <u>after</u> Adam's sin. This would further permit the possibility of weeding out the evil which had been confused within the good, so that Adam's descendants might eventually restore the universe to the perfection of Hashem's original plan. The punishment of the wicked would draw the evil from the good, thereby allowing the good to be realized by the righteous receiving their due reward. The first step was to be the Ten Plagues, the systematic compensation of evil for the Egyptians, who had contrived to eclipse the good through the wickedness of their deeds and thus bring spiritual destruction to the world.

Hashem hardens Pharaoh's heart to enable Him to bring all ten plagues upon Egypt, for only with their completion would the separation process be complete, and the world created with the Ten Utterances would be restored to a place of unadulterated good, purified of evil. And only then would it be possible for Hashem to reward the righteous Jewish people with the Torah, encapsulated in the Ten Commandments, which is the means through which we earn our true reward reserved for us in the World to Come. That world is built from the *mitzvot* we perform in this world (created with the Ten Utterances) and that we sustain through our righteousness.

Our sages teach us that Hashem created the cure before He sent the affliction, and that the Torah is the cure for all the evil in this world. It is up to us, however, to decide whether we will take the medicine, and in a dose strong enough to be of benefit.

Based upon the writings of the Sfas Emes.

⊙ Pharaoh's Amnesia
by Joshua S. Feingold

Put yourself in Pharaoh's shoes. In the past few months, a man came to you nine times, each time correctly predicting horrible plagues and destruction which befell your nation. Pretend that one morning he tells you that tonight, at midnight, every firstborn in the country will die. Would you not be a little concerned that this time, like the previous nine times, he might also be correct? If nothing else, you would probably stay up until midnight to see what happens! Yet, the Torah tells us that Pharaoh was so apathetic to Moses' warning that he "awoke at midnight" (Exodus 12:30) to the screams of his people, suggesting that he had somehow been sleeping until then. How could he have fallen asleep – was he not the least bit concerned about the future?

A similar enigma involving Pharaoh occurs in next week's Torah portion. Following his expulsion of the Jewish people from Egypt after the tenth plague, Pharaoh has a sudden change of heart and decides to chase after them, with the hope of overtaking them and bringing them back to Egypt. Why would Pharaoh want to bring back the people who had caused so much devastation to him and his empire? Has Pharaoh suddenly forgotten that every family in Egypt, including his own, is missing one child because of his stubborn refusal to let the Jews leave? Is Pharaoh out of his mind?

The answer to these questions can be understood based upon another question. Have you ever been in a dangerous situation where you felt that you had no one to turn to but Hashem? Regardless of your level of knowledge or observance, you probably prayed and asked Hashem for His help. As they say, "There are no atheists in a foxhole." When you were saved from the potentially tragic situation, Hashem's guiding hand in the world could not have been any clearer. If anybody had asked you if Hashem actively controls the world, your answer would have been an unequivocal "Yes!". So why is it that the next day things are not as clear, and a week later it was just as easy to attribute your salvation to coincidence? What happened – last week it was so clearly a miracle!

The answer is simple. This is the nature of Man. When there is nothing concrete to remind a person of what has transpired, he often cannot hold on to those single and pivotal experiences or the impressions that they made on him. Of course Pharaoh was not stupid, but he was human. While initially the plagues may have made a significant impression on Pharaoh, he quickly attributed the destruction to natural causes. The plagues had become nothing more than a series of massive coincidences.

However, all hope is not lost. This week's Torah portion teaches us the secret of how to keep the memory of the miracles fresh within our minds. Knowing the many weaknesses of Man, Hashem generously gave us daily, monthly, and yearly reminders – the *mitzvot*. The first *mitzvah* which the Jewish people received as a nation is the commandment to sanctify the new month, beginning with the month of the exodus – *Nissan*. The Torah states that *Nissan* should serve as a reference point for the rest of the months of the year. In this manner, we have a monthly commemoration of the miraculous exodus from Egypt. This *mitzvah* is followed directly by the command to offer the *korban Pesach* and to eat *matzah* every year on Passover, which the Torah tells us is also to be a remembrance of the exodus. The portion concludes with the daily *mitzvah* of *tefillin* which is to be "a sign upon your arm, and an ornament between your eyes, for with a strong hand Hashem removed us from Egypt" (Exodus 13:16). By performing the *mitzvot*, we transform the abstract "knowledge" of the good which Hashem did for us into something tangible.

So too, when we fortunately experience the profound recognition of Hashem's presence in the world, we must immediately try to materialize those feelings in order to take them with us into the future. One way to put this into practice is by keeping a running record of all the good things which Hashem does for us. This record might someday serve as a spiritual life raft, keeping us afloat when the ocean of life becomes turbulent. We know the secret. We have the power necessary to protect ourselves from Pharaoh's mistake. We <u>can</u> take it with us.

∽ The Next Generation
by Michael Alterman

"With our children and with our elders shall we go; with our sons and with our daughters, with our flocks and with our cattle shall we go, because it is a festival of Hashem for us" (Exodus 10:9).

Just before the onset of the plague of locusts, Pharaoh calls Moses and Aaron before him, prepared to finally acquiesce to their request and release the Jewish people. However, almost as an afterthought, Pharaoh asks them who they are planning to take with them, to which Moses responds that the entire nation will be going, young and old, men and women alike. Pharaoh oddly responds, "Not so – let [only] the men go and serve Hashem, for that is what you seek" (ibid. 10:11), and when Moses refuses to compromise, they are ejected from the royal chambers. It is interesting to note the excuse which Pharaoh gives for allowing only the men to leave: "For that is what you seek."

When did Moses ever give the impression that he was requesting only the men?

Pharaoh assumed that if the Jewish people were leaving Egypt so that they could serve Hashem, it would only be necessary for the grown men to participate. Based upon his knowledge of most of the world's other religions, he could not understand what place women and children had in the service of G-d. From Pharaoh's perspective, it was as if Moses had explicitly requested that only the men should be allowed to go. Moses responds that Judaism is not like those other religions. Hashem requires the service of <u>everybody</u>. In fact, not only are the children not exempt, but their education is of primary importance, for "with our children and [then] with our elders shall we go." The entire family is expected to participate.

Hashem gave us a special *mitzvah* to teach our children the Torah and to ensure their Jewish education. This *mitzvah* is so fundamental that it is included in the *Shema* prayer which we recite every day: "*v'shinantam l'vanecha* – and you shall teach [the Torah] to your children." When participating in any *mitzvah*, we must be to sure to include our children in order to teach and convey our love for Hashem's commandments to the next generation.

PARSHAT BESHALACH

eshalach *(Exodus 13:17-17:16) begins with Hashem leading the Jewish people out of the land of Egypt. Pharaoh's heart is once again hardened, and he pursues them with the Egyptian army, trapping the Jewish people on the shores of the Red Sea. When the former slaves begin to panic, Hashem reassures them and commands Moses to raise his hand over the sea, miraculously parting the waters and allowing the Jewish people to pass through safely. Pursued by the Egyptians into the sea, Moses once again raises his hand and the waters come crashing down upon Pharaoh's army. Awed by this indisputable miracle, Moses leads the Jewish people in the Az Yashir, a song of praise to Hashem acknowledging their debt of gratitude for their remarkable salvation.*

After traveling from the Red Sea, and following the miraculous sweetening of the bitter waters at Marah, the Jewish people complain to Moses and Aaron that they have no food to eat. Hashem responds by causing a daily ration of manna to fall from the sky every morning (except for Shabbat), sustaining them for their forty years in the desert, while at the same time testing their faith that they would trust in Hashem's providing for them on a day-to-day basis. They are also given a constant water source when Hashem commands Moses to strike a rock, miraculously causing water to flow from it. The portion concludes with the nation of Amalek's unprovoked sneak attack and the Jewish people's victory, followed by Hashem's promise that the memory of Amalek will eventually be erased.

ᗊ Leap of Faith
by Rabbi Daniel Estreicher

While the great miracle of the splitting of the Red Sea is well-documented, many people are not aware of the crucial factor which was necessary in order for this event to take place. Hashem was unwilling to perform this awesome miracle until He saw Man's willingness to demonstrate faith in Him. Therefore, it was not until Nachshon the son of Aminadav of the tribe of Judah bravely jumped into the water, showing unbelievable faith in Hashem, that the sea actually parted. As a result of Nachshon's great act of faith, the position of leadership and royalty was bestowed upon his tribe, the tribe of Judah. The great King David descended from this tribe, as well as the *Mashiach* who will bring the ultimate redemption.

We can learn several very important lessons from Nachshon. First of all, we must all be active members in the service of Hashem. We cannot expect to sit back and wait for miracles to happen. Hashem is willing to do many wonderful things for us, but we must first show that we are deserving by taking the initial step ourselves.

Secondly, we must realize that every one of us can make a difference. We have no idea how great our potential really is until we step forward. Even though a certain cause may be dangerous or unpopular, if we are willing to take a leap of faith, we can affect eternity. This is what Hashem wants from us, and it is up to us to meet His challenge.

ᗊ Food for Thought
by Michael Alterman

As children, we were all captivated by the mouth-watering description of the manna, as depicted in the *Midrash*. Manna was the heavenly food which sustained the Jewish people in the desert for forty years, and it tasted like whatever you wanted – pizza, ice cream, hot dogs, popcorn, etc. Our young imaginations worked overtime considering all the possibilities! However, upon analyzing the section in this week's Torah portion which describes the manna, we are provided with a less glorious perspective: "Behold, I shall rain down for you food from heaven; let the people go out and pick each day's portion on its day, so that I can test them, whether they will follow My teaching or not" (Exodus 16:4). The manna was not a free ride, nor was it merely a delightful delicacy which would provide its recipients an extended vacation during which they could enjoy life's finest pleasures. Rather, something was expected from the beneficiaries in return. What was their challenge?

Rashi explains that in exchange for their heavenly gift, the Jewish people were expected to observe the various *mitzvot* regarding the manna – not to leave any manna over for the next day, and not to go out to gather it on *Shabbat*. Most likely, our immediate reaction would be that this sounds like a pretty good deal. After all, if Hashem is willing to provide me with my daily sustenance, I will be more than happy to follow His commandments. Outwardly, this does not sound like much of a challenge. If we are assured that the manna will fall six days a week and that on Friday there will be a double portion to make up for *Shabbat's* allotment, what could possibly be the challenge?

Our rabbis tell us that the manner in which Hashem provided for the Jewish people in the desert exemplifies the means by which the Almighty provides for us even today. Just as the daily portion of manna was an absolute and indisputable miracle, so too is our daily income and sustenance a wonder directly bestowed upon us by Hashem. Of course, the miracle does not manifest itself as clearly today as it did then, but nevertheless without Hashem constantly involving Himself in our livelihood, we would never be able to put bread on our table.

Every person's yearly apportionment is determined on *Rosh Hashanah*. No amount of extra work can increase that number; no stroke of "bad luck" can deduct from the portion which Hashem assigns to us. Even life at the end of the 20th century is patterned after the circumstances which confronted the Jewish people in the desert, as described by the Torah: "Whoever gathered more [manna] had nothing extra and whoever gathered less was not lacking; everyone according to what he eats had they gathered" (ibid. 16:18).

Developing this level of faith was not a simple task for the generation in the desert. Going to sleep every night with absolutely no leftovers in the cabinets for the family's breakfast the next morning must have been an extremely nerve-racking experience. As the candles burned low on Friday night, they had to hope that the special double portion set aside for the next day would not rot, as did every morsel of manna left over on any other weeknight. Indeed, there were those who did not rise to the challenge. Some chose to leave over some manna for the next morning and it became infested with worms and rotted. Others sought to gather their portion on *Shabbat*, only to discover that the manna did not fall on the seventh day of the week. But despite the challenge, the vast majority of the nation learned to deal with the anxiety, overcoming their fears and developing their trust in Hashem.

The same challenge confronts us today, and it is certainly no easier now than it was then. However, the forty years which our ancestors spent in the desert served to implant in our national psyche the realization that everything comes from Hashem, enabling us to arrive at that same recognition, thousands of years later, when miracles are not as apparent.

Based upon the writings of Rabbi Yerucham Levovitz.

∽ # Miracle Downsizing
by Eyal Feiler

"Hashem moved the sea with a strong east wind all the night, and He turned the sea to dry land and the water split . . . The sea returned to its continuity at the turning of the morning . . . and Hashem overthrew the Egyptians in the midst of the sea" (Exodus 14:21,27).

One of the shining moments in the history of the Jewish people occurs in this week's Torah portion. The great miracle of the splitting of the Red Sea is the climax of their departure from Egypt, and this inspiring wonder forged a group of slaves into a nation.

However, a review of the verses describing the miracle raises a fundamental question. There is a well-known Jewish concept which states that when Hashem creates miracles, He performs them in a manner that follows the laws of nature as much as possible. In other words, when creating a miracle, Hashem would rather cause a minimal disturbance to the laws of nature so that its witnesses can maintain their freedom to choose whether or not to believe in G-d. In this manner, non-believers are better able to dismiss a miraculous event as being a freak act of nature or a coincidence.

If this is the case, why did Hashem create a miracle which was greater than necessary by allowing the Children of Israel to cross the sea at night while the Egyptians drowned during the day? Hashem could have created a more natural event by performing a "reduced" version of the miracle. The Children of Israel could have crossed during the day, allowing the critics to credit their success to the fact that they could easily see where they were going, or that they were able to use the daylight to find a dry bank. On the other hand, the disciplined and mighty Egyptian army could have drowned as they crossed at night because they became confused and panicked in the darkness. Why did Hashem make the miracle greater than necessary?

Rabbi Ben Zion Firer comments that the Hebrew word for a miracle, *nes*, is very similar and derives from the same root as the word for test, *nisayon*. The power and force of a *nes*, which occurs for the benefit of an individual or group of people, is directly related to the *nisayon* which they had to overcome to merit that miracle. In other words, the greater the challenge that a person must face and surmount, the larger the reward that Hashem provides for overcoming that challenge.

Not only did the Jewish people pass the test which was given to them upon leaving Egypt, but they also demonstrated their strong and steadfast belief in Hashem. The Ramban states that although the majority of the Jewish people lived together in the city of Ramses, there were small pockets of Jews dispersed all over Egypt. When the time of the exodus arrived, these small groups of Jews traveled at night so they could join the rest of the nation in Ramses, and leave together as a group. Although the dispersed Jews could have trekked across Egypt during the day, they specifically chose to travel at night, demonstrating their remarkable faith in Hashem. The night has always been a period when robbers and thieves prey on travelers walking the deserted paths between cities. The Jews in the small Egyptian communities took all of their belongings and put their faith in Hashem that they would safely arrive at their destination, knowing full well the dangers on the roads.

Because the Jewish people went out of their way to demonstrate their faith in Hashem and His guardianship by leaving at night, Hashem rewarded them by also leading them across the sea at night, thereby making the miracle so much more dramatic. This miracle not only rewarded them by completing their exodus from Egypt, but it also defied the laws of nature so that non-believers could not dismiss it as being an abnormal act of nature.

From here we can learn an important lesson. Observing the Torah and performing the *mitzvot* in a mechanical manner certainly merits some reward. However by fulfilling the *mitzvot* with zeal and excitement, and striving to do more than just the bare minimum, we not only grow in our observance and gain a feeling of satisfaction from overcoming the challenges which we face, but Hashem will even reward us by splitting the seas that impede us from achieving our goals.

PARSHAT YITRO

itro (Exodus 18:1-20:23) begins with Moses' father-in-law, Yitro, arriving at the Jewish people's camp in the desert, where he is greeted warmly by a large entourage. Yitro was inspired to join them when he heard about all of the wonders and miracles which Hashem performed for the Jewish people during the exodus from Egypt. Upon witnessing Moses serving as the people's sole judge from dawn until dusk, Yitro declares that this system will never work. He therefore suggests that subordinate judges be appointed to adjudicate the lower cases. Moses agrees to this plan.

The Jewish people arrive at Mt. Sinai and prepare to receive the Torah. Moses ascends the mountain and Hashem tells him to convey to the people that they will be to Him a treasure from amongst the nations. After three days of preparation, the appointed moment of revelation finally arrives, and amidst thunder, lightning, and the sound of the shofar, Hashem descends upon the mountain and proclaims the Ten Commandments. Moses then ascends the mountain to receive the remainder of the Torah from Hashem, both the written and oral segments. The portion concludes with several mitzvot concerning the construction of the altar in the Temple.

∞ A New Day in Every Way
by Yoel Spotts

"In the third month from the exodus of the Children of Israel from Egypt, on this day, they arrived at the wilderness of Sinai" (Exodus 19:1).

At first glance, this verse seems quite innocuous; what can be so special about telling us when the Children of Israel arrived at Sinai? However, Rashi immediately alerts us to the fact that this verse contains more than meets the eye. Rashi points out that the Torah does not write "on that day", implying "that day" in the past, when they arrived. Rather, it writes "on this day" seeming to indicate the actual day on which we are reading this verse. This usage, Rashi continues, teaches us that the Torah should be new to us every day, as on the day it was given.

If one examines the context of this verse, one finds that this lesson is very appropriately situated. As the verse states, the Jews have just arrived at Mt. Sinai and in a very short while, will receive the Torah directly from the hand of Hashem. Imagine, if you will, the scene in the camp of the Children of Israel. Cleaning, washing, bathing – everyone is busy preparing, for they all realize that this is not just an ordinary day. The revelation at Mt. Sinai marks the single greatest event since Creation. It is the climax to the events that began with the division of light and darkness. Lightning, thunder, and smoke surround the mountain – the entire world cannot help but take note of this extraordinary event. The Jews at Mt. Sinai have been permitted to approach closer to the Divine than any other people before or since. How could a Jew experiencing this incredible phenomenon not be captivated by the Torah and its laws? How could someone in such a state of euphoria not be overwhelmed with a feeling of passion to perform the will of the Creator?

Obviously, at this remarkable point in time, the Children of Israel feel an intense level of fascination and commitment to the Torah they have just received. They cannot help but run to observe its laws and commandments. But what about tomorrow? What happens when the initial excitement wears off? What happens when the lightning, thunder, and special effects are forgotten? Will the Children of Israel still perform the *mitzvot* with the same intensity? Indeed, it seems very unlikely. For exactly this reason, the Torah chose this specific moment to teach this critical lesson noted by Rashi. After the initial euphoria of receiving the Torah wears off, they must realize that their zeal to perform its *mitzvot* must not wear off. Thus, each day must be viewed as if the Torah was given <u>today</u>. By recalling that first day when they arrived at the wilderness of Sinai, the Jews can once again reach that level of exhilaration for the Torah.

If those Jews who lived just a few short days subsequent to the Revelation needed to be reminded of this message, how much more so do we living today, three thousand years later, need to take this lesson to heart. It is so easy to become entrapped by routine. Pray three times a day, recite blessings before eating food – these things easily become so habitual that we begin to perform them like robots instead of humans. The status quo is comfortable and familiar. However, this type of behavior and manner should be avoided at all costs. The dangers of mediocrity are well documented, even in the non-Torah realm – Dante reserved the hottest place in Hell for those not willing to move ahead, content with running in place. Once we begin to perform the *mitzvot* by rote rather than with the proper attention and concentration they deserve, the laws become lifeless and stale. Instead of serving as the inspiration for our everyday living, the commandments evolve into troublesome burdens that we soon tire of.

Thus, the Torah enjoins us here to break free from that vicious cycle. We cannot be content with the status quo. We must strive to move forward, to seek new heights in our spiritual lives. The first step in such a plan is a change in attitude. Like a little child overflowing with excitement at having just received a new toy, so too must we approach each new day with the same enthusiasm. With such a change in outlook, the Torah and its laws take on new meaning. Instead of being roadblocks, the *mitzvot* now become our road maps in the highway of life. Instead of restricting us, the Torah now frees us from the clutches of mediocrity. If only we heed the message of "on this day", we too can reach the same level of fervor and zeal for the Torah as the Jews at the Revelation. We too can feel ourselves receiving the Torah on Mt. Sinai.

∽ # Bottoms Up
by Rabbi Shimon Wiggins

Let us ask a seemingly ridiculous question: Where were the Children of Israel during the giving of the Torah? At Mt. Sinai, of course! But that is precisely the question. Were the Children of Israel <u>at</u> Mt. Sinai or were they <u>under</u> Mt. Sinai?

In this week's Torah portion, it says that Moses brought the Children of Israel towards Hashem and they stood at the <u>bottom</u> of the mountain (Exodus 19:17). The Hebrew word *tachtit* is translated as "bottom" in the simple explanation of this verse. However, the word *tachtit* also means "under". The Talmud (Tractate Shabbat 88a) explains that Hashem took Mt. Sinai and turned it upside down, holding it over their heads. With the threat of Mt. Sinai literally looming over the Children of Israel, Hashem said to them, "If you will accept the Torah, that's fine. But if not, then you will die!"

It seems, from the Talmud's explanation, that the Children of Israel accepted the Torah under duress. This is a mind-boggling proposition. What happened to the famous slogan and great merit of the Jewish nation: "*Na'aseh v'nishma*, we will do and we will listen"?! These words were uttered by the entire Jewish people <u>prior</u> to receiving the Torah at Sinai. By declaring that they would observe the entire Torah, before it was actually given, the Jews demonstrated deep trust and faith in Hashem. The *Midrash* tells us that Hashem found this declaration so precious that He sent angels to adorn each Jew with two crowns – one for *Na'aseh* (doing) and one for *Nishma* (listening). Therefore, how could the giving of the Torah have taken place under duress?

The Maharal of Prague gives us an essential insight to resolve this problem. Without question, the Children of Israel had free will. They had the ability to choose whether to accept the Torah or not. Furthermore, without question, they willingly chose to accept the Torah even before it was given. However, Hashem gave the Torah to the

Children of Israel in a "threatening" way to teach us an invaluable lesson. Torah is essential to the existence of the Jewish people and the world. Without Torah, the Jewish nation will cease to exist, society will collapse, and the world will self-destruct. Torah is not just for spiritual highs and for when we choose to observe it. Torah is indispensable!

This is the significance of Hashem turning Mt. Sinai over and saying, "If you choose not to accept the Torah, then you will die!" The Jewish nation understood then and for all eternity that it cannot exist without Torah.

PARSHAT MISHPATIM

ishpatim (Exodus 21:1-24:18), following on the heels of the Ten Commandments, deals primarily with civil law. The juxtaposition of the ritual with the mundane provides an enlightening insight into Judaism. From the Torah's perspective, there is no distinction between the ceremonial and the worldly activities of life – both should be infused with holiness and both must be kept completely and diligently. Included amongst the civil laws discussed in the Torah portion are the laws relating to the Jewish servant and his freedom; penalties for causing bodily injury to another person and for damaging his property; laws regarding watchmen and borrowers; the mitzvah to show sensitivity to the poor and to offer them free loans; and laws relating to the honest dispensation of justice. After mentioning the mitzvot of Shabbat and Shemittah, the portion continues with a brief discussion of the three pilgrimage festivals – Pesach, Sukkot, and Shavuot – and Hashem's renewed promise to bring the Jewish people to the land of Israel. The Torah then returns to the revelation at Mt. Sinai. The Jewish people declare their commitment to do whatever Hashem commands, and the portion concludes with Moses' ascending the mountain, where he will remain for forty days and forty nights to receive the rest of the Torah.

ↄ Please Phrase It in the Form of a Question
by Rabbi Elie Cohen

The Torah states, "When you shall see the donkey of your adversary crouching beneath its load and you shall refrain from helping him, you shall surely help him" (Exodus 23:5). The verse doesn't seem to make sense. First, the Torah seemingly commands, "you shall refrain from helping him," and then it continues, "you shall surely help him." Rashi elegantly solves the puzzle by inserting a question mark. He reads the verse as follows: "When you shall see the donkey of your adversary crouching beneath its load, will you refrain from helping him? You shall surely help him." (Note: In Biblical Hebrew, the terms meaning "you shall refrain" and "you will refrain" are one and the same, only distinguishable by context.)

It appears, though, that this interpretation is not entirely satisfactory. Wouldn't the verse have been complete without the question in the middle? The Torah, unmatched in its economy of words, could just as easily have written, "When you shall see the donkey of your adversary crouching beneath its load, you shall surely help him!"

Perhaps the simplest approach is as follows. The Torah is not just teaching us a law. It is teaching us an attitude. The Torah's question, "will you refrain from helping him?" is expressing to us that even though the person in need is an adversary, one should not only help the person, but have a sincere desire to do so.

ↄ Smoke & Mirrors
by Rabbi Yossi Lew

The stage was set. It was thundering and lightning; the sound of the *shofar* could be heard; smoke, clouds, fire – all of the drama one could possibly imagine. Hashem was about to reveal Himself and His message directly to the Jewish people. But wait! After opening with a description of the greatness of G-d, His name, and His holy day of *Shabbat*, the commandments which follow are of the most simple and mundane nature: honor your parents, don't murder, don't steal. Is this the great Revelation for which we had been waiting? Was all the drama and excitement really a necessary accompaniment to such universally accepted principles?

Continuing with this week's Torah portion, immediately following the Revelation of the Ten Commandments, we are taught *mishpatim*, simple moral and civil laws, the kind which any honorable government would implement in order to ensure efficiency and decency in its society. After the great Revelation on Mt. Sinai, shouldn't we expect commandments of a spiritual nature – perhaps relating to the construction of a temple to house the Divine presence, or prayer and the like?

The Torah is a way of life. It therefore presents us with a value system, including a moral guide for our day-to-day lives. In addition to the "spiritually illuminating" laws, the Torah also instructs us about elementary rules, because the basis of morality and our value system must be a Divine one. It cannot be something simply decided by a human mind. Values, by definition, supersede logic. For example, giving charity is a great value and a moral thing to do, but it is not necessarily <u>logical</u> to give something of yours away to someone else. On the other hand, eating lunch can hardly be categorized as a moral thing to do, although it is quite logical.

If morals and values are left up to logic, there is no telling what our thought processes could lead us to. Let's take the example of stealing. Most decent people, for moral reasons, would be horrified at the notion of stealing; however, one might be logically inclined to justify the stealing of "only" ten dollars from a wealthy person, since he wouldn't miss it anyway. Others may defend even larger thefts (or other infractions) through similar reasoning. Often the human mind will find a way to logically implement its own agenda, eventually leading to a complete breakdown of the moral fiber. Only half a century ago, such "logic" motivated a country which was supposedly the most sophisticated, advanced, and morally correct nation in the world to perpetrate the most horrifying crimes against humanity in history. The Germans "logically" convinced themselves that certain elements of the human race were unnecessary and useless to the future of Mankind, and they carried their reasoning to its ultimate catastrophic conclusion.

This is why the Ten Commandments and the immediate laws which follow are of such a common, moral, and civil nature. The Torah, in addition to informing and guiding us in all spiritual and G-dly matters, emphasizes that morality and a true value system can exist only when firmly established on a Divine base. Stealing is prohibited because Hashem so commanded; sanctity of life is affirmed because Hashem commanded us not to murder. In order to live civilly with our fellow human beings, we must first have an unwavering belief in Hashem. Only after accepting this fundamental principle, we can (and must) begin the process of understanding the laws, thus convincing our own logic of the great ethical values contained therein.

New Kid on the Block

by Stuart Werbin

"You must not abuse or oppress a stranger, for you were strangers in the land of Egypt" (Exodus 22:20).

You are a high school freshman having a great time. You have worked hard to make your way into the popular crowd, and finally you succeeded in joining that impenetrable clique. Today you're kicking back with your friends, when all of a sudden you spot the New Kid coming in your direction. The New Kid has just arrived from Cheyenne, Wyoming, and he's trying his best to get into the popular crowd.

The problem, however, is that no one likes him, and most of your friends would probably carry their dislike a step further than that. You happen to think that he is actually a nice guy, but stating your opinion would get you a one-way ticket off the wrestling team and into the National Geek Society. As the New Kid approaches with his hand raised in greeting, you know that you will have to make a decision. You have three options:

a) Take the New Kid and stuff him in a trashcan.

b) Declare, "No *haba anglais*," and return triumphantly to your amigos.

c) Say, "Hi, Maurice, it's good to see you," and introduce him to the group.

In this week's portion, the Torah commands us not to taunt converts. We usually feel most comfortable around others who are like us, such as those who come from the same country, city, neighborhood, and ethnic group. However, the Torah is telling us never to forget that we were once the "New Kid" when we were slaves in Egypt. Although we may feel uncomfortable reaching out to a newcomer, that is never an excuse for us to abuse or hurt someone. Just because he's not part of our clique of friends does not mean that we can mistreat him. Every person is created in the image of Hashem, and must be treated with the proper decency and respect.

Parshat Terumah

arshat Terumah (Exodus 25:1-27:19) begins a series of four out of five portions which discuss in detail the construction of the Mishkan, the traveling Tabernacle which would serve as a "resting place" for Hashem's presence amongst the Jewish people. This week's entire portion recounts Hashem's description to Moses of how to construct the Mishkan, beginning with a listing of the various precious materials to be collected from the Jewish people for this monumental project. Hashem describes the magnificent golden and wooden Ark which would house the tablets of the Ten Commandments, complete with its dazzling cover depicting two cherubim (angels with the faces of children) facing each other. Next, Hashem provides Moses with the blueprints of the shulchan (holy table) upon which the lechem hapanim (showbread) would be placed each week. Following the depiction of the pure golden menorah which was to be hammered out of one large piece of gold, Hashem describes the structure of the Mishkan itself, detailing the splendidly woven and embroidered covers, curtains, and partitions, and the sturdy outer walls. The Torah portion concludes with the instructions for the copper altar and the Mishkan's large outer courtyard.

∽ Mishkan: Under Construction
by Yoel Spotts

This week's Torah portion introduces us to the holy *Mishkan*. The majority of this Torah portion contains detailed descriptions of the various vessels used in the *Mishkan.* Thus, Hashem dedicates several verses to each component, describing its exact measurements and appearance so that Moses would understand exactly how to construct each vessel. Such a Torah portion, which seems to contain just a list of the different vessels, would appear to be rather uneventful. However, we are confronted with a strange discrepancy at the very outset.

At the beginning of the explanation of the holy Ark, Hashem commands Moses, "<u>They</u> shall construct the Ark" (Exodus 25:10), using the plural form, as if speaking to a group of people who are to participate in the construction of the various parts of the *Mishkan.* Now one would certainly expect that the description of each of the numerous items in the *Mishkan* would follow a parallel grammatical structure. However, this is not the case. In fact, the Ark is the only time where we find the plural form used; every other item's description is preceded by the singular command "<u>you</u> shall construct," seeming to indicate that only one person was to be involved in the erection of the *Mishkan.* How are we to resolve this contradiction? Who in fact was responsible for the actual construction of the *Mishkan?*

Before we attempt to resolve our problem, we must first preface our remarks with an important principle concerning the *Mishkan.* The commentators explain that the many vessels and *Kohanim's* garments of the *Mishkan* were not simply selected at random. Rather, each and every component represented a particular facet of Judaism and the Jewish people. Thus, each vessel and its description contained numerous messages and underlying themes for the Jewish nation. The holy Ark, the commentators further explain, corresponds to the Torah and its study; not surprising, since the Ark held the actual Torah scroll and tablets of the Ten Commandments given directly by Hashem to Moses. Therefore, the description of the Ark should provide us with some insight into the nature of the Torah and its study.

In this vein, the Ramban seeks to answer the grammatical discrepancy posed above. With regard to any worthwhile project or venture undertaken for the sake of Judaism, one may be considered a partner by simply contributing money and other resources to facilitate other people to actually complete the project. For this reason, regarding all of the other vessels in the *Mishkan*, the Torah directs its command to Moses alone, for the Jewish people have already done their part by contributing the raw materials to the building fund. Now Moses must complete the job by actually constructing the vessels.

However, this is not the case when it comes to Torah study. One can offer his money, time, and effort so that others may study the Torah, but that is not enough. <u>Every</u> member of the Jewish nation must actively involve himself in the actual study of the Torah. Therefore, the command to build the Ark, which as mentioned before represents the Torah and its study, is directed not only to Moses, but to <u>all</u> the Jewish people. Hashem wishes to indicate that although the people have contributed their gold and silver, they must nonetheless participate in the actual construction of the holy Ark – and, by extension, in the actual study of the Torah.

Of course, one who donates his resources for the sake of Torah study is to be greatly commended and congratulated. However, at the same, he must realize that he cannot simply sit on the sidelines and allow others to study Torah alone. We must all participate in this venture. Nor should we think that the Torah is a closed book, reserved for scholars and brilliant minds. The Torah can be studied on so many different levels and from so many different angles, that each individual may approach the Torah according to his own level. From the amateur to the greatest scholar, one can only gain from studying the Torah. The Torah is eternal and is there for us to study at any time – now is the time for us to open it and see what treasures it contains.

◇ If You Build It, He Will Come
by Benyamin Cohen

We can derive an invaluable lesson from a peculiar verse in this week's Torah portion. "They shall make a sanctuary for Me – so that I may dwell among them" (Exodus 25:8). At first glance, one would think that there is a misprint in the Torah. It should read ". . . so that I may dwell <u>in it</u>," meaning that if the Jewish people build the sanctuary, then Hashem will have a place to rest His presence. If they build it, He will come! Why, then, does Hashem say that He will dwell "among them" and not "in it"?

The commentaries clear up this difficulty by stating that Hashem is referring to the Jewish people themselves and not the Tabernacle. If they build the Tabernacle, then Hashem will dwell among *them*! If they participate in the construction of the sanctuary, then Hashem will reward them by dwelling among each and every one of them.

The sanctuary is portable in nature. The Torah is trying to teach us that no matter where we are – whether it be in the heart of Jerusalem or the frozen tundra of the North Pole – Hashem can and will be with us. We shouldn't be discouraged by our surroundings. As long as we immerse ourselves in the words of Torah, as long as we take time to participate in the construction of the sanctuary, Hashem will dwell among us. It is this attitude which will be the catalyst to our survival of the exile.

ᴐᴑ Golden – Inside and Out
by Michael Alterman

"From the inside and the outside shall you cover [the Ark]" (Exodus 25:11). Regarding this verse, the Talmud comments, "Any Torah scholar whose inside does not resemble his outside is not really a Torah scholar" (Talmud Tractate Yoma 72b).

Our rabbis teach us that for someone to be considered a true *talmid chacham*, a scholar and student of Hashem's holy Torah, his <u>entire</u> being must be a consistent representation of the Torah which he studies. If he presents himself to the world as a dedicated, sincere, and honest person it should not be a facade that he has deftly constructed to conceal his undesirable character traits, but rather an accurate portrayal of his true G-d fearing self. Just as the holy Ark, which was representative of the Torah that it contained, was coated with gold both inside and outside, so too must the *talmid chacham's* inner character match his public disposition and professed beliefs.

The Talmud (Tractate Berachot 28a) relates that when the great Rabban Gamliel was the prince and leader of the Jewish people, he issued a proclamation that any student whose inside did not resemble his outside would not be permitted to enter the *beit midrash*. He felt that those other students who were truly sincere should not be exposed to the negative influence of those who were studying the Torah for some ulterior motive or whose character traits were not as finely tuned as was their scholarship. It was only after the leadership was passed to someone else that the guard to the entrance to the *beit midrash* was removed and everybody who wanted to study was then permitted to enter.

The question comes to mind about who could have been so qualified that he was able to fulfill the demanding role of being this guard during the days of Rabban Gamliel. How could anybody be capable of accurately discerning which students were absolutely sincere and which were not?

It has been suggested that "the guard" which the Talmud refers to was not a person at all. Rather, the door to the *beit midrash* itself served as the guard, for it was sealed shut, locked and bolted, preventing the entrance of anybody – unless they were worthy. A student who was sincere and truly desired to study Torah would dedicate himself to somehow find the way – any way – to penetrate the sealed entrance. Everybody else who might not be sincerely motivated would be intimidated by the preeminent "guard" – the door which was sealed shut.

Studying Torah in a classroom setting is commendable, but we must transfer the teachings that we learn, from the study hall into the real world. Our goal should not be to merely broaden our horizons and expand our knowledge; rather, we should apply the lessons of the Torah in our everyday life, transforming ourselves into a true *mentsch*. If we sincerely want to improve, nothing – not even a bolted door – can stand in our way.

PARSHAT TETZAVEH

ollowing the detailed commandments in last week's portion concerning the construction of the Mishkan, Parshat Tetzaveh (Exodus 27:20-30:10) begins with the daily mitzvah given to Aaron and his sons to kindle the menorah in the Mishkan with pure olive oil. Hashem describes to Moses the special garments which are to be worn by the Kohanim during their service, woven and crafted from materials donated by the people. The ordinary Kohanim would wear four special garments, while four additional vestments were to be worn exclusively by the Kohen Gadol. The Torah portion then shifts its attention to Hashem's commandments regarding the melu'im, or inauguration ritual for the newly constructed Mishkan, to be performed exclusively by Moses for seven days. The melu'im included Moses' adorning and anointing the Kohanim, and his bringing korbanot (offerings). On the eighth day, Aaron and his sons would assume their offices as the Kohanim. After then describing the korban tamid (daily offering), the offering to be brought in the Mishkan every day of the year in the morning and afternoon, the portion concludes with the command to build the last of the Mishkan's structures, the golden altar upon which the ketoret (incense) would be offered every morning and afternoon. All of these commands are actually carried out in the concluding portion of Exodus, Parshat Pekudei.

∞ Menorah Torah

by Ranon Cortell

This week's portion begins with the familiar proclamation of Hashem to His loyal servant Moses, "You shall command the Children of Israel that they shall take for you pure, pressed olive oil for illumination, to kindle the lamp continually" (Exodus 27:20). Hashem then proceeds to divulge the methods by which Aaron and his sons will light the holy *menorah*. Immediately afterwards, Moses at long last is told to appoint his brother and sons official *Kohanim* of the sanctified *Mishkan*, and only then does the Torah delve into the other myriad responsibilities conferred upon the saintly *Kohanim*. "Why," one asks in sudden heart-stopping anticipation, "was the *menorah* singled out as the only priestly command to precede the *Kohanim's* appointment?"

Rabbi Moshe Feinstein explains that it is a well-known tradition that the *menorah* represents our most precious source of wisdom and guidance, the Torah. Just like the *menorah* was a constant and unerring source of light in the inner sanctums of Hashem's earthly palace, so too, the Torah must serve as a valiant torch to guide us through the pitfalls of our existence. It is for this reason that the *mitzvah* of lighting the *menorah* was separated from the other priestly commands – to teach us that the lessons which are inherent and symbolized by the *menorah* pertain to every Jew. The *menorah* teaches us many important methods of learning Hashem's precious Torah, as well as how to spread its wisdom to others.

For instance, the Torah exhorts us that the oil used must come from olives which were "*katit*", explained by Rashi to mean that they must be hand-pressed, rather than squeezed by a machine or olive press. This seemingly minor detail teaches us that in order to truly acquire Torah learning, a person must utilize all of his energies and potential and truly exert himself in eager pursuit of Hashem's gift of wisdom to the Jewish people. There are no shortcuts or crash course seminars for attaining a true understanding of the Torah. Secondly, just like a candle is lit by holding the flame to the wick long enough so that the fire will catch and burn by itself, so too a teacher must imbue his students with wisdom until they are able to grasp the information and desire further wisdom on their own initiative, the ultimate goal of the teacher.

Finally, the *Kohanim* were commanded to fill the cups of the *menorah* every night with five *lug* (a measurement) of oil, regardless of the length of the night. This simple law also teaches us a crucial point in our methods of instruction. No matter what the intellectual capabilities of the student may be, the teacher must be willing to dedicate equal time to each student's education. The teacher should not reason that the bright student can figure it out on his own, because this inattention by the teacher may cause the student to turn his intelligence to other pursuits. And the student with comprehension difficulties must never be dismissed as lacking the potential to become something great.

In summary, if one is looking for insight into wisdom and Torah, one should turn to the *menorah*. As the Talmud stipulates, "One who desires wisdom should turn south (the location of the *menorah* in the Temple)" (Tractate Baba Batra 25b).

∽ For Whom the Bell Tolls
by Ezra Cohen

Every *Kohen* who served in the Temple wore four special garments, including a shirt, pants, belt, and turban, all of which were made of white linen. The *Kohen Gadol* wore an additional four golden garments, including the mantle, the apron, the breastplate, and the headplate. Attached to the bottom of the mantle were 72 hollow ornaments in the shape of pomegranates alternating with 72 golden bells. The bells tinkled to announce the arrival of the *Kohen Gadol* to the sanctuary. There are several lessons we can learn from the tinkling of the bells.

The Chasam Sofer comments that the bells remind us that the leaders of Israel, at times, must make their voices heard. Although silence is certainly a highly valued trait in the life of a Jew, sometimes the leader has to make his view known – he has to make noise – especially when the holiness of the Torah is under attack. He must speak in a loud voice against any possible desecration of Hashem's name.

The mantle and its bells, as stated by the commentators, were an atonement for the sin of *lashon hara*, evil speech. When we examine the purpose and nature of the bells we see how this is possible. The sound of bells announces one's presence before entering, and this demonstrates sensitivity to others. If one is responsive and empathetic to another's feelings, he will surely refrain from speaking evil against him.

The bells also teach us a general lesson of *derech eretz*, good manners. The *Midrash* comments on the tinkling of the bells prior to the entrance of the *Kohen Gadol* into the *Mishkan*: This teaches that we should give advance notice of our visits to people, not entering someone's house unexpectedly. This applies even upon entering one's own home.

Furthermore, Rabbi Chaim Shmulevitz adds that even if we are doing a praiseworthy deed, whether it be the priestly service in the Temple or collecting charity (outside it), we must demonstrate sensitivity towards others by informing them of our arrival ahead of time. The *Kohen Gadol* was dressed in clothing which represented these good manners. He only entered the *Mishkan* with advance notice – by the sounding of the bells on his hem. We see from here that not even a worthy cause supersedes the imperative to have good manners. One should realize that the *Kohen's* bells toll with a message for us all.

All Work and No Play
by Michael Alterman

The Torah does something very puzzling towards the end of this week's Torah portion. After a lengthy discussion of the *melu'im*, consecration service of the *Mishkan*, the Torah immediately begins to describe the *korban tamid*, the offering which was to be brought in the *Mishkan* (and in the subsequent Temples) twice a day for as long as it existed. It was completely unrelated to the *melu'im*, yet the two sections are separated by only a few blank spaces (called a *stumah*) in the Torah scroll, after chapter 29, verse 37. One can almost imagine Moses and the Children of Israel saying to Hashem, "We just consecrated the *Mishkan* so how about giving us a break before we start the daily service."

Rabbi Samson Raphael Hirsch explains that the Torah's decision to juxtapose the inaugural consecration service to the daily *korban tamid* was no accident. Hashem was teaching us a crucial lesson for all eternity. Hashem had promised the Jewish people (in last week's Torah portion), "Make for Me a sanctuary, and I will dwell amongst you" (Exodus 25:8). Any Jew could have easily assumed that simply building the structure was the goal and ultimate accomplishment. Hashem had promised to dwell amongst the Children of Israel if they built Him a sanctuary – end of story. After one had contributed to the building fund, helped collect the supplies, and maybe even hammered in some nails, he might think that he could go home, completely satisfied with what he had accomplished. Some individuals may have felt that they had fulfilled their obligation to the point that they had no further desire to participate. After all, they had built Hashem's sanctuary as Hashem had requested.

To prevent people from making such a grave error, the Torah places the commandment to perform the daily *korban tamid* immediately following the initial consecration of the structure itself. Hashem was telling us that the construction of the *Mishkan* was not the end, but rather the means to serve Him to our utmost capabilities. We cannot go home, satisfied that the *Kohanim* will perform our duties in the sanctuary. Similarly, we cannot refrain from participating and attending services in our respective synagogues, satisfied that the rabbis will fulfill <u>our</u> requirement.

Judaism is a participatory religion with *mitzvot* designed to bring the morals and ethics of our Torah into action; it is not a spectator sport. Notably, it is only after the commandment of the *korban tamid*, when we begin to participate in Hashem's service on a daily basis, that Hashem reiterates His promise to be our G-d, directly involved in our daily lives. As Hashem says in Exodus 29:45 after describing the *korban tamid*, "I will dwell amongst the Children of Israel, and I will be for them a G-d."

PARSHAT KI TISSA

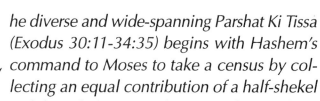he diverse and wide-spanning Parshat Ki Tissa (Exodus 30:11-34:35) begins with Hashem's command to Moses to take a census by collecting an equal contribution of a half-shekel coin from every adult male between the ages of 20 and 60, the profits from which will go to the Mishkan. Hashem describes to Moses the copper kiyor (wash basin) with which the Kohanim would sanctify their hands and feet before serving in the Mishkan. Also discussed is the annointment oil which would be used to sanctify the Mishkan's various vessels for regular use. This is followed by the recipe for the aromatic ketoret to be burned twice daily. Hashem designates Betzalel, of the tribe of Judah, and Oholiav, of the tribe of Dan, to supervise the upcoming construction of the Mishkan. The mitzvah of Shabbat is then repeated to caution the nation that even the construction of the Mishkan does not supersede the observance of the weekly day of rest.

The Torah returns to the narrative of the Revelation at Mt. Sinai and describes the horrible sin of the golden calf. Hashem relents to Moses' prayer that the Children of Israel should be spared from annihilation for this grievous transgression, and Moses descends from the mountain with the two tablets of the Ten Commandments in hand. Upon witnessing a segment of the population dancing around the golden calf, Moses smashes the tablets and burns the idol, initiating the process of repentance. As a result of the people's fall from their lofty spiritual plateau, Hashem announces that

His presence cannot reside amongst them, and Moses is forced to temporarily move the Tent of Meeting out of the camp so that Hashem can continue to communicate with him. Moses again ascends the mountain to pray to Hashem that the Jewish people should be forgiven and regain their status as the chosen people. Moses eventually returns with the second set of tablets and a renewed covenant with Hashem, his face radiant as a result of his Divine experience.

⬯ # Gold Rush
by Rabbi Elie Cohen

It is the opinion of Rashi that the *Mishkan* was erected as a means to atone for the great sin described in this week's Torah portion – the golden calf. One who studies Rashi's commentary to both the sin of the golden calf and to the section of the Torah dealing with the *Mishkan* notes the following peculiar similarity: As Aaron relates to Moses what occurred to precipitate the sin of the golden calf, he states, "I threw [the gold] into the fire and this calf emerged" (Exodus 32:24). Rashi points out that the calf was formed by itself, without Aaron's effort.

A similar phenomenon occurs with regard to the *menorah* in the *Mishkan*, about which the Torah states, "hammered [out of a single chunk of gold] shall the *menorah* be made" (ibid. 25:31). Rashi explains that the passive wording "be made", as opposed to the more common active form, indicates that the *menorah* was also formed by itself. He continues to explain that Moses had difficulty with the construction of the *menorah* because of its complicated nature, so Hashem told him to throw a chunk of gold into the fire and the *menorah* would emerge on its own. Thus, both the *menorah* and the golden calf were made by casting gold into a fire, forming by themselves. What significance does this correlation have?

The commentaries state that the root of the sin of the golden calf was not an overt desire to worship idols. In fact, the Jewish people originally intended for the calf simply to act as a replacement for Moses (whom they thought had died while atop the mountain), an intermediary between them and Hashem. If so, what caused their grievous transgression? The root of the sin was that the Children of Israel were prepared to innovate a new form of relating to Hashem without properly consulting with Aaron.

Therefore, when the *Mishkan* is actually constructed (in next week's portion), the Torah continually stresses that everything was made "as Hashem commanded Moses." Although the master builders and craftsman certainly had their own ideas for the construction of the *Mishkan*, they simply followed the Divine directives without incorporating any of their own changes. In a general way, we can see how the *Mishkan* was an atonement for the sin of the golden calf.

This lesson is demonstrated more acutely in the specific instance of the *menorah*. The Talmud (Tractate Baba Batra) informs us that the *menorah* could not be fashioned even by Moses, but instead had to be produced through a miracle of Hashem. This symbolizes the idea that all wisdom, represented by the *menorah*, can ultimately be attained only through Hashem. Even Moses, the greatest man alive, was unable to comprehend everything, and had to turn to Hashem, the source of all wisdom, for assistance. If this is true, then to attempt to innovate changes in His service, contrary to His wisdom, is illogical. How can we be wiser than the source of all wisdom!

Therefore, the *menorah* was made in the same way as the golden calf. We are being told, "If you would like to make innovations in the service of Hashem by casting a chunk of gold into the fire to make an idol which you consider to be an improvement, then consider the *menorah*. Its lesson lies in the fact that it too could not be made without Divine assistance and was formed in the fire by itself." It doesn't pay to try to be smarter than Hashem. It is He to whom we turn for wisdom and understanding. Let us try to use this gift in congruence with His Torah.

Misplaced Priorities

by Benyamin Cohen

While perusing this section of the Torah, it is quite interesting to note that the *mitzvah* to construct the *Mishkan* came after the Revelation at Mt. Sinai. The focal point of the *Mishkan* was the holy Ark which held the two tablets. Wouldn't it have made more sense to first prepare the place to keep the tablets and then receive them? Why wasn't the *Mishkan* built first?

From this seemingly simple question, a powerful life-lesson emerges. When we go to the nearest Judaic gift shop, we often spend a great deal of time examining the beautiful artwork on the *mezuzah* cases, but do we spend as much time inspecting the quality of the scroll that goes within the case? All too often, we immerse ourselves in the secondary purpose, totally forgetting the main objective. We spend time and money purchasing an exquisite *talit* and *tefillin* bag, yet we do not show nearly as much enthusiasm for the contents therein. By placing the construction of the *Mishkan* <u>after</u> the revelation at Mt. Sinai, the Torah is reminding us not to lose sight of the true purpose. The tablets and Ten Commandments engraved upon them are what's important; the holy Ark which contains them is secondary. More time should be spent learning and honoring the Torah than crafting the Ark which holds it. Will it be the *challah* cover or the *challah*, the beautiful synagogue sanctuary or the prayers said within? We must never lose sight of our priority to fulfill Hashem's *mitzvot* to our utmost capabilities.

PARSHAT VAYAKHEL/PEKUDEI

 his week we read the final portion of Exodus, a book which began with the Jewish people enslaved to Pharaoh in Egypt and now ends with the completion of the construction of the Mishkan *in the desert. This second book is referred to by the commentaries as the book of redemption, and that is the theme which runs throughout, from the beginning of Parshat Shmot to the end of Parshat Pekudei. Redemption was not achieved solely by escaping from slavery; receiving the Torah at Mt. Sinai gave purpose to that freedom, and the resting of Hashem's presence amongst His nation (the result of the completion of the* Mishkan*) marks the climax of that salvation.*

Parshat Vayakhel (Exodus 35:1-38:20) begins with Moses assembling the entire nation of Israel to transmit to them everything that Hashem commanded him about the construction and fabrication of the Mishkan *in the previous three Torah portions. However, Moses first cautions them yet again about the fundamental* mitzvah *to observe* Shabbat, *reminding them that although the construction of the* Mishkan *is of transcendent importance, it does not take precedence over the weekly observance of* Shabbat. *Only a day earlier, on Yom Kippur, Moses descended Mt. Sinai with the second set of tablets in hand, informing the people that they had been forgiven by Hashem for the horrible sin of worshipping the golden calf. In response to Moses' call, the Children of Israel come forward with their generous contributions for the construction of the*

Mishkan, *producing a surplus of supplies. The craftsmen are selected and the building begins, as the Torah describes in detail the fabrication of every aspect of the* Mishkan.

Parshat Pekudei (ibid. 38:21-40:38) begins with a complete accounting of the gold, silver, and copper contributed by the people for use in the Mishkan. *The Torah goes on to describe the weaving and crafting of the various vestments to be worn by the* Kohen Gadol *during his service. Following Moses' inspection and approval of the many utensils and unassembled parts, Moses sets up the* Mishkan *on* Rosh Chodesh Nissan *as each part is anointed and arranged in its proper location. And as Hashem promised, His glory fills the* Mishkan.

∞ **Backdraft**

by Benyamin Cohen

At the beginning of Parshat Vayakhel we learn about the prohibition to light fire and the general rule of refraining from work on the holy day of *Shabbat.* Many commentators expound on this idea and note that when we refrain from work, we are presented with such an abundance of free time that we don't even know what to do with it. Picture this scenario: While relaxing with friends in the gazebo in the backyard, the conversation turns to remarks about other people – "Did you hear what happened to . . . ?" or, "I heard that. . . ." When people have nothing better to do, it is very easy and quite tempting to start a discussion about David, Michael, Debbie, or Ruth. What ends up happening is that "fires" are lit. And before the first fire of ill will is extinguished, it has become a blaze that can rage out of control.

Gossip and slander turn into a fiery ball that consumes anything and everybody in its path. What the Torah is hinting to us is not only must we refrain from starting an actual fire on *Shabbat,* but also prevent ourselves from igniting a fire of the mouth, where sparks fly all over the place. We must try to contain ourselves from speaking evil and continuously be aware of where the fire extinguisher is at all times.

∞ Divine Architecture
by Eyal Feiler

The beginning of Parshat Vayakhel sounds a lot like an inventory at the Sinai Home Depot. A detailed list of the hardware donated to the *Mishkan* by the Children of Israel is provided, and not only are the raw materials mentioned, but also the individuals who donated the items. One group which is specifically singled out is the twelve princes, each of whom represented one of the twelve tribes of Israel. We are told that "the princes brought the *shoham* stones and the stones for the breastplate" (Exodus 35:27). Rashi states that the princes declared that they would make their donation to the *Mishkan* last, in order to supplement any shortage of donated goods. However, since the nation's contributions were more than enough for the construction, the princes were left with nothing to give except for the above-mentioned stones. Learning from their mistake, they were first in line several months later to present gifts for the *Mishkan's* dedication.

The *Midrash* points out that during the construction of the *Mishkan*, Moses did not want to take any advice from the princes. They therefore sat silently and passively on the sidelines, reckoning that Moses would call upon them if and when he needed their help and advice. However, when they heard the announcement in the camp of Israel that no more donations were needed, the princes became concerned that they had missed the opportunity of participating in the building of the *Mishkan*. Therefore, they made a big financial commitment on their own by donating the precious stones for the *Kohen Gadol's* breastplate.

This commentary seems problematic. Could it be that Moses, the most humble of all people, insisted that the princes sit idly during the *Mishkan's* construction? Was Moses too arrogant to accept advice from the distinguished representatives of the twelve tribes? Although Moses may have been a great leader, he certainly was not an experienced building contractor. Furthermore, Moses himself later told his own successor, Joshua, that when he takes over the reins of leadership he should seek the counsel of the nation's elders, following their opinions and suggestions. To that advice, Hashem responded to Joshua that the burden of leadership was on his own shoulders: "There can be but one leader for the generation" (Rashi on Deuteronomy 31:7). Did Moses think that Joshua was not as capable as himself to lead the Jewish people?

According to Rabbi Ben Zion Firer, Moses and Joshua faced two different types of situations. Moses was occupied with building holy objects. In this endeavor there can be no room for input from Man. Everything is built according to the specifications outlined in the Torah by Hashem. Even the plans of Betzalel, the *Mishkan's* architect, were governed by Divine stipulations. Moses' participation in the construction of the *Mishkan* was also dictated by Hashem, as Hashem says to Moses, "You should build the *Mishkan* according to the fashion which I showed you on the mountain" (Exodus 26:30).

Moses believed that unlike the building of the *Mishkan*, Joshua's primary mission of settling the land of Israel was not entirely dictated by the Torah. In fact, Moses himself listened to the demands of the Jewish people in the desert by sending the spies to scout the land of Israel before they entered it. Therefore, he felt that when conquering Israel, Joshua could accept outside advice by following the guidance of the elders.

However, contrary to Moses, Hashem declared that issues concerning the settlement of Israel are similar in nature to matters regarding the *Mishkan*. Only Hashem can dictate the Holy Land's settlement and there can be no human deliberation in the matter. Thus, when Moses told Joshua to seek the guidance of the elders, Hashem in turn told Joshua the exact opposite by stating that there can be only one leader for the generation – Joshua, by himself without the elders.

The *Mishkan's* assembly highlights one aspect of the relationship that the Jewish people have with Hashem. Although there was no human input in the design of the *Mishkan*, it was up to Moses and the Jewish people in the desert to build Hashem's dwelling place. Rather than create the holy vessels Himself, Hashem requires Man to exert his own effort in creating and fashioning the *Mishkan*. Similarly, Hashem gave us the Torah so that we can use it as an instruction manual for building our lives. It is up to us to develop ourselves so that we can withstand the trial and tribulations of life. Fortunately, just as Moses was successful in building the *Mishkan* by following Hashem's command, we are assured that by following the Torah step by step, we too will be successful in our own personal construction.

☞ Order in the Tabernacle
by Joshua Gottlieb

"I don't have time!" This statement is an all too common aphorism in today's society. We have many things to accomplish each day, yet by nightfall we are inevitably behind in completing our tasks. How might we better manage our time and thereby accomplish more every day?

With regard to the construction of the *Mishkan* in this week's portion the Torah states, "Betzalel, son of Uri the son of Chur, of the tribe of Judah, did everything that Hashem commanded Moses" (Exodus 38:22). This verse raises a formidable question: How was Betzalel able to make everything Hashem commanded Moses? Betzalel wasn't present when Hashem directed Moses to build the *Mishkan*!? Rashi, the fundamental commentator on the Torah, explains that the verse teaches us that through *ruach hakodesh*, Divine inspiration, Betzalel knew even those things which Moses did not tell him. Although he was not present when Hashem issued the commands to Moses, Betzalel was still able to construct the *Mishkan* exactly according to Hashem's specification. Rashi proves that Betzalel knew everything through *ruach hakodesh* from the fact that when Moses told Betzalel to make the vessels of the *Mishkan* first, and only then construct the *Mishkan* structure itself, Betzalel corrected Moses and informed him that it was to be done the other way around.

The Kli Yakar agrees with Rashi that the verse in fact teaches us that Betzalel knew how to build the *Mishkan* through his own *ruach hakodesh*. However, he refutes Rashi's proof and maintains that, in reality, Moses told Betzalel everything in its correct order.

Why does it matter whether the *Mishkan* structure or the vessels were made first? Rabbi Yerucham Levovitz explains that from here we see the importance of putting everything in its proper order. We will never have enough time each day to accomplish all that we would like. Therefore, we must establish priorities in our lives so that we may achieve as much as possible in the time allotted to us.

Hashem, M.D.
by Michael Alterman

If one were to quickly glance through this week's second Torah portion of Pekudei, one may notice that there is a phrase which seems to recur time and again. Repeatedly, the Torah informs us that the parts of the *Mishkan* were constructed and assembled "as Hashem had commanded Moses", in accordance with the blueprints and specifications delineated and taught by Hashem to Moses. In fact, this phrase appears in one form or another eighteen times throughout the Torah portion. Why did Hashem find it necessary to repeat such a detail so many times?

Our rabbis taught that the *Mishkan* was meant to serve as an atonement for the horrible sin of the golden calf. As we know, the Jewish people did not initially intend for the calf to be a form of idol worship. It was supposed to be a "go between", an intermediary in their worship of Hashem; a tangible object through which their service of Hashem would be enhanced and revitalized. They believed this to be necessary because they mistakenly thought that Moses, their representative to G-d, had died while upon the mountain. Failing to take into consideration the second creed of the Ten Commandments, "Thou shalt not make a graven image," the Children of Israel used their own judgment, deciding to introduce an unsolicited addition to their relationship with Hashem. It was for this error in judgment that Hashem reacted so zealously, threatening to destroy the entire nation, because the concept of one G-d is the central and primary tenet in Judaism.

Hashem commanded the construction of the *Mishkan* to provide the Jewish people with a much-needed physical structure from which to serve Hashem and also to stand in stark contrast to the golden calf which they had recently worshipped. The *Mishkan's* outward appearance would seem to the casual observer to be very similar to the golden calf, since several of the *Mishkan's* structures were made from pure gold just like the calf. The golden *cherubim* which rested upon the Ark were magnificent physical structures, comparable to the golden calf which the Children of Israel had so recently formed.

However, with all of their apparent similarities, the one major difference between catastrophe and sanctification lay in Hashem's command to Moses. The golden calf was an attempt by the people to gain proximity to Hashem through their own method, failing to take into consideration that they had been warned specifically and clearly against such action. Conversely, the construction of the *Mishkan* was precipitated by Hashem's command and supervision. It is for this reason that our Torah portion repeats and emphasizes at every step of the construction that the *Mishkan* was being made "as Hashem had commanded Moses."

LEVITICUS

PARSHAT VAYIKRA

his Shabbat *marks the beginning of our reading the third book of the Torah,* Sefer Vayikra, *which deals primarily with the services and responsibilities of the* Kohanim. *This (and next) week's portion focuses on many of the* korbanot *to be brought in the newly-constructed* Mishkan. *Parshat Vayikra (Leviticus 1:1-5:26) begins with Hashem calling Moses into the* Mishkan *where he will receive the many relevant* mitzvot *to be ultimately passed on to the Jewish people. The first half of the Torah portion describes the various optional* korbanot *brought by individuals. They can be classified into three general categories, each one comprised of several gradations in size and expense: the* korban olah *(elevation offering) which is completely consumed on the altar; the* korban minchah *(meal offering) which, because of its inexpensive contents, is usually brought by someone of modest means; and the* korban shelamim *(peace offering) partially burned on the altar, with the remainder divided between the owners and the* Kohanim. *The second half of the portion (beginning with chapter four) discusses the required* chatat *(sin) and* asham *(guilt) offerings to be brought in atonement for unintentional transgressions.*

∞ Quality vs. Quantity
by Rabbi Chaim Goldberger

Of all the *korbanot* introduced in this week's Torah portion, the only one that does not require the sacrifice of an animal is the *korban minchah*, an offering of flour mixed with oil and incense brought as a low-cost alternative to the more impressive bullock or fowl offerings. Yet, when the Torah describes the people who bring each of the various offerings to the Temple, the only one singled out and identified as being a *"nefesh* – soul" is the person who brings the lowly *korban minchah* (Leviticus 2:1). The Talmud (Tractate Menachot 104b) elaborates: "Why is the *korban minchah* distinguished in that its bearer is termed a *nefesh*? Hashem declares: 'Who generally brings a *korban minchah*? The poor man. I will consider his act as if he sacrificed his entire soul.'"

It can be assumed that to one who is impoverished, the act of parting with fine flour which he might otherwise eat to silence his hunger is an even greater act of sacrifice than that of the rich man giving up an expensive animal. To the pauper, the flour is more than a large portion of his possessions. It is his very life. The Torah is teaching us that it is not the size of the gift that determines the magnitude of the sacrifice; rather the importance lies in the giver's intentions and circumstances.

When Jacob dispatched his sons to encounter the mysterious ruler in Egypt, he sent them with a gift. This tribute was indeed a small one – "a bit of balsam, a bit of honey, wax, lotus, pistachios, and almonds" (Genesis 43:11) – but its significance lay not in its size. These items had been carefully deliberated upon and specially selected. They were delicacies that were unavailable in Egypt at the time. Their message was one of painstaking care and thoughtful concern. And quite appropriately, Jacob called the gift a *"minchah"*.

Of all our daily prayers, the one that is the shortest is *Minchah*, the afternoon service. It contains neither the long introductory and closing segments of the *Shacharit* morning service, nor the *Shema* and *Barchu* prayers of the *Ma'ariv* evening service. It is basically just the *Shemoneh Esrei*, yet the afternoon service is the only one which we call by the name *"minchah"*. Why? Because, as "impoverished" as this service appears, it is the only one that comes right in the middle of our workday; it is the only one that asks us to drop whatever we are busy doing and remind ourselves that we are merely subjects of our great Almighty Master. *Minchah* is the only prayer service that asks us to disconnect ourselves from our mundane and worldly mindset and retreat into a sudden and total encounter with the Divine. It may take just fifteen minutes, but it is a *minchah*. It reminds us of the motivation necessary in gift-giving of all kinds, that it is not only the size that counts. The meaning and the intentions are equally significant.

∞ Sacrifices 101
by Rabbi Danny Gimpel

The third book of the Torah, *Sefer Vayikra*, which we begin to read this week is also called by our sages "*Torat Kohanim* – the law of the priests". This name is very appropriate because of the tremendous number of laws and details of the *Kohanim's* sacrificial services in the *Mishkan* elucidated in this book. For many in our Western society, the concept of animal sacrifice is difficult to comprehend, and most people simply attribute such practices to primitive civilizations. Perhaps to better understand the role of animal sacrifice we should try to determine the purpose of a sacrifice. The first step would be to understand the Hebrew word for sacrifice, "*korban*", which comes from the same root as the word "*karov* – to come close." A *korban* is a means through which we draw close to Hashem.

When someone upsets us, our usual reaction is to become angry, and as a result we distance ourselves from that person. We are displeased with him until we eventually forgive and forget or until we are appeased. Similarly when we sin, we distance ourselves from Hashem because of our displeasing actions which damage our relationship with Him. *Korbanot* provide a means for repairing this impaired relationship, bringing us close to Hashem once again. Still, how are we to understand on some level that sacrificing an actual animal can lead to this proximity to Hashem?

Many commentators explain that the killing of an animal is meant to represent what the transgressor himself actually deserves for violating Hashem's command, and the animal serves as a substitute for the transgressor's punishment. When a person sees the *korban* resting on the altar, he is supposed to envision himself in the animal's place, a thought which should arouse feelings of *teshuvah*. The act of slaughtering an animal also plays a role in the retribution of the sinner in the heavenly courts, achieving a degree of forgiveness.

Perhaps by utilizing a different approach to understanding the animal sacrifice, we might gain some sense of appreciation for what was expressed by such an act. To develop a successful relationship between a husband and wife, each one must be concerned for the other's needs and possess the ability to give one to the other. This giving may very often conflict with one's personal needs and desires, yet the "sacrifice" of self-interest to support and provide for the other strengthens the relationship with feelings of love, dependence, and dedication. If we could imagine living in an agricultural society and livestock are our major possessions, then if required to part with our most prized assets by offering it to Hashem, we would indeed feel the sacrifice. This sacrifice would be viewed either as a punishment or, if voluntarily brought, would cultivate feelings of love through the giving of oneself to Hashem. It is difficult to understand Hashem's "pleasure" from the sacrifice, but the human dimension of giving draws us closer to Hashem in a very real sense.

This same closeness can be accomplished today, even without sacrifices, through a different means of giving of ourselves. The Rambam writes that the greatest positive *mitzvah* in the Torah is the giving of charity because it brings unification to the Jewish people, which he says will lead to the eventual coming of the *Mashiach*. From the lesson of the sacrifices, let us resolve to assist our fellow Jews in need, while at the same time helping ourselves become better human beings.

PARSHAT TZAV

*P*arshat Tzav *(Leviticus 6:1-8:36) begins with Hashem continuing to teach Moses many of the various laws relating to the* Mishkan *service. However, while last week's portion described the* korbanot *from the perspective of the giver, this week the Torah focuses more directly on the* Kohanim, *providing further detail about their service. After first describing the maintenance of the fire which burned on the altar, the Torah discusses in detail the various kinds of* korbanot *which Aaron, his sons, and the succeeding generations of* Kohanim *would be offering. The offerings must be brought with the proper intentions and eaten in a state of spiritual purity. Finally, Moses performs the lengthy* melu'im, *consecration service of the* Mishkan, *and Moses anoints and inaugurates Aaron and his sons for their service in the* Mishkan, *in front of the entire congregation of Israel.*

⊂∂ ## Body & Soul

by Rabbi Shimon Wiggins

If this week's Torah portion was to be accompanied with sound effects, a rousing alarm would be heard, motivating us to take action, for it begins with Hashem telling Moses to command Aaron and his sons regarding the *korban olah*. The language of the verse that instructs Moses to do so is peculiar. Usually Hashem tells Moses, "Speak to the Children of Israel" or "Say unto them". However, here the Torah uses the term "*tzav* – command [Aaron and his sons]". This word indicates that there is an urgency and importance regarding what will follow. What is so important and urgent about the *korban olah?*

Furthermore, Rashi quotes the *Midrash*, pointing out that the Hebrew word *"tzav"* connotes urgency to action in the present <u>and</u> in the future. Why does this *mitzvah* require such strong language to ensure its fulfillment in future generations while no such emphasis is utilized for most *mitzvot* of the Torah?

The key to resolving this mystery lies in Rashi's next statement – the Torah uses the word *"tzav"* when a monetary loss is involved in performing a *mitzvah*. In our case, it is a financial obligation upon the Jewish nation to bring the *korban olah* twice daily. Therefore, the Torah uses the word *"tzav"* to strongly charge us in this *mitzvah's* fulfillment despite the monetary loss. But is the monetary loss really so great? After all, the entire Jewish nation shares in the obligation to bring the daily offerings. Aren't there other *mitzvot* that result in a greater monetary loss?

Rabbi Shimon Schwab offers an enlightening analysis of the Jewish nation's relationship to *korbanot*. There are two aspects to *korbanot*. The first is the physical animal which is being offered to Hashem, while the second aspect is the intent of the person bringing the *korban*. These two aspects are not given equal value. In Hashem's eyes, the essential aspect of a *korban* is the intent, motive, and attitude of the person offering it; the physical component is only of secondary importance. Throughout history, it has been Man's challenge to properly combine these two aspects.

Being overly concerned with the physical aspect of the offering is completely missing the point. According to the Sforno, this is why Cain's offering was rejected by Hashem (Genesis 4:3-7). Cain thought that Hashem was only interested in the physical gift. Since his intent was not to come closer to Hashem, his offering was rejected.

Overemphasis of the physical aspect of *korbanot* was the Jewish nation's error during the period of the First Temple. Numerous verses in the Prophets reprove the Jewish nation for merely bringing animals without any sincere intent to become closer to the Divine.

However, later during the period of the Second Temple, the exact opposite occurred. The Jewish nation completely ignored the physical aspect of *korbanot*. They reasoned that if the essential aspect of a sacrifice is to grow spiritually, then why bother with the physical aspect. Does it really matter if the animal does not come from the best of the flock?

Once again, the Jewish nation is reproved by the Prophets. Indeed, one's intent is the essential factor when bringing a sacrifice. But one cannot overlook the physical aspect. As human beings composed of a body and a soul, we must serve Hashem on both physical and spiritual levels. Just as we cannot ignore the physicality of our own being, we also cannot ignore the physical aspect of serving Hashem.

Now we can understand the Torah's concern of there being a monetary loss with regard to *korbanot* and especially with regard to the *korban olah*. Since a *korban olah* is completely burned on the altar, and knowing that Hashem is essentially concerned with a person's intent, one could easily assume that the physical aspect doesn't matter, precipitating a desire to limit the monetary expense. Therefore, the Torah stresses the word "*tzav* – command" which connotes urgency now and for future generations. The Torah is telling us that even when we realize the importance of sincere intent in serving Hashem, we must also be sensitive to the physical aspect.

A practical example of this challenge faces us every day during prayer. If I have proper intent to accept Hashem's sovereignty, then does it really matter if I pronounce the words of prayer correctly? Doesn't Hashem know what I am thinking? The answer is a resounding yes. But there is an equally resounding imperative to serve Hashem with our physical being as well, and thus use the totality of our existence in Hashem's service.

❧ A Single Scoop
by Micah Gimpel

Like much of the portion, the beginning of Parshat Tzav is involved in the instructions to the *Kohanim* regarding their daily service in the *Mishkan*. The Torah appears to offer technical and practical advice on how to deal with the accumulation of ashes remaining on the altar from the offerings of the previous day: "[The *Kohen*] shall separate the ash of what the fire consumed of the *korban olah* on the altar, and place it next to the altar" (Leviticus 6:3). Since the ashes from the offerings will amass on the altar as each day passes, we need a method of clearing space to allow for the next day's services. Therefore, at first glance we would assume that the Torah is wisely recommending that we remove the ashes every morning.

Surprisingly, the rabbis understood this statement not as a requirement to clear the <u>entire</u> altar, but merely as an obligation to remove a <u>single scoop</u> of ashes every day and place it on the side of the altar. This nullifies the practical benefit of the separation, since the rest of the ashes will remain on the altar until the accumulation makes further offerings impossible. Many commentators speculate about the significance of this obligatory separation which seems to have no practical benefit. Rabbi Samson Raphael Hirsch suggests that by taking a portion of yesterday's service and placing it on the side of the altar before continuing with today's service, symbolically the *Kohen* is making a national declaration that today we will continue to serve Hashem as we did yesterday, according to the dictates of His will.

Rabbi Ze'ev Zechariah Breuer, grandson of the above-mentioned Rabbi Hirsch, develops an alternate explanation along the same lines. This separation of the ashes begins the service in the Temple every day. When the *Kohen* reaches his place to start a new day of work, he stands before all of the remains from the previous days, piled high upon the altar. The ashes are symbolic of our past, complete with our many errors and mistakes. If it were possible for a person to begin every day fresh with a clean slate, without an accumulation of "ashes", we would perceive the future to be free of any foreseeable failures, as if our mistakes of the past had never actually occurred.

The Torah, however, instructs us otherwise. The ashes of the past are still there. We must reflect on the past as we move toward the future. Our relationship with Hashem and our fellowman should not remain static. All of our relationships carry a certain amount of baggage and nothing eases that load overnight. If we choose to ignore our problems from the past, then they will remain problems, obviating the relationship's continual growth. The *Kohen*, therefore, leaves most of the ashes on the altar, as a reminder.

However, we are certainly obligated to attempt to rectify matters as much as possible. Just as we cannot sweep our problems under the carpet, so too we must realize that our faults cannot be remedied all at once. We can, however, work on our faults, little by little. The lesson of the daily separation of the ashes is that when confronted with the buildup of remains from the past, we are expected to make corrections by removing a little ash everyday, gradually yet continuously.

℘ Hashem's Fragrant Perfume
by Rabbi Dov Ber Weisman

Since the first two Torah portions of Leviticus deal almost exclusively with the sacrificial service, we may wonder of what relevance are these offerings to us. We unfortunately do not have a holy Temple today, and consequently no longer have the opportunity to perform these services. Perhaps the following insight can help us relate better to the *korbanot* of old and, in turn, to our current service of Hashem.

With regard to many of the offerings, the Torah states that they shall be "a pleasing aroma to Hashem", regardless of whether the offering was a valuable bullock brought by a wealthy businessman or its inexpensive alternative – a meal offering brought by a destitute pauper.

Our rabbis comment, "It is the same whether one does more or less, provided that he intends it for the sake of Heaven" (Talmud Tractate Berachot 5b). The question, however, could still be raised that if both the rich and the poor are giving equally for the sake of Heaven, then isn't the one who is making a greater contribution accomplishing more than the one who is giving less? How can the rabbis say that they are equal?

The Sfas Emes resolves this dilemma by teaching us an extremely important lesson about what it is that Hashem expects from us. He explains that our main task in life is to perform our particular commitment wholeheartedly and to fulfill our potential in our service of Hashem. If we are doing all that we can and are truly incapable of anything more, then although our contribution may be minimal, it is just as good as somebody with greater potential who is doing more. Both individuals are working with a sincere heart, striving to fulfill their potential. It is irrelevant that one is actually giving more than the other. People have different strengths, different potentials, but they are all essentially doing the same thing – using everything that they have in order to serve Hashem. And that is all Hashem wants from us – to serve Him in sincerity and in truth to the best of our abilities.

With this in mind, a person should never despair in what he is doing, as Hashem views everyone individually, realizing their unique characteristics and position in life. This means that each and every prayer, *mitzvah*, and act of kindness that we do is cherished by Hashem as He sees His beloved children yearning to serve Him wholeheartedly, in truth and love. Therefore, no matter what your sacrifice may be, know that it shall always be "a pleasing aroma to Hashem".

PARSHAT SHEMINI

his week's Torah portion, Parshat Shemini *(Leviticus 9:1-11:47), begins by discussing the events which occurred on the eighth and final day of the* melu'im, *inauguration service in the* Mishkan. *After months of preparation and anticipation, Aaron and his sons are finally installed as* Kohanim *in an elaborate service. Aaron blesses the people, and the entire nation rejoices as Hashem's presence rests upon them. However, the excitement comes to an abrupt halt as Aaron's two eldest sons, Nadav and Avihu, are consumed by a heavenly fire and die in the* Mishkan *while offering the* ketoret *on the altar. The Torah states that they died because they brought a "strange fire" into the inner sanctum of the* Mishkan, *the meaning of which is discussed by the commentators at great length. Aaron is commanded that the* Kohanim *are forbidden to enter the* Mishkan *while intoxicated, and the Torah continues to relate the events which occur immediately after Nadav and Avihu's tragic deaths. The portion concludes with a listing of the kosher and non-kosher animals, and various laws about* tumah, *ritual contamination.*

☜ Death in the Family
by Joshua S. Feingold

Put yourself in Aaron's shoes. You have just been informed that two of your precious sons have died. Imagine the trauma of losing two beloved children in one day, and then amplify this grief with the knowledge that at the time of their death they were trying to serve Hashem. The *Mishkan* had just been erected, and they were bringing the *ketoret* for the first time in what could have been long careers of service to Hashem. Think about the pain and suffering that Aaron must have felt.

Most people would question Hashem's justice. They would ask, "Why did they die? They were trying to do good! They were trying their best to serve You!" This essentially would be asking the most fundamental question ever posed in history: Why do bad things happen to good people? In light of this, Aaron's reaction to the horrible news is enigmatic. The Torah relates that "Aaron was silent" (Leviticus 10:3) – he did not respond. Apparently, Aaron did not question Hashem's actions; rather he remained quiet and accepted their death as the will of G-d.

We find a similar phenomenon in Aaron's behavior upon considering the passage in the Torah where Hashem initially sends Moses and Aaron to request from Pharaoh that the Jewish people be freed from slavery. Instead of releasing the slaves, Pharaoh responds by increasing their workload. Moses could not comprehend how Hashem could have commanded them to ask for freedom, knowing that nothing good would come from it. Moses therefore asks Hashem, "Why have you done evil to this people, why have you sent me?" (Exodus 5:22). In essence, Moses was also asking the question of why bad things happen to good people. It is interesting to note that although Aaron was also present when Pharaoh increased the burden, and even though Aaron was mentioned in the previous verse, the Torah only reports that Moses asked this basic question. The Torah does not mention whether Aaron also asked Hashem why He "did evil to this people." Did Aaron not also have the same question? From the reaction he has to his sons' deaths, it would seem that although the question may have bothered Aaron, he did not ask. What gave Aaron the strength not to question Hashem when things turned sour?

By examining Aaron's childhood, perhaps we can discern how he learned this important lesson. Aaron grew up in Egypt during a period when every Jewish newborn baby boy was drowned in the Nile. Imagine his thoughts when he found out that his mother had given birth to his brother Moses. Young Aaron must have wondered why Hashem would be so cruel as to bring a child into the world merely to be cast into the river. However, he soon learned that Moses was saved from death by Pharaoh's daughter, and destined to become the redeemer of the Jewish people from Egyptian bondage. Through experience, Aaron learned that everything that Hashem does has a purpose. He discovered that bad things do <u>not</u> happen to good people. Rather, with the narrow outlook on the world which humans intrinsically possess, we cannot fathom the real good that surrounds us.

So what about us? It is very difficult for a person of non-biblical proportions to realize that Hashem does only good. The Zoroastrians of the second Temple period could not comprehend that something which appears bad could really be good. Instead, they claimed that there must be two separate entities running the world, both a good force and a separate evil force. How can we come to the profound recognition that everything, even what appears to be bad, is really good?

Be a student of Aaron. Look back on your life and consider some of the things which appeared to be bad at the time, and then developed into something good. Of course, because of our narrow outlook on life, we will be unable to answer all of our questions. Many of us will still feel like Rabbi Yannai (*Pirkei Avot* 4:19) who said, "We cannot grasp neither the tranquillity of the evildoers nor the suffering of the righteous." However, eventually we will receive answers to all of our questions. As we say three times a day in the last line of the *Aleinu* prayer, the prophet Zachariah foretold that there will come a time when ". . .His name will be one." The prophet meant that when the *Mashiach* comes we will realize that everything, both the good and the bad, was really determined by the one caring G-d and was in fact all for the best.

∞ Soul Food

by Rabbi Norman Schloss

In this week's Torah portion we are taught many of the parameters for the laws of Kashruth. The Rambam explains that these laws of "clean" and "unclean" animals are *chukim*, decrees which Hashem gave us for the betterment of ourselves. While we may not understand the reasons and intentions behind these particular laws, we nevertheless adhere to them as we would to any other *mitzvah* from Hashem.

Rabbi Yitzchak Abarbanel adds that many people may think that the laws of Kashruth were given to us for health reasons. He refutes this theory for two reasons. First, if the purpose of these decrees was merely for reasons of health, then this section of the Torah could be reduced to a brief medical book and the rest discarded. Secondly, we clearly find that gentiles eat all kinds of foods and do not seem to be any less healthy from a medical standpoint.

Rather, explains Abarbanel, the Torah is not teaching us about physical health, but about spiritual health. The reason for the Kashruth laws is in order to refine our special souls and keep them in a pristine state. For the non-Jew, eating is a way of sustaining himself from day-to-day; therefore, he may eat whatever he wants. This is not so for the Jewish people who have a special place at Hashem's side and whose souls cannot tolerate spiritually harmful foods.

Many times when I do Kosher supervision, I am asked the reason why we keep Kosher. I explain as follows: Let us suppose that a person went to a doctor for a regular examination. The doctor calls him into his office and explains that the patient has contracted a serious disease and that for the rest of his life he must adhere to a very limited and strict diet. Failure to comply with this special diet could be disastrous and the person could die. Of course, any rational person would immediately comply with the strictures imposed upon him by the doctor.

In much the same way, the Supreme Doctor, Hashem Himself, prescribed for us those foods that are beneficial to our spiritual well-being and forbade the detrimental ones. In the same way that we would follow "doctor's orders" for physical ailments, so too must we follow Hashem's orders without question.

Still another theory behind the laws of Kashruth is that we become what we eat. An example of this can be seen in the explanation of Rashi for the prohibition of eating stork. The Torah calls the stork "*chasidah*" (Leviticus 11:19), from the Hebrew word *chesed*, kindness. Citing the Talmud, Rashi explains that the stork is called by this name because it displays kindness towards other members of its species by sharing food with them. The question therefore begs itself, if the stork is so compassionate, why then is it not Kosher? The Rizhiner Rebbe explains that this is because the stork only shows compassion towards those of its own species, while it ignores all others. To the Jewish people, this is not an admirable trait, for we have an obligation to be charitable to all.

In conclusion, we see that for the Jewish people, chosen by Hashem, the laws of Kashruth are much more than just dietary ordinances to ensure our physical health. They are a way of improving ourselves as we strive to come closer to Hashem.

PARSHAT TAZRIA/METZORA

fter the discussion at the end of last week's portion regarding tumah *resulting from dead animals, Parshat Tazria (Leviticus 12:1-13:59) introduces the various categories of* tumah *emanating from human beings, beginning with a woman upon giving birth. The rest of the portion describes in great detail the varying and numerous manifestations of the disease called* tzaraat. *Although it has been commonly mistranslated as leprosy, this skin disease has little resemblance to any bodily ailment transmitted through normal exposure. Rather,* tzaraat *is the physical manifestation of a spiritual malaise, a punishment from Hashem primarily for the sin of speaking* lashon hara, *amongst other transgressions and anti-social behavior. Known as a* metzora, *someone afflicted by a* tzaraat-*like patch on his skin is subject to a series of examinations by a* Kohen, *who declares the patient to be either* tahor *or* tamei. *If* tamei, *he is isolated outside of the camp, an appropriate punishment for someone whose foul tongue caused others to become separated from one another. After describing the various forms, colors, and manifestations of the disease on a person's skin, head, and beard, the portion concludes with a discussion of garments contaminated by* tzaraat.

Parshat Metzora (ibid. 14:1-15:33) continues the discussion of tzaraat, *detailing the three-part purification process of the* metzora *administered by a* Kohen, *complete with immersions,* korbanot, *and the shaving of the entire body. After a lengthy description of* tzaraat *on houses and the command to demolish the entire residence if the disease has spread, the final chapter of the portion discusses several categories of natural human discharges which render a person impure to varying degrees.*

⤜ Labor Pains
by Yoel Spotts

When writing a novel, one would surely be careful to arrange the storyline in a logical and orderly fashion, inserting smooth transitions between different topics. Likewise, one would certainly expect the Torah, serving as the very lifeblood of the Jewish people and bearing much more significance than a mere novel, to follow similar guidelines. However, the introductory section of this week's Torah portion seems to diverge from this demanded consistency. Parshat Tazria commences with a discussion of the laws concerning the status of a woman who has recently given birth, and the various procedures which must take place with regard to her and the child. The Torah then immediately proceeds with a detailed description of the different types of spots and discolorations which may render an individual a *metzora*. These two subjects – a woman who has just given birth and a person who is suffering from *tzaraat* – would appear to be totally unconnected. Why then are they placed in such close proximity?

In order to answer this question, it would seem logical that we must first examine the details of these two laws. In Leviticus 12:7 we find that a woman who has just given birth must bring a *korban*: "The *Kohen* shall offer it before Hashem and <u>atone for her</u>, and she becomes purified from the source of her blood; this is the law of one who gives birth to a male or to a female." This law raises an obvious question: What sin has this woman committed that requires atonement?

The rabbis of the Talmud provide an interesting answer to this problem: While under the stress and intense pain of childbirth, this woman very likely may have sworn never to return to her husband, the cause and source of her present suffering. Therefore, when the woman fully recovers, returns to her husband and thereby neglects her previous oath, she has in fact broken this vow. While the Torah recognizes that this oath was taken under great anguish and distress, nonetheless this woman cannot be totally absolved from performing any sort of penitence. After all, she has taken a vow and it cannot be disregarded. Therefore, the Torah affords this woman the opportunity to obtain complete atonement by bringing an offering.

If we now shift our attention to the second issue in question, that of the affliction of *tzaraat*, we discover that the Torah initiates its discussion of the person stricken with this disease without any sort of introduction; the reader is immediately propelled into a comprehensive discussion of the various forms and manifestations of *tzaraat*. The Torah in no place makes mention of the cause of *tzaraat*, thus leaving one to wonder what sin could possibly prompt this disease to afflict one's body and/or property. Rashi offers an answer based upon the Talmud that the primary cause of *tzaraat* is the grievous crime of *lashon hara*. In order to appreciate the gravity of his actions, the speaker of *lashon hara* is afflicted with *tzaraat*. Not only must the affected person deal with lesions covering his body, he is also forced to separate from the general community and undergo a lengthy healing process marked by repeated visits from the *Kohen* to determine the status and development of the disease. It is hoped that all of this misery and torment will help him recognize his misconduct and lead him to repentance.

At this point, we can readily understand the juxtaposition of these two seemingly disconnected subjects. The Torah here wishes to teach us the power of speech. While Western society espouses beliefs such as "sticks and stones may break my bones but names will never hurt me," Judaism attributes much more importance and significance to the spoken word. Every word uttered must be carefully measured. Even an oath taken in the throes of childbirth must be accounted for. Even a seemingly harmless comment about a fellow Jew must be dealt with. Words do mean something. We cannot allow our mouths to run free without any concern for what may result. Just as the Torah was given to us on Mt. Sinai, not by a scroll that fell from the sky, but through the holy word of Hashem, so too must we purify and sanctify our own speech.

≈ Gossip Column
by Benyamin Cohen

Parshat Tazria and Parshat Metzora deal mainly with the laws regarding the *metzora*, one who is afflicted with the spiritual disease of *tzaraat*. As mentioned above, the chief cause of *tzaraat* was the evil sin of *lashon hara*. Those who contracted the coarse lesions covering part of the skin were sent out of the camp for an extended period of time. Just as the disease was of a spiritual nature, so too was the cure. When Hashem saw that the individual had truly repented, the disease vanished and he could once again return to society.

Let us take a closer look at this disease. An individual has just been afflicted with a terrible illness. He has been forced to leave his family and live outside the camp in a state of embarrassment and shame. What is the purpose of this punishment? Wouldn't a public apology in the local Jewish newspaper have been more appropriate?

We must realize that Divine punishment is not motivated by revenge, but is rather a form of therapy. The *metzora* is banished from the camp because he spoke evil about other people. In his current state, outside the confines of the campground and away from human contact, the afflicted individual cries out for companionship. In a sense, he is in solitary confinement. Consequently, he will come to appreciate the sound of a human voice and how fortunate we are to share this world with other people. Once he comprehends the importance of brotherhood and unity, the *metzora* will understand the true power of words and the catastrophic effects they can wield on others if used improperly. He will experience a moral awakening.

As you've probably already figured out, this disease is not around today. Perhaps Hashem knew that most of us would always be afflicted with it. However, the lesson still remains. How careful must we be regarding our daily contact with other people. Unfortunately, we have become accustomed to hearing slander and listening to gossip. The next time someone says, "Did you hear what happened to. . .?", we should try to change the subject or walk away, for as the sages teach, one who listens to gossip is just as guilty as the one who speaks it. Let us take the lesson of the *metzora* to heart and appreciate the veritable meaning of human companionship.

Outbreak

by Michael Alterman

Among the numerous details of *tzaraat* discussed in Parshat Tazria, we find one in particular which seems to run completely counter to human logic. The Torah tells us that if a person is covered completely, from head to toe, with the white patches indicative of *tzaraat*, he is considered not to be afflicted with that dreaded disease and remains *tahor* (Leviticus 13:13). Any lesser affliction limited merely to one area of the body renders him completely *tamei*, and the laws of *tzaraat* become applicable. How can it be that someone having a limited dose of a disease is considered completely afflicted, while one with the largest outbreak imaginable remains totally healthy?

We know that the main purpose of Hashem's causing someone to contract *tzaraat* is to serve as a warning that he isn't being sufficiently scrupulous in his observance of one of several *mitzvot*, including the injunctions against speaking *lashon hara* and behaving arrogantly. The person, therefore, contracts a horrible disease which results in his removal from the camp for an extended period of complete isolation. This can be the perfect opportunity for him to reflect on his path in life and reassess his deeds. Such treatment and isolation is necessary, particularly to uncover "smaller" errors in judgment, the mistakes which would otherwise remain unnoticed. Therefore, for a minor case of *tzaraat*, isolation is required to induce significant introspection. However, if the case of *tzaraat* is so serious that it covers him from head to toe, thereby publicizing his evil ways both to himself and everybody else, an extended period of isolation is not necessary to evoke repentance.

Today, when we do not merit having such clear signs from Hashem, it is incumbent upon us to examine our deeds, constructing our own litmus test to determine whether we are in fact in compliance with the guidelines provided by the Torah. While the correct path is often as clear to us as the *tzaraat* which covered one from head to toe, frequently decisions must be made by carefully evaluating and eliminating many of our inner tendencies and biases – the small patches of *tzaraat*. It is only upon our ultimate internalization of these values that we can assuredly avoid the pitfalls of the *metzora*.

PARSHAT ACHAREI MOT

*he commandments described in Parshat Acharei Mot (Leviticus 16:1-18:30) chronologically follow the tragic deaths of Aaron's two oldest sons, Nadav and Avihu, which we read about in Parshat Shemini several weeks ago. This week's portion begins with a lengthy description of the special* Yom Kippur *service to be performed in the* Mishkan *by the* Kohen Gadol. *The service included the* Kohen Gadol's *confession on behalf of himself and the entire nation; the lottery selection from amongst two identical goats, one of which would become a national sin offering and the other would be pushed off a cliff in the desert as the bearer of the people's sins; and the complex incense and blood-sprinkling ceremonies to be performed in the* Kodesh HaKedoshim *(Holy of Holies). Following the command that* Yom Kippur *and its laws of fasting and refraining from work will be observed eternally by the Jewish people as a day of atonement, the Torah prohibits the offering of* korbanot *outside of the* Mishkan *complex. Blood may not be eaten, and during the* shechitah *(ritual slaughtering) process a portion of the blood spilled must be covered. The Torah portion concludes with a listing of the immoral and forbidden sexual relationships, and the command that the Jewish people maintain and ensure the holiness of the land of Israel.*

Fringe Benefits

by Micah Gimpel

It's *Yom Kippur*. The whole nation has been reflecting on their short-comings of the previous year and planning a strategy for improvement in the coming one. Everyone is in the synagogue praying for a merciful judgment. No one is eating or drinking, no one is wearing leather shoes, and everyone is dressed in white. Our rabbis tell us that on *Yom Kippur* we reach a level of purity like that of angels. What words would a person expect to hear emanating from the pulpit? Considering the gravity and solemnity of the day, one might expect to hear words of retribution, yet instead we read in the Torah something that seems to be completely out of place. Isn't it shocking that in the afternoon service of *Yom Kippur* we read the section from this week's Torah portion about forbidden sexual relations? Why, on the holiest day of the year, are we reading about these specific prohibitions?

In his commentary on the Talmud (Tractate Megilah 31a), Rashi explains that the reason we specifically read this section about forbidden relationships is because "the transgressions of the sexual prohibitions occur because the evil inclination of one's soul desires them and this desire is overwhelming." We read this specific passage since we are constantly challenged regarding promiscuity and, all too often, we falter. Especially on a day and at a time when we are thinking in such holy terms, we need to be reminded of situations when we may likely fail – particularly in the area of physical temptations. This specific reading, considering the atmosphere of the day, should shock us, and that jolt will hopefully last throughout the year whenever we are faced with temptations.

The Talmud (Tractate Menachot 44a) relates a story that exemplifies this idea. A man who was very careful about the *mitzvah* of *tzitzit* heard that the most beautiful woman in the world happened to be a prostitute. In his weakness, he arranged a time to meet her. When the scheduled time came, the man arrived and the temptation to act on his desires was enormous. As he removed his shirt, the fringes of his *tzitzit* slapped him in his face, causing him to remember the Divine prohibition and refrain from committing this illicit act. The *mitzvah* helped him overcome his base desires.

The purpose of this reading on *Yom Kippur* is to give everyone a reminder that is intended to last throughout the entire coming year. The rabbis recognize Man's tendency to rationalize these issues of sexual relationships, and they therefore demand that specifically at a time when we are all thinking of how to improve, we should be reminded about these prohibitions.

We all must examine the reasons why we act in certain ways and analyze our motives to see if they are noble and sincere. Everyone is a genius at rationalizing their conduct, but not everyone is sensitive enough to recognize that rationalization. The rabbis wanted to ensure that, on the day when everyone is most concerned about their daily conduct, we remember the prime example when people often justify their ill behavior.

Animal Instinct
by Yoel Spotts

In this week's Torah portion we find several commandments that seem to have very little in common. We begin with a run-down of the laws and practices of *Yom Kippur*, then proceed to the prohibition of eating blood. Finally, the portion concludes with a discussion of the forbidden relationships. Disregarding the possibility that these particular commandments were haphazardly tossed together to form the Torah portion of Acharei Mot, we most certainly should be able to discover a common theme linking these various topics.

Interestingly enough, we see that the Torah prohibits the consumption of any animal's blood, even those which are kosher. Thus, not only does the Torah exclude the vast majority of creatures from our diet, it even limits our scope with regard to the permissible ones.

Furthermore, the Torah demands of us a day of total and absolute abstinence from all nourishment. The restrictions and regulations seem almost overwhelming.

Indeed, we discover a very similar structure with regard to the forbidden relationships. In this week's portion, the Torah outlines for us the unsuitable individuals whom we may not select as mates. However, that is not all. The Torah strictly regulates the relationship of even those people permitted to us. A proper union must be preceded by *kiddushin*, the sanctification of marriage. An unsuccessful marriage must be terminated by the giving of a *get*, or divorce document. Extramarital relationships are viewed with disdain and disgust. And although the Torah itself does not prohibit polygamy, it has been the recommendation of the rabbis and the practice of the masses to limit ourselves to only one spouse. Thus, we see that the Torah places severe restraints and limitations on the food we eat and on our relationships.

The similarities do not end there. This week's portion is not the only place we find these two topics grouped together. In fact, the Rambam places the Laws of Forbidden Relations and the Laws of Forbidden Foods in the same section in his code of Jewish law. The Rambam names this section, curiously enough, *Kedushah*. While "*kedushah*" is usually translated as "holiness", many commentators note that the term also connotes the notion of "separate" or "distinct". Thus, it would appear that the Rambam wishes to convey to us that these two areas of law empower and enable us to separate and distinguish ourselves.

Now, the pieces are finally falling into place. When Hashem created the universe, He placed both Man and beast on this planet. At first glance, Man appears to be no different than any other creature. After all, both eat, both procreate, both engage in the same mundane physical activities. Are we, then, no different than the animals that roam the earth? The gifts of speech, rational thought, and free will are all indications that Man is indeed different and separate from animals.

However, when we allow our animal desires free reign, acting without any restraint, we are in fact demonstrating that we are no better than our pet cat or dog. When we continue to satisfy our gastronomic cravings and submit to our carnal appetite, we have reduced ourselves to a mere conglomeration of flesh and bones.

For this reason, the Torah contains so many prohibitions in the areas of food intake and sexual relations. The Torah enjoins us to control our base desires in order to "separate" and "distinguish" ourselves from all other creations. By displaying our willpower and self-discipline, we can rise above the level of mere physical beings. No wonder that after having introduced these laws in this week's Torah portion – fasting on *Yom Kippur*, refraining from eating blood, and avoiding forbidden relations – the Torah commences next week's portion with the admonition "*kedoshim te'heyu* – you shall be holy and distinct", for only by sanctifying the physical aspects of our life can we achieve success in our spiritual quest as well.

∞ Hindsight is 20/20

by Michael Alterman

"Behold – days are coming – the word of Hashem – when the plower will encounter the reaper, and he who treads upon the grapes will meet the one who brings the seeds . . ." (Haftorah for Acharei Mot – Amos 9:13).

The Dubno Maggid explains the above prophetic line referring to the days of the *Mashiach* with the following parable: A city dweller who had never before seen a farmer at work, happened upon a man in the countryside who was plowing the ground and dispersing seeds in the newly-produced furrows. He immediately ran over to the farmer and chastised him for throwing such excellent seeds into the ground and allowing them to rot. The farmer responded patiently that the city dweller should wait to see what would eventually occur.

Several months later, the city dweller was thrilled to see that the seeds had sprouted into beautiful stalks of wheat, but was horrified when the farmer ruthlessly cut down the wonderful sheaves. Perceiving the city dweller's concern, the farmer assured him that, with time, he would understand what was being done. The farmer then proceeded to grind the wheat, mix it with water, knead the dough, and place it in a hot oven. The city dweller once again could not understand why the farmer insisted on destroying the kernels of grain by grinding them and placing the mixture in a hot oven. Once again, the farmer reassured the city dweller that he must wait patiently to see what the end product will be.

When we examine and ponder our seemingly haphazard and upside-down world, we are perplexed and dismayed by what appears to be an unjust existence where evil prevails and the righteous live lives of hardship and toil. We cannot fathom what is occurring behind the scenes because we are trapped in the finite element of time, rendering us unable to view the big picture. Unfamiliar with the process of planting seeds, nurturing them, and allowing them to develop, we only see the afflictions of the righteous by the random elements of nature and are not witnesses to the final result, the main point.

However, this should not cause us to despair. In the future, all will be revealed and our understanding of the many occurrences throughout history will be as clear as is the pleasure the city dweller derives from eating the warm, delicious, freshly-baked loaf of bread produced after months of hard work. Our prayer, as expressed by the prophet Amos in the above verse, is that we will one day achieve total clarity by witnessing both the beginning and the end of the story – to see the plower encounter the reaper, standing together as one.

PARSHAT KEDOSHIM

edoshim *(Leviticus 19:1-20:27) begins with Hashem's command to the entire nation of Israel to be holy, emulating the supreme sanctity of Hashem Himself. The Torah goes on to delineate a multitude of* mitzvot *through which we can achieve sanctity, covering a wide variety of subjects, both positive commandments and negative injunctions, dealing both with our unique relationships to Hashem and our fellow man. We are commanded to fear our parents, to guard Shabbat from desecration, and to refrain from the worship of idols. Hashem instructs us to leave various gifts from our harvest for the poor and downtrodden, including the edge of the field and the sheaves which were unintentionally dropped while being gathered. We must maintain justice, have honest dealings with our neighbors, refrain from tale-bearing, and generally care for others as we do ourselves. Following a description of several categories of* kilayim *(forbidden mixtures) – crossbreeding animals and plants, and the wearing of* shatnez *(a mixture of wool and linen in one garment) – the Torah discusses* orlah, *the prohibition to consume fruits from the first three years of a newly-planted tree. The portion continues with a listing of the punishments to be meted out against people who transgress and participate in the various forbidden relations discussed in last week's portion. Parshat Kedoshim concludes with the commandment, once again, that we be a holy and distinct people from amongst the nations of the world.*

Hair Do's and Don'ts

by Daniel Lasar

There is an important correlation between the Torah portion of Kedoshim and its predecessor, Acharei Mot. In Acharei Mot, Hashem commands the Jewish people, "Do not perform the practice of the land of Egypt in which you dwelled, and do not perform the practice of the land of Canaan to which I bring you, and do not follow their traditions" (Leviticus 18:3). In the subsequent portion, Kedoshim, Hashem directs the Jewish people, "You shall be holy, for holy am I, Hashem, your G-d" (ibid. 19:2). These two verses provide an illuminating emphasis on not only how we live as Jews, but on the way we live in the context of where we live.

In *Pirkei Avot* (1:7) the sage Nittai articulates, "Distance yourself from a bad neighbor, and do not associate with a wicked person." One need not read too many newspapers or listen to too many talk shows to be aware of the serious morality problems confronting our society today. It is human nature to be influenced by the character traits and standards of value present amongst one's peers. However, it is incumbent upon us to strive to conform to the eternal code of conduct that Hashem prescribes in the Torah.

A subtle, yet vital symbol of avoiding the influence of Western society is found even with regard to the way we cut our hair. Many people today have their sideburns shorn, a reflection in many ways of the ever shifting styles of the contemporary world. The Torah states otherwise in this week's portion: "You shall not round off the edge of your scalp and you shall not destroy [with a razor] the edge of your beard" (Leviticus 19:27); Jewish men are neither permitted to shave off their sideburns nor to shave their faces with a razor blade. Thus, in as simple a thing as going to the barber, we must remain cognizant that it is the Torah that guides our behavior, not what society says is "cool". Many of our visible practices, such as wearing a *kippah* or dressing modestly, help us remember our distinctiveness and special role in this world.

Unfortunately, the last century has seen an alarming rate of inter-marriage, ignorance, and assimilation. Not surprisingly, this can be largely attributed to the inviting society in which we live. Unlike yesteryears, when our mothers would trek miles to go to the *mikveh*, or when our fathers would scrape together just enough money to honor *Shabbat* with wine for *kiddush*, we thankfully have endless opportunities to perform *mitzvot* without hardship. Tragically, though, it is very tempting to "do like the Romans do" and attempt to fit in like everyone else. We are commanded, however, not to emulate values that are antithetical to the Torah. Rather, we are to be holy – to follow the Torah lifestyle. Hashem has His reasons for the optimal manner in which we should live our lives.

We are now in the period between the holidays of *Pesach* and *Shavuot*, the seven week interval in which the Jewish people purged themselves of their Egyptian ways and prepared to receive Hashem's Torah at Mt. Sinai. So, too, should we take inventory of our own attitudes and values, noting that not the ephemeral fads of Western culture, but the everlasting standards of the Torah should embody who we are. If we remember this, then we will truly be a light unto the nations.

❧ Fortune 500
by Rabbi Elie Cohen

One of the many *mitzvot* listed in this week's portion is the prohibition to not "make a cut in your flesh for the dead" (Leviticus 19:28). We are not permitted to injure ourselves in response to the loss of a loved one, something which in fact was an ancient pagan custom. As innocuous as this law may seem, King Solomon uses it to make a very valuable point in his "Song of Songs" in which he likens the relationship of Hashem and the Jewish people to that of a husband and wife. In one praise of Hashem the Jewish people state, "The words of His palate are sweet and He is all delight" (5:16). Rashi interprets this verse that the Jewish people are expressing to Hashem that His words – the Torah – are sweet and pleasant to them.

As an example of this sweetness, Rashi cites the above-mentioned prohibition that we not injure ourselves. What makes this particular *mitzvah* so sweet? It can be found in the concluding words of that verse – "I am Hashem". This formulation is used throughout the Torah as a means of conveying the concept that Hashem is the one Who is trustworthy to pay us our reward for the *mitzvot* we do. Thus, the verse is understood, "You shall not make a cut in your flesh for the dead . . . I am Hashem, the one Who is trustworthy to pay you your reward for the observance of this *mitzvah*." How could earning a reward be any easier!

This theme of how little effort is necessary to receive reward recurs in Rashi's commentary to Deuteronomy 24:19. The Torah speaks of the requirement for a farmer to leave for the poor any sheaves that he drops or forgets while reaping his field, "in order that Hashem your G-d will bless you in all the works of your hand." Rashi comments that one is blessed for doing this *mitzvah* even though it came about accidentally. The farmer did not intend to drop anything. Thus, deduces Rashi, a person who inadvertently drops a quarter which is subsequently found by a poor person is himself blessed.

All this having been said, it is still possible for a skeptic to challenge King Solomon's assertion that the Torah's words are sweet. Perhaps punishment is equally easy to achieve. Why, one might ask, are we only looking at one side of the coin?

The Talmud addresses itself to this query. In the second of the Ten Commandments, Hashem is described as one Who "watches kindness for thousands of generations" and Who "visits the sins of the fathers upon the children, the third, and the fourth generations [if they follow their fathers' wicked ways]" (Exodus 20:5-6). Hashem <u>continually</u> "watches" kindness in order to reward a righteous person's descendants for thousands of generations, but only carries the punishment for sins up to four generations. From this, our sages derive that Hashem's attribute of reward is 500 times as great as is His attribute of punishment. (Since any plural word must refer to a minimum of two, "thousands" refers to at least 2000 generations of reward, 500 times more than the four generations of punishment.)

We now clearly see that although it is not always apparent in this world (which is not the prime place for reward anyway), Hashem's attribute of reward is far greater than His attribute of punishment. Let us use this lesson to strengthen our effort in the performance of His *mitzvot*.

PARSHAT EMOR

ollowing on the heels of the command given in last week's portion to the entire Jewish population to be sanctified and holy, Parshat Emor (Leviticus 21:1-24:23) begins by discussing various laws directed specifically to the Kohanim and the Kohen Gadol whose Divine service requires them to maintain a higher standard of purity. Included is the command for the Kohen to refrain from becoming ritually impure through contact with a dead body (except for close relatives) and increased restrictions on whom they may marry. A Kohen with any one of a series of physical blemishes is forbidden to perform the service in the Temple until he is cured. The subject matter then returns to the entire nation: Anyone who is tamei is told to stay away from places and things which are especially holy. After discussing the laws of terumah (the small percentage of food which must be separated from the harvest in the land of Israel and given to a Kohen before the remaining portion can be eaten) and the various blemishes which render a korban unfit, we are warned to always be mindful of not desecrating G-d's name and, on the contrary, to sanctify Him at all costs. The Torah goes on to discuss the festivals of the year (Pesach, Shavuot, Rosh Hashanah, Yom Kippur, Succot, and Shemini Atzeret), followed by two constant mitzvot maintained in the Mishkan: the lighting of the menorah every day and the displaying of the lechem hapanim each week. The portion concludes with the horrible incident of a man who cursed G-d's name and was subsequently punished with the death penalty at Hashem's command.

In Sickness and in Health
by Matthew Leader

Unfortunately, people are not always fair. If someone informed you that you couldn't have a certain job because of a physical disability, whether it be a doctor, lawyer, or Native American Chief, most people would say, "Hey mister, that's just not fair!". However, everyone expects Hashem to be fair, at least in the written rules if not always in obvious practice. That is why many sages throughout the ages have discussed the seemingly non-egalitarian part of this week's Torah portion that deals with the laws of the *Kohanim*. After describing several details of how a *Kohen* should keep himself especially holy, Hashem tells Moses that a *Kohen* with any physical blemish, such as blindness, eczema, or even a broken foot may not approach the *Mishkan* to perform the priestly service or bring offerings, for that would "profane My holy place" (Leviticus 21:23).

How can this be? Isn't our religion one of internal improvement, where Hashem judges us by our thoughts and actions, not by our personal appearance? In the fundamental *Shema* prayer, it is written that we should serve Hashem "with all of our heart and all of our might" and He will be pleased with us. The *Aishet Chayil* psalm, recited every Friday night as a praise to the women of the house, informs us that "charm is falsehood and beauty is nothingness, but a woman who fears Hashem, she is to be praised." So how can a person unfortunate enough to go blind or develop a skin disease be excluded from serving Hashem if he has a good heart?

Conveniently, Rabbi Meir Simcha HaKohen of Dvinsk asks the very same question, and gives us an answer in two parts. The first is the most obvious – since Hashem is the arbiter of what is true justice, then whatever He does is by definition just. The laws regarding offerings are *chukim* and we can only guess the reasons why Hashem wants certain people to be involved in this service and others to be excluded. This teaches us that we should not apply our limited human ideals of "fairness" and "justice" to Hashem's actions. This answer is most comprehensible in the case of a *Kohen* who is born with a defect. However, this is not really understandable in the case of someone who Hashem apparently did deem deserving when they previously performed the priestly service, but now has been stricken from the roster. We must therefore assume that this person has made himself unworthy to serve through some sin or action that he committed. But surely, there are injured people who are more righteous than others who are healthy?

Rabbi Meir Simcha answers this in classic Judaic fashion by asking another question: If there were to be disqualifications, why didn't Hashem just tell the prophet of the era which people had sinned and have the prophet disqualify them from the priestly service? Rashi states that the fact that the Torah writes the word "blemishes" an extra time (ibid. 21:21), after already listing several examples, teaches us that any physical blemish is cause for disqualification, even one which is not readily apparent or visible. Therefore, explains Rabbi Meir Simcha, the physical blemish is a way for Hashem to send a direct message to the afflicted person that even if his actions seem to be pristine outwardly, there may be an internal flaw or character trait that he needs to remedy. The blemish in no way means that he is "evil" or a "sinner"; rather it suggests that there is some small attribute or activity that he needs to work on before he can resume his priestly service. Perhaps only the *Kohen* himself can discover this flaw through his own dedicated introspection, while the "religious authorities" of the time may be unable to detect the internal problem.

This lesson of personal responsibility does not apply only to the *Kohanim*. Each of us, on our own level, must maintain our unique relationship with Hashem and respond to the subtle messages which He sends our way.

∽ Baker's Dozen

by Micah Gimpel

One of the most interesting features of the *Mishkan* was the *lechem hapanim*, the special showbread which was always kept on display. Baked every Friday and changed each *Shabbat*, the loaves would miraculously remain oven-fresh for the entire week until they were distributed to the *Kohanim* and replaced by a new batch. Interestingly, when the Torah describes the *mitzvah* to prepare the twelve loaves of bread for the *lechem hapanim*, Hashem makes a point of commanding not only the baking of the bread, but also the gathering of the flour for its preparation. "You should take fine flour and bake it into twelve loaves. . ." (Leviticus 24:5). The Netziv points out that although the primary focus of the *mitzvah* was the actual baking, nevertheless the gathering of the flour was also included as an important part of the commandment. Our taking the flour for this *mitzvah* increases the holiness of the *lechem hapanim*, for it shows that we consider the activity important enough to dedicate our time to every one of its details.

This principle is not only true with regard to the *lechem hapanim*; the preparations for any *mitzvah* or holy endeavor begin and, to a certain extent, become a part of that *mitzvah*. The significance of the *mitzvah* is intensified by the extent to which a person prepares for its performance. For example, the *mitzvah* of *Shabbat* begins well before sunset on Friday night. Friday, known as *Erev Shabbat*, is designated specifically for the many preparations which need to be made to ensure the sanctity of our day of rest. The Rambam in his code of Jewish law lists many advisable preparations to be made <u>before</u> *Shabbat* in order to better appreciate the day once it arrives. We should shower, prepare appetizing food, and wash our clothes; we should clean and organize the house, and set the table for *Shabbat*. One could view this as merely pragmatic advice in order to have everything ready by the time *Shabbat* arrives. However, the Rambam clearly lists this preparation as a *mitzvah*, in a separate category from the other *mitzvot* of *Shabbat*, calling it *kavod Shabbat*, respect for *Shabbat*. When we prepare, we can better appreciate the experience and, in turn, develop a greater love for the holy day. The Rambam elaborates and declares that any additional preparations made for *Shabbat* are praiseworthy.

Another application of the importance of dedicating time to prepare for the performance of a *mitzvah* involves studying and concentrating before prayer. For a person to walk into the synagogue just as the service begins (or even later) provides no opportunity to reflect and set the proper tone for prayer. Therefore, Jewish law recommends that a person should arrive at the synagogue early to provide him the opportunity to realize that prayer is a personal conversation with Hashem that cannot be taken lightly. Prayer is a remarkable opportunity, a time when finite Man has an opportunity to speak with the Infinite, and it must be approached with proper concentration.

Similarly, the Talmud advises that we should begin studying the laws pertaining to a forthcoming holiday a month in advance. Again, this injunction can be viewed on practical grounds as insurance that we will be ready when the holiday arrives. However, another benefit is derived from this practice. If we understand the holidays and their significance, which manifest themselves in the laws pertaining to the day, the holiday itself develops a deeper meaning for us. The preparation is critical to achieving this deeper understanding and relationship with the festivals.

🔗 Death Row
by Benyamin Cohen

Although this week's portion deals primarily with complex and intricate laws, towards the end the Torah returns to the narrative and tells the story of a man who blasphemed the name of Hashem in the camp of Israel. At the time of the incident, Hashem had not yet informed Moses how the judicial system would deal with such a case.

In the meantime, Moses placed the perpetrator in confinement (Leviticus 24:12). Rashi reveals that this man was not the only one in prison at this moment in time. Also incarcerated was a man named Tzlaphchad who had deliberately desecrated *Shabbat* and was imprisoned for his sinful action while awaiting the death penalty (see Numbers 15:32). However, when Moses incarcerated the blasphemer until his punishment was decided, he placed him in a separate cell from Tzlaphchad. Why were the two inmates put in different cells? Was the warden afraid of a riot?

The Sifsei Chachamim explains that had the blasphemer been placed together with the desecrator of *Shabbat*, the one who cursed Hashem would have naturally assumed that his penalty was also death, a ruling which was not yet certain. This would have unquestionably placed an excessive degree of anguish on the individual. Even though he had transgressed in such a serious manner, there was no reason to cause him any unnecessary suffering. He was therefore placed in a separate cell.

This is not only an interesting story, but one that should deliver a powerful message to us all. If we are required to be so concerned about the feelings of a possible death-row inmate, how much more so should we take into consideration the feelings of our friends, family, and colleagues. This episode exemplifies how we must concentrate our efforts into maintaining the human dignity of our fellowman and not cause any undue pain. In the fast-paced dance of life, we must be ever so careful not to step on anyone's toes.

PARSHAT BEHAR

ehar *(Leviticus 25:1-26:2) focuses primarily on* mitzvot *concerning the land of Israel, beginning with the command to observe* Shemittah – the mitzvah *to allow one's fields to remain uncultivated every seventh year, refraining from the normal cycle of planting and harvesting. Similarly, the earth in Israel is to remain unworked in the* Yovel, *or 50th year, at which time the ownership of all land automatically returns to its ancestral heritage. Hashem promises that He will bless the land in the sixth year so that it will produce enough food to last throughout the* Shemittah *period. After describing the process by which original land owners can redeem their ancestral property in the years before* Yovel, *the portion shifts to speak about the poor and downtrodden. Not only are we commanded to give them* tzedakah *and to do acts of loving kindness for them, but ideally we are to pro-vide them with the means to raise themselves out of their poverty-stricken state. We are prohibited to receive and pay any interest on loans made to other Jews. The Torah then discusses the various details regarding Jewish and gentile servants working for Jews, and the* mitzvah *to redeem Jews who are servants to gentiles. All Jewish servants are to be set free at the onset of the* Yovel *year. The portion concludes by repeating the prohibition of worshipping idols, and the* mitzvot *to guard the* Shabbat *from desecration and revere Hashem's sanctified places.*

☙ Gimme a Break

by Yoel Spotts

In this week's portion the Torah paints quite a grim picture for the farmers of the world. After having been commanded in Parshat Kedoshim (Leviticus 19:9) that certain portions of the harvest must be left for the poor (e.g. the corners of the field, the produce that is forgotten at the time of harvest, etc.), this week the Torah informs the farmer that he must also observe *Shemittah*, allowing his field to lay fallow every seventh year. Certainly, this is a bitter pill to swallow: Keeping Kosher and celebrating *Shabbat* are one thing, but to sacrifice one's livelihood for an entire year seems tantamount to financial suicide. Why has the Torah demanded so much from the simple farmer?

Although several commentators offer interpretations of the commandment of *Shemittah*, the Kli Yakar rejects most of these explanations out of hand and instead offers his own hypothesis. He proposes that the Torah has demanded the cessation of all agricultural activity in order to inculcate the Jewish people with a sense of trust and faith in Hashem. If they were permitted to plant and harvest at will, they would arrive at the mistaken conclusion that their livelihood and sustenance may be attributed to their own toil and effort. The Jews would erroneously deduce that their own control over the natural forces of the world dictates their fortune and success. Therefore, Hashem instituted the *Shemittah* cycle so that the Jewish people will realize that their achievements and accomplishments are totally dependent upon the grace and goodwill of Hashem. When faced with the reality of the nonexistent harvest, the Jews will have no choice but to turn to Hashem for sustenance and support. The *Shemittah* cycle serves as a constant reminder to the Jewish people that they must rely not on themselves, but on Hashem above.

Although most of us, as non-farmers, cannot fully appreciate the gravity of a *Shemittah* year, we can nonetheless derive an important lesson for our own lives. All too often we become entrapped by our success, patting ourselves on the back and congratulating ourselves on a job well done. We fail to realize the true source of our prosperity. We delude ourselves into thinking that "my strength and the might of my hand made me all this wealth" (Deuteronomy 8:17). Only when we fall on rough times do we finally take note of our own inadequacy. In order to remind us of the true Provider of our needs, Hashem must take harsh steps that will force us to re-examine our self-reliance. By enduring these trying and demanding times, we can arrive at a total and complete appreciation for the kindness and compassion of Hashem.

The Big Picture
by Michael Alterman

Perhaps one of the most difficult *mitzvot* in the Torah to properly observe is *Shemittah*. Allowing your field to remain fallow for an entire year, completely cutting off your livelihood for an extended period of time, requires an incredible amount of faith. This is compounded by the fact that the entire nation plans to do the same thing at the same time. Because of the inherent difficulties involved, Hashem renders a special pledge to the observers of *Shemittah*, as described in this week's Torah portion: "The land will give its fruit and you will be satisfied; you will dwell securely upon it" (Leviticus 25:19). Hashem tells them not to worry – nobody will go hungry.

Following that promise, the Torah speaks of a logical, yet seemingly inappropriate hypothetical question that may be raised by the people: "What will we eat in the seventh year – behold! We will not plant and we will not gather our crops!" (ibid. 25:20). A question like this would have been totally understandable and even expected had it been asked when the *mitzvah* of *Shemittah* was first presented a dozen verses before. Indeed, that may have been our initial reaction upon hearing about this *mitzvah*. However, in the preceding verse Hashem had just given His guarantee to the people that they <u>would</u> have enough food to eat. After hearing such a promise, what could they possibly be worried about?

To complicate matters even further, Hashem responds to their concern with what would appear to be the ultimate blessing conceivable: "I will ordain My blessing for you in the sixth year and [the land] will yield a crop sufficient for <u>three years</u>" (ibid. 25:21). What a great assurance! Can you imagine the fields producing three times the regular crop in one year, every single time the *Shemittah* cycle comes around – an open miracle for all to see and none to dispute. However, if Hashem was planning to make such a remarkable promise, why did He not do so in the first place? If this pledge is going to satisfy everybody's concern, then why not preclude their fears by telling them the wonderful news <u>before</u> they panic?

The Dubno Maggid answers by analyzing the passage in the following manner: If we take a moment to ponder the situation, we will realize that there are several ways in which Hashem could potentially solve the "dilemma" of what they will eat during *Shemittah*. While Hashem could easily arrange for the fields to produce outstanding crops in the year immediately preceding *Shemittah* (similar to what occurred before the famine in Egypt during the days of Joseph), in reality that would be slightly less than ideal. After all, if the fields produce extra grain, somebody must harvest, process, prepare, and store the surplus so that it can be used when it is most needed. Conversely, the ultimate blessing would be one in which the recipients would not be required to do any extra work. This blessing would occur not in the fields, but in the stomach. Conceivably, Hashem could arrange for a smaller amount of food to last for a longer period of time, i.e. for people to be content with less than usual; a regular crop could provide more satiation than normal, satisfying the people throughout the *Shemittah* period and thereby requiring no extra work on the part of the *Shemittah* observer.

Indeed, that was the promise in the first verse: "The land will give its fruit and you will be satisfied . . ." Hashem was telling them not to worry. No blatant miracles, no record-setting crops, no extra work, yet everybody will be satisfied. However, such a blessing carries with it one possible setback. Since the extra grain cannot be physically seen and identified, one may always find himself feeling insecure and uncertain about the source of his next meal. "Will I have enough to feed my entire family? The pantry is only half full!" Those who did not have faith in Hashem's promise that He would provide them with ample sustenance immediately came forward to voice their concern. Consequently, Hashem answered by promising <u>those people</u> the lesser of the two options – the surplus of grain in the fields, coupled with increased toil and labor. Ideally, Hashem had intended to bestow upon everyone the greater of the two options – miraculously satisfying them with a smaller amount of food and no extra work involved. However, due to the doubts of the less faithful sector, Hashem was forced to settle with providing that group with the secondary blessing. They had to actually <u>*see*</u> the good in order to appreciate it.

Often, we fail to recognize the special blessings that Hashem graciously bestows upon us. It seems that when things don't go exactly as we hoped, we immediately assume the worst. The fundamental Jewish principle of "*gam zu l'tovah* – everything is for the best" goes completely unnoticed, as we are unwilling to wait and see how things will turn out. While absolute faith that everything is for the best is difficult to acquire, making a conscious effort to adopt the proper attitude is an attainable goal. Additionally, as demonstrated by the increased blessing to those who trusted Hashem with regard to *Shemittah*, the reward makes it well worth the effort.

☙ The $50,000 Bar Mitzvah
by Benyamin Cohen

Money can be a funny thing. One minute we have it and the next we don't. Throughout the course of our lives, we may ride the roller coaster of financial fortune – several times. In this week's Torah portion, we read about the seemingly strange laws of *Shemittah*, which basically require farmers to let their land lay fallow for an entire year.

At first glance, this injunction seems ludicrous. Why would any sane-minded farmer agree to leave his land, his sole source of income, for a whole year?

Many commentators agree that one of the major lessons which can be learned from the laws regarding *Shemittah* is the ability to acknowledge that everything comes from Hashem. In reality, <u>everything</u> we own belongs to Hashem. We are custodians just taking care of things during our sojourn on earth. If Hashem tells us to leave our farmland for a year and not do any work on it, then it is imperative for us to heed His call, since ultimately it is Hashem Who decides how bountiful the land will be.

Once we reach that understanding that we are not the real owners of our possessions, our wealth, and our money, then we must ask ourselves an important question. If this money really is on loan to me from Hashem, then how does He want me to spend it? Does he want me to spend $50,000 on a car? Is that why He gave me so much money? Should I spend a year's salary on a Bar Mitzvah party or on a home theater surround sound system?

In Chinese, the characters for the word "challenge" are very similar to the characters for the word "opportunity". Prosperity, whether it be moderate or the kind that allows you to have a car for each day of the week, is a tremendous challenge. Knowing what Hashem wants us to do with our money can often be difficult. Yet, this challenge brings with it opportunity. We can give to Torah causes, support educational institutions, and care for those in need. Hashem is giving us an incredible chance to do a *mitzvah* – don't let the opportunity pass!

PARSHAT BECHUKOTAI

arshat Bechukotai (Leviticus 26:3-27:34), the last Torah portion in the book of Leviticus, begins by briefly listing some of the blessings and rewards that the Jewish people will receive for diligently following the Torah and performing Hashem's mitzvot. The portion then shifts to the subject matter which has made it famous – the tochachah, Hashem's harsh rebuke. Step by step, the Torah describes the tragedies which will befall the Jewish people, often in graphic terms, as they abandon the observance of Hashem's Torah and mitzvot, providing an eerie account of what has been our history to this day. The portion then goes on to speak about the sanctification of voluntary gifts to the Temple and the process by which a person can monetarily redeem those sanctified items for his own use. The book of Leviticus concludes with a brief discussion of tithes, including a portion which the farmer must himself consume within the city of Jerusalem called ma'aser sheni.

☙ Did Hashem Forget?

by Micah Gimpel

This week's Torah portion contains the *tochachah*, the famous harsh rebuke of the Children of Israel for not following in the ways that Hashem commanded. However, though the lengthy passage begins on a negative note, it ends in an inspiring manner. Hashem tells us that He will forgive the Children of Israel once they repent and change their ways. This uplifting section begins with an interesting verse: "I will remember My covenant with Jacob, and also My covenant with Isaac, and also My covenant with Abraham will I remember, and I will remember the Land" (Leviticus 26:42).

Linguistically, this verse is quite difficult for a number of reasons. Rashi quotes a *Midrash* that asks an obvious and enlightening question: Why does the Torah only use the language of "remembering" regarding Jacob and Abraham, but not in relation to Isaac? Could it be that Hashem remembers Isaac less than the others?

The *Midrash*, as quoted by Rashi, presents an answer that requires some clarification. It states that Hashem sees the ashes of Isaac as if they were gathered and placed on the altar; therefore remembering is unnecessary in Isaac's case. This statement is making reference to the *akeidah*, Isaac's near-sacrifice at his father's hand described at the end of Parshat Vayeira (Genesis 22:1-19). Aside from the apparent irrelevance of the *akeidah* to the question being discussed, we must first understand what the *Midrash* is talking about, for as you may recall, Isaac was never sacrificed and therefore never burned on the altar. At the last moment Hashem rescinded His command. If that's the case, how can the *Midrash* give such a seemingly erroneous answer speaking about Isaac's non-existent ashes?

The *akeidah* was a tremendous test of faith which serves as the paradigm of Isaac's greatness. Already 37-years-old and mature in his character development, Isaac was willing to act in accordance with Hashem's command to give up his life. This faithful attribute stemmed from Isaac's passive nature. Throughout his life, his greatness was demonstrated by his lack of action. He went back to the same cities to which Abraham had previously gone in order to reinforce or strengthen what his father had already done; rarely did he do anything on his own initiative. It was at the *akeidah* that Isaac's passivity is most strongly displayed and it characterizes his whole life and personality. Hashem, therefore, views Isaac as if he actually was sacrificed at the altar, since he was willing to give his life even at the very last moment. The ashes would have represented the fulfillment of the sacrifice and remain before Hashem as a permanent reminder of Isaac's greatness. Therefore, the Chofetz Chaim explains, since Isaac's ashes are always seen, there is no need for remembering.

This understanding of Isaac clarifies both questions. The reason why Isaac is not "remembered" in the verse is simply because he was never forgotten. It is unnecessary to remember something which constantly remains in the forefront of one's consciousness. Therefore, in answering the question, the *Midrash* refers to the *akeidah* – the means by which he was never forgotten – to express Isaac's greatness, his passivity.

Hashem is telling the Children of Israel about their punishments for their sins and how Hashem will forgive them. The actions of the Children of Israel were so offensive that they could not ask for mercy from their iniquities. But through the merit of Isaac, who represents greatness through lack of action, the Children of Israel could repent and ask Hashem to overlook their horrible sins by focusing on their lack of action. Isaac's passivity allows us to be great through our own passivity. Our avoiding a negative situation can sometimes be tantamount to performing a positive act.

☞ Microwaves, Jets, & Hashem's Rebuke
by Rabbi Dov Ber Weisman

Parshat Bechukotai is known as the Torah portion of admonishment. It describes the age-old formula that "If you go in My decrees and observe My *mitzvot* and perform them, then I will bring you rain in its proper time. . ." (Leviticus 26:3-4). In other words, if you keep the commandments, you will be blessed spiritually and materialistically, while if you abandon them, G-d forbid, the opposite will be true.

Interestingly, upon analyzing the series of curses found in Parshat Bechukotai, we see an amazingly accurate depiction of today's society. The verses tell us that if you disdain My statutes, I will bring upon you confusion (see ibid. 26:14-17). This means that you will have no peace of mind, no tranquillity. Since you had no patience while performing the *mitzvot* and were instead thinking, "when will services be over?" or "when will *Shabbat* be over so I can get back to my 'real' life and to my materialistic pleasures," then *midah k'neged midah* you will have no patience, tranquillity, or true enjoyment even in your physical pleasures.

As a result of this curse, one finds that despite all of our technological advancements that do everything faster and more efficiently – from cars and jets to computers and microwaves, to instanteverything – even so, Man has no time! He is always running and has no time to stop and think, "Who am I? Why am I here? Where am I headed?" And with all of these twentieth century comforts, how can one explain the phenomenon that more people have mental and emotional problems, have more worries, anxieties, and ulcers than ever before! More people are under psychiatric care and are turning to drugs and suicide. The bottom line is that with all of these time-saving discoveries, Man in fact has less time, less patience, less sensitivity, and less peace of mind and happiness than in any other generation. We always seem to be late, racing to every meeting or event. We simply have no time – and this is called progress! We may see in this phenomenon the fulfillment of the verse: "You will flee, but there will be nobody chasing you" (ibid. 26:17).

All of this results in a strange paradox that, although we have more material wealth and comforts than any other generation in history, nevertheless we live in the most impoverished society when it comes to actual satisfaction. We are never satisfied! We simply are not happy with our lot. We are witnessing the result of the prophetic verses in this week's Torah portion: "You will eat and not be satisfied" (ibid. 26:26) and "I will cast upon you confusion . . . causing eyes to long and souls to suffer" (ibid. 26:16).

But all of this need not apply to the Torah Jew. The Jew, seeking spiritual wealth and using the materialistic world as a means to that end (as it was meant to be used), sanctifies the physical world into a *Mishkan* to Hashem. The choice is ours and the formula is and has always been the same: "If you observe My *mitzvot*" then you will enjoy this world and the next.

NUMBERS

PARSHAT BAMIDBAR

arshat Bamidbar (Numbers 1:1-4:20), the first portion of the fourth book of the Torah, is primarily involved with the census taken of the Jewish people in the second month of their second year in the desert. After listing the leaders of the twelve tribes of Israel, the Torah presents the totals of men between the ages of twenty and sixty for each tribe, the overall count being 603,550. The encampment structure is then described, with the tribe of Levi in the middle, safeguarding the Mishkan and surrounded by the twelve tribes of Israel, each in their own designated area. The appointment of the tribe of Levi as the spiritual leaders of the Jewish people is presented, and their own census is taken, apart from the rest of Israel. The Torah portion concludes with the instructions given to the family of Kehat, the second son of Levi, for their role in dealing with the most sacred parts of the Mishkan.

The Triple Crown
by Rabbi Daniel Estreicher

In this week's Torah portion of Bamidbar, we find a fascinating *Midrash* on the very first verse: "And Hashem spoke to Moses in the wilderness of Sinai." The *Midrash* expounds that the Torah was given in association with three things – fire, water, and in the wilderness.

Rabbi Meir Shapiro gives a beautiful explanation as to why these three things are so important. He explains that the character trait which has distinguished the Jewish people from the very beginning is the spirit of self-sacrifice. It has always been evident in our observance of the Torah's laws and in our adherence to its faith.

Abraham, the first of our Patriarchs, allowed himself to be thrown into a <u>fiery</u> furnace for having broken his father's idols, and was saved only by an open miracle from Hashem. By this act, he imparted to all future generations the will and strength to die for their Judaism. Now some people may argue that this was one isolated act of heroism by a great individual. They should then consider a second instance involving the <u>entire</u> Jewish people. When the Red Sea was divided, the Jewish people marched as one nation into the midst of the raging <u>waters</u> at the command of Hashem.

Of course some may further argue that this test took place over a relatively short period of time. Then let them finally consider the third instance, the fact that the entire Jewish nation willingly entered the <u>wilderness</u> without food or drink, not knowing how long they would have to remain there. They only did this out of love and loyalty to Hashem, as it says in Jeremiah, "I remember the affection of your youth . . . how you followed Me in the wilderness in a land that was not sown" (2:1).

It was by virtue of these three tests – through fire, water, and wilderness – that the Torah was given to the Jewish people as their eternal possession. The willingness to give up their lives for their belief in Hashem and His Torah has ensured our survival even to this day.

∽ Multiplication Through Division?
by Rabbi Reuven Stein

"The Children of Israel shall encamp, each man by his banner according to the insignias of their father's household, at a distance surrounding the Tent of Meeting shall they encamp" (Numbers 2:2).

In this week's portion the Torah records the divisions of the Jewish people by tribe, each one under a separate banner. It is interesting to note that, as the Torah mentions at the beginning of the portion, these events took place in the second year after the exodus from Egypt. Why did Hashem wait until the second year to divide the tribes under separate banners? If this was the optimal way of traveling and assembling, the division could have easily been made earlier. What is the significance of the division taking place in the Jewish people's second year in the desert?

Rabbi Yaakov Kamenetzky explains that separate groups normally are a source of divisiveness and strife. Numerous factions will lead to differing opinions, as each group struggles to accomplish their individual objectives. Without a central focal point, the tribes could have potentially divided into competing factions and fought amongst each other. However, just before Passover in the second year in the desert, the *Mishkan* was completed and put into operation. Service of Hashem in the *Mishkan* was the rallying point around which the entire nation could focus its attention. When various groups have a central focal point, their differences serve to enhance the group as a whole. The human body has eyes that see and ears that hear – are they jealous of one another? The fact that they serve one central body allows their differences to complement each other and enables it to function optimally.

When Jews are united around the Torah and the service of Hashem, then our differences complement one another and help us reach our goal. The Chofetz Chaim asked why we find so many different kinds of Jews with different strengths – some who excel in constant Torah study, some in doing acts of loving kindness, some in prayer. He explained that to function effectively in battle, an army needs to have many types of soldiers: infantry, cavalry, scouts, and medics. The various tasks discharged by each group are all necessary. If every soldier performed the same function they would not be effective in battle. It is only as a team of multiple forces, rallying around a common banner, that they can defeat the enemy in battle – as long as they are working together towards a common goal. If we unite to serve Hashem, then our individual unique strengths can help us achieve our common service of Hashem.

∽ Census, But Who's Counting

by Eyal Feiler

This week's Torah portion opens with a familiar scene. Hashem tells Moses to once again count the Jewish people in the desert: "From twenty years and above, all those who are capable of fighting, you should number them, you and Aaron" (Numbers 1:3).

According to Jewish law, however, while counting the people Moses had to follow specific Torah-mandated guidelines. As explained in the Talmud (Tractate Yoma 22b), it is prohibited to conduct a census of the Jewish people by counting individuals directly (see Exodus 30:12). One reason provided by the Talmud is that Hashem blessed our forefather Abraham with many descendants, as many as the grains of sand on the seashore, so it would be inappropriate to attempt to count his descendants. Just as grains of sand cannot be counted, so too the Jewish people are uncountable.

To that end, Rashi, commenting on the above verse, explains that a direct census was not taken. Rather, each person contributed a half-shekel coin which in turn were counted to determine the number of people. Ramban takes a position similar to that of Rashi's, pointing out that the above verse uses the Hebrew term "*tifkedu* – to list or highlight" rather than the more common word "*tisperu* – to count".

Ramban offers three reasons for Hashem's command to count. First, Hashem wanted the Jewish people to have greater contact with Moses and Aaron. In a nation of millions, not everybody had the opportunity to encounter the great leaders on a daily basis. During the counting process, each individual would have the chance to meet Moses and Aaron, since they personally made the count and collected the coins. Second, Moses needed to know the size of each tribe for military purposes and land rights once the Jews arrived in Israel. Finally, through the census Hashem's greatness and kindness to the Children of Israel would be highlighted, since only seventy people came down with Jacob to Egypt and now there were more than 600,000 males encamped in the desert.

Ramban, however, raises an important question regarding the census. King David took a similar count of the Jewish people during his reign hundreds of years later, and as a result, Hashem punished the people with a raging plague that wiped out 70,000 men. As the Talmud in Tractate Berachot states, King David was at fault. Surely as king of Israel he knew that Jewish law required him to count only by indirect means, so we must assume that he did so. Why then was he punished? Ramban explains that King David had no real reason for counting the Jewish people. On a certain level, he took the count to give himself the satisfaction of knowing that he was ruler over so many. But if this in fact is true and King David was the only one who committed the sin, then why did 70,000 men deserve death by plague?

Rabbi Yaakov Ruderman explains that to answer this question we must first understand why the Torah forbids an unnecessary counting in the first place. Rabbeinu Bachya states that the danger we face in taking a census is that we are turning the group into a gathering of individuals rather than one cohesive unit. While together as a group, the weaknesses of individual members are overshadowed by the strengths of others. However, when people are viewed as individuals, they lose the benefits they received from the strengths of the other members of the group. When King David counted the people for no reason, he was singling them out as individuals. Those who deserved to be punished for their sins were no longer protected by the group and therefore were killed in the plague. When viewed as individuals, they were unable to stand alone on their own merits.

The census teaches us the power of a *kehillah*, or group. This lesson is one of the reasons we always try to pray with a *minyan*, or quorum of at least ten, since the power of the group is stronger than the individual. When we pray to Hashem without a *minyan*, we are judged individually based upon all our deeds, good and not-so-good. How many of us would be comfortable being judged daily on our own merits? However, when we pray to Hashem in a *minyan*, those who are more worthy protect the weaker individuals, making our prayers as a group much more effective. We should all strive to be among those who are meritorious.

PARSHAT NASO

aso (Numbers 4:21-7:89) continues delineating the responsibilities and tasks of the three Levite families – Gershon and Merari in this week's portion, Kehat in last week's – and counting all of the Levites who were of age to serve in the Mishkan. After Hashem commands Moses to purify the camp so that it will be a worthy home for the Divine presence, the Torah describes the process to be carried out with a sotah, a wife who was warned by her husband not to seclude herself with another man and was subsequently found doing so, providing good reason to suspect her of adultery. She is taken to the Kohen in the Temple and, if she doesn't admit her guilt, she is given sacred bitter waters to drink which will lead to one of two results: The waters will either establish her innocence, removing the doubt from her relationship with her husband by blessing her with children, or the waters will prove her guilt through a miraculous, grotesque death. The Torah then describes the laws of the nazir, a person who has voluntarily accepted upon himself to adopt a special state of holiness, usually for thirty days, by abstaining from eating or drinking any grape products, from taking a haircut, and from becoming contaminated through contact with a corpse. After relating the blessings by which the Kohanim will bless the people, the Torah portion concludes with a lengthy listing of the offerings brought by each of the twelve tribal leaders during the dedication of the Mishkan for regular use. Each prince makes a communal gift to help transport the Mishkan, as well as donating identical gifts of gold, silver, animal, and meal offerings.

To Drink or Not to Drink

by Yoel Spotts

While the "tastes great" vs. "less filling" debate rages on in barrooms across America, we are confronted with a somewhat similar dilemma in Judaism concerning another intoxicating beverage: Wine. Although our sages have offered numerous observations about wine and its effects, many of their comments appear contradictory, and we are left with no clear consensus on the matter. On the one hand, the Talmud (Tractate Berachot 40a) states unequivocally, "Nothing brings lamentation to the human race like wine." Additionally, we find that Noah is criticized for choosing to plant a vineyard as his first undertaking following the flood, an action he is subsequently punished for via the incident with his son Cham. On the other hand, we find statements from the sages that clearly extol the virtues of wine, including the Talmud (Tractate Pesachim 109a) which declares that one cannot experience true happiness on the festivals without wine. Even more startling is the injunction on the holiday of *Purim* to become intoxicated with wine in order to achieve a level of holiness and closeness with Hashem matched only by *Yom Kippur*.

As if to add to the confusion, in this week's Torah portion we find seemingly paradoxical remarks by our sages concerning the nature of wine only a few verses apart! Interestingly, the section describing the *nazir* follows directly on the heels of the section about the *sotah*. As nothing is random in the Torah, the Talmud (Tractate Sotah 2a) explains this juxtaposition with the advice that one who has witnessed the horrifying death of the *sotah* woman should take a lesson from her crime and abstain from wine, since wine can cause a person to behave inappropriately in the same manner as the *sotah*. Certainly this comment indicates a negative sentiment towards the evils of wine. However, that is only half of the story. Later in the *nazir* narrative, as the *nazir* concludes his period of abstention, he is instructed by the Torah to bring an offering of atonement. The Talmud (Tractate Nedarim 10a), in seeking to understand what sin this person has committed that requires atonement, reasons that since he has separated himself from the pleasures of wine for 30 days, he is therefore categorized as a sinner. Unbelievable! Within a span of several verses, the sages have seemingly reversed their position entirely! How are we to interpret these mixed messages sent to us by our sages?

The truth is that we can easily resolve this paradox if we keep in mind a very important principle espoused in Judaism. Almost none of the physical pleasures in our world can be classified as inherently virtuous or evil. The physical world was placed here by Hashem for us to use. Judaism does not advocate asceticism; with the right intentions and motivations, the physical world can serve as a spiritual springboard, elevating us to new heights of holiness.

Conversely, used in the wrong way, the physical delights can propel us downward into the depths of spiritual depravity. This duality is especially true with wine, one of the most potent and powerful pleasures of the physical world. Used in the correct context, wine can raise us to a spiritual level on par with *Yom Kippur* when we are compared to angels. However, wine also contains the power to lead us to complete and utter spiritual destruction. Thus, in reality, there is no contradiction in the *nazir* section. On the one hand, the Torah wished to show the potential pitfalls of the physical world, and in particular with wine, and thus placed the *nazir* immediately following the description of the *sotah*. However, on the flip side, the Torah reminds us of the incredible potential the physical world possesses to enhance our spirituality. With the representation of the *nazir*, the Torah has masterfully enlightened us about the true nature of the physical world we live in, a powerful lesson to keep in mind in every move we make.

☙ Diamonds, Rubies – and Milk?
by Michael Alterman

"A man's sanctified items shall be his" (Numbers 5:10).

Once there was a hard-working man who was having a difficult time making ends meet. Unable to earn enough money to support his family, he decided to go on an extended business trip in a far away land where he hoped to be more successful. Upon his arrival, he quickly became involved in the sale of dairy products. Milk brought a high return since it was scarce in that land, and he soon became quite wealthy.

When, after several years, he was satisfied that he had made a fortune which would provide comfortably for his wife and family for the rest of their lives, he prepared to return home with his newly-acquired wealth. However, reasoning that he could also sell his milk at home, he decided against transporting his treasure chests of gold and silver coins and instead repurchased many barrels of milk. He promptly loaded them onto his ship, hoping that he could increase his profits even further. At the last minute, just before his ship was to set sail, a merchant selling diamonds and precious stones for an extraordinarily low price approached him. Using every method of persuasion available, the merchant finally convinced the man to exchange a small portion of his valuable milk for some of the precious, yet inexpensive gems.

After many days of travel, the man finally arrived at his home port. His family excitedly came out to greet him, anxious to discover what treats he had amassed over the long years of separation. When they began to unload the hundreds of chests of merchandise, they were immediately overcome by an overpowering stench. It soon became apparent that his thousands of gallons of milk had spoiled during the long voyage. Frustrated by the many years of separation and unable to believe her husband's stupidity, his wife began crying bitterly. "How could you invest your entire savings in milk, something which anyway sells here for next to nothing. You should have purchased chests of precious gems for a cheap price, and sold them here for millions. With what will you support us now!" Realizing his horrible blunder, the man could not respond. Eventually he remembered that he had, at the last minute, purchased a few boxes of precious stones, and he used those to support his family for some time.

So is the life of Man. We come to this world for a short time, thinking we will turn a huge profit by investing in its many fleeting pleasures. Food and drink are cheap; glory, honor, and pleasure await us at every corner. We fail to consider the valuable diamonds and precious gems, the Torah and *mitzvot*, which can be acquired here for so little. And when our time comes to leave this world, all we have to take with us are our fun and games – our spoiled milk. Of course we amass a few precious gems over the years, but our hearts yearn for the many lost opportunities when we could have made millions and prepared for ourselves a wonderful place in the real world, the World to Come.

With this parable, the Chofetz Chaim homiletically explained the above verse in this week's Torah portion. Not our money and not our fame – only the *mitzvot* that we do and the Torah that we learn are really ours to take with us.

∽ Spiritual Technology
by Rabbi Mordechai Pollock

The Jew of the 90's is aided in many ways by the technology of the times. Not only do we benefit from the conveniences, efficiencies, and medical advances that our technology provides for us, but we, Hashem's children, can benefit in other ways as well. Technology often enables us to understand and appreciate certain concepts that would otherwise have been more difficult to grasp.

One example of this phenomenon is our fundamental understanding that it is unnecessary for one of the five senses to be stimulated in order to appreciate that something is present. We understand that there are forces such as gravity and magnetism which we cannot feel, see with the naked eye, smell, hear, or taste. We take for granted that the paper and ink from which we are now reading are not simply paper and ink. In our study of science, we learn that there are an incredible number of molecules, atoms, and atomic particles that make up this seemingly simple piece of paper.

We understand, then, that within the physical world there are at least two types of existences. There are those realities which we can relate to through the use of the five senses, and then there are those realities which the five senses cannot possibly relate to without assistance. In truth, there is a third type of existence, totally different and yet interestingly similar to the first two. This third level consists of spiritual realities. These are as real and as factual as any physical existence. However, they are one step further removed from our senses. While some physical existences can be sensed unaided and others need some kind of tool, spiritual existences cannot be experienced without having a connection to the spiritual. As real as the spiritual is, we often find it very difficult to connect with it.

"Command the Children of Israel that they shall expel from the camp everyone with *tzaraat*, a *zav* (a person who had an emission), and everyone contaminated by a human corpse" (Numbers 5:2). All those people that have a specific level of spiritual impurity are required to leave the population center until such time that they have purified themselves. An impure person doesn't necessarily look different on the outside, nor does he act differently than a pure person. In all ways a pure person and his impure friend could appear to us exactly the same. In truth, they are not. Spiritual impurity, while not noticeable to the unlearned, untrained, and spiritually disconnected, is actually as real as any concrete physical existence. Like someone who is physically ill with a contagious disease, the spiritually contaminated person's presence in the camp is an impossibility. They must be removed in order to prevent an outbreak.

We must appreciate that we cannot understand everything by simply looking at the surface. A much deeper understanding is necessary to truly relate with the world within which we live. While physical realities may be detectable with technological tools, the only way to connect with spiritual realities is through studying the guidebook given to us by our Creator – the Torah. Hidden in our Torah lie the secrets upon which the entire world is based.

PARSHAT BEHA'ALOTCHA

eha'alotcha *(Numbers 8:1-12:16) begins by briefly discussing the daily lighting of the golden* menorah *in the* Mishkan, *followed by a description of the Levites' consecration ritual. The Torah then describes the celebration of Passover in the second year in the desert, complete with the bringing of the* korban Pesach. *Those who are* tamei *on the regular date of Passover and therefore unable to participate in the offering, are commanded to celebrate* Pesach Sheni, *a quasi-Passover celebration held one month later, at which time the Paschal lamb is eaten with* matzah *and bitter herbs. After mentioning the cloud and fire which alternated resting above the* Mishkan, *the Torah describes the standard procedure by which the Children of Israel would break camp to continue their travels in the desert. Soon after leaving Mt. Sinai and journeying to the Wilderness of Paran, the people begin a series of bitter complaints. Spurred by the* erev rav *(the "mixed multitude" who joined the Jewish people upon leaving Egypt), the Children of Israel are dissatisfied with the manna, their daily miraculous portion of heavenly bread. As Moses begins to despair, Hashem commands him to select seventy elders to form the* Sanhedrin, *the court which would assist him in leading the nation. Almost immediately, two of the newly-elected members announce a prophecy in the camp. Hashem sends a massive flock of quail which the people gather to eat; those who had complained about the lack of food overstuff themselves and die during this supernatural event. The portion concludes with*

Miriam's speaking lashon hara *to Aaron about their brother Moses. She is punished by Hashem with* tzaraat *and is quarantined outside the camp for seven days.*

∞ Just What the Doctor Ordered
by Daniel Lasar

This week's Torah portion of Beha'alotcha recounts how the Children of Israel were despondent about the manna that Hashem had provided them to eat during their journey in the wilderness. After being prodded by the incessant murmurings of the *erev rav*, the Children of Israel complained, ". . . Who will feed us meat? We remember the fish that we ate in Egypt free of charge; and the cucumbers, melons, leeks, onions, and garlic. But now, our life is parched, there is nothing; we have nothing to anticipate but the manna!" (Numbers 11:4-6).

A lesson that can be learned from this incident is that old habits are hard to break. Not long after leaving behind the misery and spiritual bankruptcy of Egypt, the Jewish people experienced the most significant Divine encounter in history at the giving of the Torah at Mt. Sinai. They had embarked on a journey far from Egypt's shores into the spiritual crucible of the wilderness. There, the people accepted the privilege of living their lives in accordance with Hashem's *mitzvot*. Unfortunately, after departing from Sinai, the nation regressed somewhat to the mentality that they had become so accustomed to in Egypt.

Hashem had brought them out of Egypt through wondrous plagues; He split the Red Sea, drowning their pursuers; sheltered their journey in the barren desert; and He bestowed upon them the holy Torah. The manna was a special food that would take on the taste of whatever the consumer desired. It was served directly to the people from Hashem. What was there to gripe about? Why the concern for food? Rashi, quoting the *Midrash*, explains that the people who complained weren't really concerned with food. Rather, this complaint which centered around the delicacies of Egypt was a pretext for them to vent their frustrations toward the discipline required by the *mitzvot*. Instead of a privilege, they viewed the *mitzvot* as a burden. They reminisced about the nostalgic days in Egypt when the food was "free" – they were not "constrained" in Egypt by the *mitzvot*, as the Torah had not yet been given. The complainers were entrapped in their slave mentality, viewing with disdain the obligations and responsibilities incumbent upon an independent people.

They seemed to prefer slavery to freedom: ". . . Why did we leave Egypt?" (ibid. 11:20). In Egypt, "anything goes" was the creed; there were no restrictions on behavior. After the Torah was given, however, they were expected to behave as the chosen people. Those who complained – much the same as children who whine about bedtime, taking a bath, and keeping their room neat – yearned for the days when their behavior was not regulated, when there was no curfew.

Today, are we really free or are we still slaves? Do we act as if we've left Egypt spiritually, or are we still craving those melons, leeks, and onions? Sure, today's society is enormously enticing with its "anything goes" maxim, but what about the manna? It tasted like whatever a person wanted. Similarly, we can make of our lives what we want to – we can choose to pursue the corrupt and the temporary, or the lofty and the infinite. The taste, the manner in which we conduct our lives, will reflect this choice.

If someone is sick, he will go to a doctor. The doctor tells the patient what is the proper regimen to follow to become healthy again. If a physician prescribes something for us, we listen to him – even if it isn't pleasant to take the medicine and adhere to the regimen designed to make us better. Likewise, we need to dutifully follow the prescription given to our people over 3,300 years ago and take the "tablets" given at Sinai! Granted, it may be difficult at times to break away from certain behaviors that one finds pleasurable, but just because one is accustomed to certain types of conduct, does that make it right?

The complainers, imbued with a reluctance to conform their conduct to that which the Torah demands, preferred the unrestricted society of Egypt. As we are now "leaving Sinai" (*Shavuot* was a couple of weeks ago), we should strive to improve our fulfillment of the Torah's *mitzvot*. Why don't we simply listen to Hashem, our "Life Doctor"? After all, He knows what's best for us.

∽ Working 9 to 5
by Micah Gimpel

"Speak to Aaron and say to him: 'When you kindle the lamps, towards the face of the menorah shall the seven lamps cast light'" (Numbers 8:2).

Were this command to have been given alone, Aaron would have certainly encountered great difficulty in fulfilling Hashem's request, for he is not provided with enough information to even begin this *mitzvah*. When should he light the candles and what does the service entail? Assuming that candles are only needed at night, the *menorah* should presumably be lit before sunset. However, to know the procedure with certainty, we must refer to an earlier passage in the Torah where this *mitzvah* is originally given in greater detail.

At the conclusion of Parshat Tetzaveh (Exodus 30:7-8), Hashem informs Aaron about the details and schedule of this *mitzvah*. Of prime importance is the surprising command to arrange the candle wicks and prepare the *menorah* in the morning. While we could intuitively expect the *menorah's* preparation to precede nightfall so that it will be ready to illuminate the dark and empty Temple at night, why must Aaron prepare the *menorah* in the morning, so many hours before it will be kindled? He could easily set up the *menorah* in the afternoon closer to the actual time of lighting. Furthermore, why is this technical and pragmatic preparation infused with so much significance by giving it its own command from Hashem?

Presumably, the Torah is offering a symbolic gesture to teach us an important lesson, namely, that we must set and organize our priorities. Today, understandably, we often get lost in the fast-paced life and quest for the dollar. We are constantly exposed to realities that challenge our ideals and standards, and for some reason, the word "idealistic" becomes synonymous with "nonrealistic". The Torah here advises us to constantly alert ourselves to the dangers inherent in routine practical life.

We must fight the tendency to view the essentials of living as an end in themselves. The necessities of work are only tools and devices with which to achieve our goals. What we occupy ourselves with during the day is only there to enable us to take advantage of life at night. All too often, we spend our time exhausting ourselves at work or school only to come home and collapse. When we finally reach our daily goal of returning home to be with the family or to personally grow, we are drained of energy to do more than watch the news and retire for the night. Through the *mitzvah* of preparing the candles, the Torah teaches us to recognize the difference between working to live and living to work. Aaron must prepare the wicks as his work in the morning to teach us this lesson. The *menorah* is prepared during the day, even though it only serves its function at night when it is lit. Similarly, we prepare during the day in order to fulfill our task at night. We must work in order to live!

PARSHAT SHELACH

helach (Numbers 13:1-15:40) begins with the pivotal incident of the spies' bad report about the land of Israel. As the Jewish people prepare to enter the land of Israel, they send twelve eminent leaders to survey the Promised Land, ten of whom return and deliver a bad report to the people, claiming that it would be impossible for the Jewish people to conquer the powerful nations living there. Refusing to listen to Caleb and Joshua's good report, the entire nation cries and complains throughout a night of total hysteria. Hashem threatens the Jewish people with extermination, at which point Moses pleas successfully that they not be totally annihilated. Even so, Hashem declares that they would be punished with forty years of wandering in the desert, during which time that entire generation would die out. Realizing their grave error, a group insists on advancing into the land immediately, against Hashem's will, and is wiped out by the notorious nations of Amalek and Canaan. The Torah then shifts gears to describe the wine libations which would accompany many of the korbanot brought in the Mishkan. After teaching the details of challah – (not to be confused with the bread we eat on Shabbat), this refers to the portion to be separated from every batch of dough and given to a Kohen – the Torah mentions several laws dealing with the prohibition of idol worship, and the unfortunate case of the man who received the death penalty for desecrating Shabbat. Parshat Shelach concludes with the third paragraph of the Shema prayer containing the mitzvah to wear tzitzit which serve as a constant reminder to us of Hashem and His commandments.

☙ No Strings Attached

by Rabbi Lee Jay Lowenstein

The tragic affair of the spies is one of the most frustrating and perplexing events the Torah records. Frustrating, because as casual observers we sit with our hands tied as the story painfully unfolds, bringing with it such disastrous results whose shockwaves continue to haunt us throughout time. Perplexing, because it is almost unimaginable that a nation which had collectively witnessed the glory and might of Hashem's outstretched arm as He brought them forth from Egyptian bondage should question His ability to safely settle them in their Promised Land. How do we justify their loss of faith and of what consequence does it have for us today?

The Torah portion closes with the commandment to adorn all four-cornered garments with the *tzitzit* strings. Rabbi Mordechai Gifter makes a fascinating observation regarding the Torah's description of the function of *tzitzit*. We are commanded to meditate on the *tzitzit* which remind us of the rest of the *mitzvot*, so that we should not be led astray by the passions of our <u>hearts</u> or by the desires of our <u>eyes</u> (Numbers 15:39). Rashi explains that the heart and eyes require special protection since they are naturally inclined to lead one into sin. The sinning process, Rashi continues, first involves the eyes detecting an object of desire. The heart is then set aflame with a craving for this object, and together the eyes and the heart propel the body into action. Asks Rabbi Gifter: If the snare of sin is first laid by the eyes and then by the heart, as Rashi would have it, why then does the Torah write them in the opposite order, stating that *tzitzit* are first a prescription against following one's <u>heart</u> and then one's <u>eyes</u>?

Classically, we understand Man's hierarchical position as the last created entity as symbolic of the dominant role Mankind plays vis-à-vis the universe. The stage is set; all the raw materials are in order and Man is thrust upon the scene to harness the raw power, elevating it by putting it into his service. However, in a more metaphysical sense, perhaps the placement of Man is meant to indicate that all of creation itself has no reality whatsoever, that it is in a totally incomplete state until Man is at last created.

We humans are indeed peculiar. Have you ever shared an event or experience with another and, upon comparing notes, discovered that the two of you had radically different interpretations of what transpired? You felt enlightened, stimulated, and took full interest in the occasion, whereas your companion was "hung up" on the imperfect minutiae and found it to be trivial and boring. Reality is, in fact, quite elastic. It takes the shape of whatever interpretation we wish to ascribe to it. Our attitude and self-concept dictate the way we relate to external stimuli and what kind of value or meaning we attach to them. In the highest sense, Man is a partner with Hashem in creation because each and every one of us, according to our unique personalities and character composition, "create" our own world in which we live.

Rabbi Gifter explains: It is true that the eyes are the first to entice the individual to sin; however, the eyes will only see what the heart wishes to see! *Tzitzit* demand that we reflect upon our duties of the heart, that we question and challenge our values and clarify the way we view ourselves. The wearing of the *tzitzit* aids us in defining ourselves by identifying the greater cause to which we adhere. Just as the bellhop at the posh metropolitan hotel is identified as belonging to its ranks (and indeed is accorded a great sense of dignity and honor) by the uniform and insignia which he wears, *tzitzit* serve to brand us as loyal servants of the Almighty Creator of the universe. They are the garments of royalty.

Out of their own mouths the spies reveal the underlying decay which precipitated this disastrous event. In their report to the people, they interject a self-denigrating quip which would appear to be out of consonance with the tone and tempo of their story. In the midst of describing the land of Israel as a land whose climate produces nations of gigantic proportions, they add, "We were like grasshoppers in <u>our own</u> eyes and so we were in their eyes" (Numbers 13:33). That the inhabitants regarded the Jews as puny insects would certainly evoke feelings of dread and fear. However, what of their own feelings of inferiority? What could they have possibly expected this remark to accomplish?

The answer is crystal clear: The Jewish people did not lose faith in Hashem; they lost faith in themselves! They lost the proper healthy perspective of what their true value was, of who they really were. Had they understood the great love which Hashem felt for them, they would have believed themselves to be worthy beneficiaries of the most precious of gifts, the land of Israel. Instead of looking at themselves as spiritual giants who would effortlessly crush the Canaanite tribes, they saw a nation of hopeless, miserable grasshoppers who did not deserve the love showered upon them.

The truth is, Hashem loves us more than we will ever know. Like a compassionate father, He wants only the best for us. It is our job to be His children; we have to only believe in ourselves and reflect upon the noble identity to which the *tzitzit* serve as a constant reminder. As long as we wear His "royal emblem", proudly calling ourselves His faithful children, then we <u>are</u> His children and He will open to us His boundless love. Hashem's love assuredly comes with <u>strings</u> attached!

∞ # Spies Like Us
by Yoel Spotts

The incident of the spies recorded in this week's Torah portion represents probably the greatest tragedy that befell the Jewish people in their forty-year sojourn in the wilderness. As a result of this great disaster, death was proclaimed on all adults over the age of twenty, and the Jewish nation was forced to endure an additional 38 years in the desert. The sin of the spies seems even more catastrophic when we consider the stature of the spies themselves. The Torah states that the people chosen for the task were among the leaders of the Jewish people, and Rashi notes that even immediately preceding their appointment, the spies were of pure heart and intentions. How could these righteous men have succumbed to the evil of speaking negatively and pessimistically about the land of Israel – the land that our forefathers had prayed and longed for, the land that "flows with milk and honey" where one lacks nothing? How could the good intentions of the spies transform so quickly into evil strategies and conspiracies? How could they have sunk this low so fast?

Rabbi Yaakov Kanievsky provides a simple yet profound solution. He answers that those selected to spy out the land had overestimated their own significance. The spies had assumed that they had been commissioned for an absolutely vital and critical task – to inspect and analyze the various features of the land, and based on their observations, to decide if entry and subsequent conquest of the land was prudent or even possible. They believed that the entire fate and future of the Jewish people lay on their shoulders. However, in reality, they had been designated for a much less meaningful assignment. They were simply to report on the various sights and sounds of the land that the Children of Israel could expect to see upon their arrival in Israel. In fact, the successful conquest of the land of Israel had already been promised and assured by Hashem, so any conclusion reached by the spies as to the propriety of invading the land would not only be trivial and irrelevant, but utterly inane and ludicrous.

However, the pride that the spies allowed into their hearts and minds clouded their vision and perception. The exaggeration of their own self-importance propelled them into a downward spiral of corruption. The spies' haughtiness, as little and insignificant as it may seem, resulted in one of the greatest calamities and catastrophes in the history of the Jewish people.

Of course, if the vice of pride can wreak such incredible havoc on the intellect and rationale of men of such prominence, how much more destructive are the effects of haughtiness on less virtuous people like ourselves. No wonder that Rabbeinu Yonah, commenting on *Pirkei Avot* (4:4), advises that concerning every other characteristic and trait, one should adopt a policy of the Golden Mean, yet one should refrain totally from any haughtiness and vanity. Although all other attributes are necessary in some measure in order for one to grow and develop, even a minuscule amount of arrogance can lead to devastation.

PARSHAT KORACH

arshat Korach (Numbers 16:1-18:32) begins with the infamous rebellion led by Korach against his cousins, Moses and Aaron, claiming that the two of them had usurped power from the rest of the Jewish people. After attempting to convince the rebels to retreat, Moses tells the dissenters and Aaron to each offer up ketoret to Hashem. The true leader's offering would be accepted by Hashem, while the rest of the people would die an unnatural death. At Moses' request, Hashem causes the earth to miraculously open up and swallow Korach, while the rest of the leaders of the rebellion are consumed by a flame from Hashem. When the survivors complain about the mass death, Hashem threatens to destroy them as well, and a plague breaks out. Once again, Moses and Aaron intervene, using the ketoret service to prevent the demise of the rest of the nation. In this way, and through the wondrous blossoming of Aaron's staff from amongst those of the other tribal heads, Moses and Aaron are proven to be the chosen leaders. Aaron's role as the Kohen Gadol is reiterated, and the Torah describes the gifts to be given to the Kohanim as reward for their service in the Mishkan, including the right to eat certain portions from the korbanot. The Levites are also to be supported for their dedication by receiving ma'aser, or one tenth of all crops produced by the Jewish people in the land of Israel.

Race for the Presidency
by Joshua S. Feingold

"The leaders of the rebellion stood before Moses with two hundred and fifty men from the Children of Israel, leaders of the assembly, those summoned for meeting, men of renown" (Numbers 16:2).

Pretend that you are one of the 250 men who were fighting for "equal rights" under Korach. Since these men were Jewish leaders, it is a fair assumption that they were intelligent people; most of our leaders throughout history have been. So put yourself in their shoes. Korach comes over to you and asks you to join in a rebellion against Moses and the *Kohanim*. You would probably ask, "What are we fighting for?" His answer would have been, "It is not fair that the *Kohanim* are the only people who can perform Hashem's service in the *Mishkan*. I feel that everyone should be allowed to participate." If I was one of those smart men, I imagine I would say, "Korach, you have a great idea, but I think I'll let you rebel and if and when you win, I'll be happy to do the service along with all the others. After all, Hashem has said that any non-*Kohanim* who perform the service will die, so why should I take any chances?" Remarkably, they all did agree to participate in the rebellion and perform the forbidden service, and they all died. What led these intelligent people to do something so foolish?

Further, it seems that this week's Torah portion goes out of its way to point out the importance of those people who rebelled against Moses. If they had been men of ill repute, it would make sense that the Torah would tell us who they were in an effort to demonstrate that it was only the lowly members of the nation who dared to rebel. However, it would seem to be very bad P.R. for the Jews to eternally mention that it was some of their great leaders who sinned. Why does the Torah tell the world derogatory information about our ancestors?

To find an answer to our questions, we must first understand the situation of the leaders of old. Imagine that in addition to your high

I.Q. you are tremendously wealthy, imagine that you have one billion dollars at your disposal. (Or for the more flamboyant, ten billion dollars.) After you buy everything your heart desires, you are still left with a hefty sum. You have everything that money can buy, but no real power, so you purchase a very powerful company. You are feeling on top of the world when one day you flip on the television and there it is, something you do not have – the presidency. The feeling of jealousy begins to slowly eat away at your insides and you become awfully depressed. Noticing you are down, one of your close friends suggests that you run for president. A grand idea, you think, but after a few months of campaigning you realize that although you might have the money to buy some votes, you will not receive enough to put yourself in office, so you are forced to drop out.

This scenario is exactly what the Torah is warning us against. Korach and his group had everything that they could have possible wanted – wealth, honor, prestige – everything except for the coveted right to participate in the Temple service. This was reserved for the *Kohanim*, and nobody could buy that position.

The rabbis in *Pirkei Avot* (4:28) teach that "Jealousy, desire, and honor remove a person from the world." It makes sense that these leaders would be jealous of the *Kohanim*. Imagine how hard it must have been to see the *Kohanim* doing the Temple service, while they had to stay away from the holy area. "I'm sorry, no non-*Kohanim* past this point," the guard always said. The desire to do the work of the *Kohen* and have the honor reserved for *Kohanim* surely fueled their jealousy. So, like the doomed presidential candidate, Korach's followers also tried to gain the unobtainable.

Now we can appreciate why they acted, but we still do not know what motivated such smart people to ignore the obvious truth, that they could go so far as to throw away their life with seemingly little thought. Perhaps these men were blind. Of course, not the normal physical loss of eyesight, rather a self-inflicted unintentional blindness. Many things can blind a person, but it takes something potent, like jealousy, to prevent a person from ever realizing that he has been blinded. Jealousy is often compared to a flame which burns up the insides of a person. Like a small flame, jealousy eats away at a person and quickly grows into a raging uncontrollable fire. Of course, these men were not stupid. In fact they were really quite brilliant, but they <u>were</u> blind.

With this idea in mind, we can understand why the Torah goes out of its way to tell us how great they were. The Torah wants to make the point that even great people can be blinded by their desires. The Torah is warning every one of us, even our greatest leaders, not to be fooled into thinking that we are any better than Korach's clan which succumbed to the vice of jealousy. If they could ignore the obvious, so can we.

So what can we do to protect ourselves? The Talmud (Tractate Sanhedrin 109b) tells an interesting story about one of Korach's cohorts, Onn ben Pelet (mentioned in the first verse of the Torah portion) who had planned to participate in the rebellion with the rest of the leaders. However, his wise and righteous wife persuaded him not to participate, arguing that even if the rebellion would be successful, Korach would be the one in charge and Onn would remain subservient to him, just like he already was to Moses. This brought Onn to his senses and with his wife's help, his life was saved.

As humans, we often fall prey to the "where are my glasses?" dilemma. Often we will search desperately for them to no avail, only to discover later that they were on top of our head the whole time. Something which takes another person a split second to find causes us so much trouble and for an extended period. It would seem that the way to protect ourselves is to have other people who can tell us if our ideas are good. Seek council before acting, bounce the ideas off someone else, ask for advice. By internalizing the lesson taught to us by the many great, yet unfortunate men in Korach's group, we will be better prepared to face life's great challenges – and we might even have better luck finding our missing glasses.

ᴐᴐ Won't You Be My Neighbor
by Avi Lowenstein

Korach had many followers, among them heads of the tribes, but most of his supporters came from the tribe of Reuben. Why was Reuben lured into Korach's movement more than any of the other tribes? Rashi explains this phenomenon with the Talmudic maxim, "Woe is to the wicked, woe is to his neighbor." Since the tribe of Reuben camped beside Korach's Levite family of Kehat, the Reubenites were greatly influenced by Korach.

Because of their close contact with Korach, the Reubenites tragically erred. However, by the same token, the Talmud states that close contact with a great person can enrich a person's life: "Good is to the righteous, good is to his neighbor." The Rambam writes in his classic code of Jewish law, "It is the nature of a person to be pulled in his views and actions after his loved ones and friends, and to act according to the custom of the people of his land. Therefore, a person must attach himself to the righteous and sit with the wise always, so that he will learn from their ways. He should distance himself from the wicked who walk in the dark so that he will not learn from their ways" (Hilchot Dei'ot 6:1-2).

In discussing the locations of the cities of refuge which were established upon the Jewish people's arrival in the land of Israel, the Talmud (Tractate Makkot 9b) comments that although three cities sufficed for the nine and a half tribes in Israel proper, the same number of cities was needed for the two and a half tribes on the other side of the Jordan River, for there were many murderers there. However, this explanation is difficult. The cities of refuge were only for accidental killings, so why should a high homicide rate require more cities if someone who murders intentionally doesn't flee to them anyway? The Maharal of Prague explains that people who live in a place where there are many murders become desensitized and lose sight of the value of human life. When this happens, they become less concerned about preserving human life and eventually, carelessly, destroy it. Therefore, the prevalence of deliberate homicides also led to an increase in unintentional killings.

No matter how much we think that we can resist being influenced by our peers and environment, we cannot remain unaffected. Good fences do not keep out bad neighbors. It is up to us to choose the people with whom we associate. If we surround ourselves and associate with people striving to come closer to Hashem, we too will grow tremendously. Every morning in our prayers we ask Hashem to rescue us from an evil companion and an evil neighbor. With our own efforts and Hashem's help, we can reach great heights by learning from others.

PARSHAT CHUKAT

hukat (Numbers 19:1-22:1) begins with the quintessential decree of the Torah, Chukat HaTorah, *a mitzvah we are asked to perform even though we are unable to understand its purpose and reason –* parah adumah, *the red cow, whose ashes are used to purify people who have become contaminated through contact with a corpse. The narrative then jumps 38 years to begin the description of what transpires just before the Jewish people enter the land of Israel. The prophetess Miriam dies and the people are left without water, since the miraculous well which had accompanied them throughout their sojourn in the desert existed only in her merit. Hashem commands Moses and Aaron to speak to a particular rock so it will miraculously produce water; Moses strikes it with his staff instead, and Hashem tells the two leaders that they will not enter into the Promised Land. After this, the king of Edom refuses to let the Jewish people pass through his borders, causing them to take a more circuitous route. Aaron dies and is buried on Mount Hor, and Elazar his son succeeds him as* Kohen Gadol. *The Children of Israel sing a song of praise about the miraculous well that Hashem had provided in Miriam's merit, and the portion concludes with the battles and victories over Sichon the king of Emori and Og the king of Bashan.*

∽ Shopping for Righteousness

by Kevin Rodbell

Stepping into the modern shopping mall near the central bus station in B'ersheva, Israel you feel quite at home. The dozens of modern shops look distinctly American; you note the familiar sight of people riding escalators, traveling up and down the multi-story atrium that occupies the mall's central section; and, yes, you can sigh a deep breath of relief and fill your lungs with the cool, soothing, air-conditioned air that fills this wonderful shopping center. The actual experience of shopping may not even be so enthralling – after all, the Middle East shopping mentality is not exactly what we're used to, and the customer is not always right – but the mere fact that you are sheltered in a calm, hospitable, <u>cool</u> environment puts your mind at ease. The temperature outside is approaching 105 degrees and you have learned to appreciate the air conditioner which provides this mass of cold air.

Thanks to modern innovations like air conditioners, efficient long-distance water conveyances, and improved food storage, large cities like B'ersheva have begun developing on the edges of deserts. But their existence is tenuous and only possible in the mildest areas. In essence, the desert remains defiantly harsh to human habitation; so much so that it makes you wonder how the Jews – a nation with a seven-digit population – survived wandering in the desert for forty years before they entered the land of Israel.

No, the Jews were not sustained by air conditioners, piped water, and shipped food. Instead they benefited from some rather miraculous devices provided by Hashem. Special clouds surrounded and covered the traveling nation; they maintained a kind of ultimate climate-control, cooling the air and removing obstacles on the path ahead. Plus, the Jews didn't have to worry about sunburn. The clouds also offered protection from predators. Furthermore, manna descended six days a week. The perfect food substitute, manna provided 100% RDA of everything. In fact, the manna was so perfect that all of it was absorbed by the digestive tract, obviating the need to relieve one-self. And a well, flowing from a large rock, rolled along with them to supply water. With most of their physical needs provided for, the Jews had plenty of time to immerse themselves in the study of the Torah which they had received at the beginning of their journey.

However, the gifts that made this ideal and protective environment possible were not gratuitous. Rather, the Jews received them in the merit of several devoted, motivated, and righteous individuals who dwelled amongst them. The Talmud (Tractate Ta'anit 9a) relates that Israel had three great leaders – Moses, Aaron, and Miriam – and three wonderful gifts were given through them. In the merit of Miriam, a well continuously overflowed with water; Aaron was responsible for the Clouds of Glory; and the manna fell in Moses' merit.

Although these associations – Miriam with the well, Aaron with the Clouds, and Moses with the manna – are not mentioned explicitly in the Torah, each one can be detected with some basic, careful observations in the flow of the text. Hashem records in our Torah portion that Miriam died and was buried in Kadesh, a place in the Desert of Tzin. The description continues, "And there was no water for the congregation, and they gathered [to complain] to Moses and Aaron" (Numbers 20:2). Why are these seemingly unrelated events placed back to back? The water from the well flowed in Miriam's merit. She was a *tzadeket*, a righteous woman, who dedicated herself to serving Hashem. Her presence and involvement with the Jews brought them special consideration from Hashem; her passing left a great void for the Jewish people. Since her unique qualities that had merited the well were absent, the well ceased to function.

The deaths of Aaron and Moses left similar gaps, leaving the Jewish people bereft of the Clouds of Glory and of the manna. In fact, whenever a *tzadik* or *tzadeket* leaves us – whether to the next world or to another location in this world – we feel a great sense of loss. When the Torah describes Jacob's traveling from Canaan to Charan (where his uncle Laban lived) it makes a very revealing addition:

"Jacob left B'ersheva and went to Charan" (Genesis 28:10). The Torah could have conserved words by combining the two verbs as follows: "Jacob went from B'ersheva to Charan." Obviously, the act of leaving is inherently significant. In this regard, Rashi quotes a *Midrash* which states, "A *tzadik's* departure from a place leaves an indelible impression." The Yafeh To'ar explains that wherever a *tzadik* goes he enlightens his surroundings (both spiritually and physically) with his Torah wisdom. He bestows a sense of dignity upon all those in his presence by honoring and being honored by them and he offers invaluable advice from a Torah perspective. As a Torah role model, the *tzadik* sets an influential and positive example for those around him.

Perhaps this can help clarify the *mitzvah* of "And to Him you shall cling" (Deuteronomy 10:20). We cannot physically cling to Hashem because He is not physical. Our rabbis therefore explain that we must seize every opportunity to associate with righteous and pious individuals, Jews who are immersed in Hashem's Torah and whose every action reflects that immersion. Certainly *tzadikim* are mortal, but their powerful, penetrating influence can help us grow closer to Hashem. A practical lesson emerges from all of this. Every time you encounter such a person, opportunity is knocking – even the most basic interactions have a guaranteed effect. You can grow Jewishly by conducting business with, eating lunch with, or simply introducing yourself to this person. Beyond the gifts that a community receives in the merit of a *tzadik,* the *tzadik* himself benefits the community; his mere presence is a gift in its own right.

☞ Torah from the Desert?

by Avi Lowenstein

Towards the end of this week's Torah portion, in singing praises of the well which followed them in the desert, the Children of Israel list their travels. The list begins with their journey from a place called

Midbar (desert) to a place called Matana (literally meaning gift) (Numbers 21:18). The *Midrash* understands Matana to refer to the Torah, the ultimate gift from Hashem to the Children of Israel. According to this interpretation, this passage referring to their travels also alludes to the receiving of the Torah in the desert. The question arises: Why was the Torah given in the desert, a barren and desolate place? A possible answer could be that the desert represents the great potential of every person. When left alone it is nothing more than a wasteland, but when cultivated it can produce a lush oasis.

The *Midrash* says that not only did the well provide water for the Children of Israel to drink, it also irrigated the ground which, in turn, grew abundant vegetation. The key ingredient necessary to develop one's potential to the maximum is "water". The Torah is compared to water, for just as water will always seek the lowest ground level at which to settle, so too, the Torah settles in a person who humbles himself and makes his ego low. Similarly, just as a desert needs water to become productive and flourish, so must the Jew have "water" (Torah) to develop and thrive.

We can learn from the Torah being given in the desert that, as human beings, we have tremendous potential. To develop that potential we must saturate ourselves, through and through, with the Torah. However, before we can absorb the Torah, we must humble ourselves to a level at which the Torah will rest. Then, as Hashem will one day "make the desert like Eden and the wilderness as the Garden of Hashem" (Isaiah 51:3), so too with Hashem's help will we blossom and achieve our potential.

PARSHAT BALAK

arshat Balak (Numbers 22:2-25:9) shifts from the Jewish people's travels in the desert to relate the story of Bilam, the gentile prophet who attempted to curse the Children of Israel. Commissioned by Balak, the king of Moav, Bilam agrees to embark on a journey to the Israelite encampment; however he first asks Hashem for permission, and goes on the condition that he would speak only what Hashem places in his mouth. While on the road, an angel brandishing a sword blocks Bilam's path, causing his donkey to repeatedly swerve off the road. Unable to see the angel, Bilam responds by striking the disobedient donkey three times. Miraculously, Hashem causes the donkey to speak to Bilam, and G-d uncovers the humiliated prophet's eyes so that he can see the angel standing in the path. The angel then reminds Bilam once again that he may only speak the words that Hashem places in his mouth. Upon his arrival near the Jewish camp, Bilam repeatedly attempts to curse the people; each time Hashem prevents him from doing so, and instead he ends up uttering several sets of blessings and praises, much to Balak's dismay. The Torah portion concludes with the Jewish men's debauchery with the promiscuous daughters of Moav and Midian, and the public licentious act of Zimri (a prince of the tribe of Simeon) with a Midianite princess. Pinchas, Aaron's grandson, zealously responds by piercing them to death with a spear, halting a plague from Hashem which had broken out in the camp.

☞ **Lion Around**

by Rabbi Dov Ber Weisman

The Talmud (Tractate Berachot 12b) states that the sages wanted to include this week's Torah portion of Balak in our daily recital of the fundamental *Shema* prayer. The question, of course, is why? What is so special in the Torah portion of Balak to justify its daily recital in one of our most important prayers? The answer can be found in one particular verse – "They are a nation that arises like a young lion" (Numbers 23:24).

The Sfas Emes explains that the rabbis considered this verse to be so important because it represents one of the highest acclamations of the Jewish people. Like the lion, we are a nation that always arises; no matter how low we have sunk, we always get back up. This is what Jews are all about, and it is our proudest character trait. We are a people that arises from the ashes. It is a quality that is expressed by anyone who has any connection to a family who went through the Holocaust and survives today to call themselves a Jew.

In the concentration camps, Eichmann took the curtain off of an *aron kodesh* (holy ark) and placed it over the entrance to the gas chamber. On it was written the verse, "This is the gate to Hashem; righteous ones will go through it." He meant it as a mockery – a mockery of Hashem, the Jewish people, and of anything beyond the realm of this physical world. But the message was truly accurate – the Jews who went through that curtain did become righteous. Eichmann and the Nazis are long gone, but we put that curtain back up on our arks. We rose back up like a lion, and there are now more ark curtains and more synagogues to put them in than ever before. No matter how many times we fall down, we always get back up. This is the hallmark of the nation of Israel. The prophets called us "a nation of survivors".

King Solomon writes, "A righteous one falls seven times and gets back up" (Proverbs 24:16). Who exactly is a righteous one?

A righteous individual is not necessarily one who never sins, but rather a person who sins and gets back up.

This is the message that Rabbi Yitzchak Hutner wrote to one of his students who was discouraged about his apparent lack of spiritual attainment and growth. Rabbi Hutner told him, "Do not give up. That's what life is all about – the battles, the struggles. Our sages say that the only way to become a righteous individual is after falling. That is what makes you better. Growth comes only through struggle. It isn't automatic. Sometimes you've got to lose some battles before winning the war."

This is what *teshuvah* is all about. There are going to be battles, regressions, struggles, and losses. But we have to get back up. It is a lesson in Jewish history and a lesson to each and everyone of us. Sometimes, we as Jews can be sleeping. We can go for years without doing *mitzvot*. And then we get up like a lion and change. We are a nation that is not beaten, a nation of survivors. It is because of this trait that we are still here today.

Based in part on a class from Rabbi Yissocher Frand.

∽ Environmental Concerns
by Daniel Lasar

In last week's portion, the Torah describes how the Children of Israel were advancing towards the land of Israel. Before entering the land, the people encountered enemy armies along the way that they subsequently defeated. In this week's portion, the Torah narrates how the Moavites and Midianites, hearing of the Israelites' victories, conspired to defeat the Jews through a method apart from conventional warfare. They realized that a physical challenge to the Jews would be in vain. It was not through armed combat, but rather through spiritual malfeasance that they would attack the Jewish people.

Balak, the Moavite king, summoned a renowned gentile, Bilam, to issue a curse on the Jewish people. However, Hashem thwarted Bilam's efforts, and ultimately Bilam could only bless the Jews. Noting their modesty even in the layout of their camp, he uttered the famous blessing, "How goodly are your tents O' Jacob, your dwelling places O' Israel" (Numbers 24:5).

Nonetheless, Bilam remained undaunted in his resolve to bring harm to the Jews. He instructed the representatives of Moav/Midian that the Jewish people could be defeated another way: Luring the Jewish people to serve false gods by using gentile women to entice the Israelite men. Thus, Bilam's advice was to wean the hearts of the Jews away from Torah and toward idol worship. Sadly, some Israelites succumbed to the temptations of the gentile women. The debauchery ended only when Pinchas, Aaron's grandson, killed a tribal leader who was publicly engaged in this sinful conduct.

The sequence of the above events has stark relevance to the condition of the Jewish people today. After nearly two millennia of triumphantly struggling to survive amongst a multitude of physical persecutions, the Jewish nation is today waging a crucial spiritual battle. It is not the guns or knives of an oppressor, but rather the allures and temptations of Western society that so grievously threaten our very existence. One of the most tragic problems the Jewish people face today is intermarriage. Disastrously, the result of most mixed-marriages is that within the next two generations, most remnants of Judaism are completely obliterated and substituted with the "false gods" of Western culture. Too many of our brethren do not see the importance of marrying a Jewish mate, of building a Torah household, or of continuing our spiritual mission in the world. Yet, the very foundation of the Jewish people is the Jewish home. For this core unit to productively convey Hashem's beautiful value-system to the world, it is essential that both partners in this task – husband and wife – be dedicated to the Torah dictates that they will transmit.

We should take heed of the zeal with which Pinchas acted to save the nation from further spiritual calamity. So too must we not be afraid to reach out to someone straying from our people. We should work to create an atmosphere whereby intermarriage will be less prevalent, and ultimately, non-existent.

As we approach the beginning of the three-week period of mourning for the destruction of the Temples, consider that one of the reasons for the destruction of the first Temple was because the Jewish people engaged in, among other things, forbidden relationships. Interestingly, Rashi cites a *Midrash* on Bilam's earlier mentioned blessing to the Jewish people which has great relevance to this time of year. The word "tents" in the verse, refers to the Temples when they were in existence, while "dwelling places" alludes to the period of time when the Temples are destroyed. This is because the Hebrew word for "dwelling place – *mishkan*" is also closely related to the Hebrew word "*mashkon* – collateral". This suggests that rather than destroy the Jewish people for their sins, instead Hashem destroyed the Temples, venting His anger on the inanimate bricks in place of the people.

Thus, we should endeavor to rectify our people's errant ways by lovingly seeking out Jews who have strayed from the path of Torah. We should delicately point out to them the tremendous rewards of a Jewish lifestyle. As the great sage Hillel said, "Be among the disciples of Aaron, loving peace and pursuing peace, loving people and bringing them closer to Torah" (*Pirkei Avot* 1:12).

PARSHAT PINCHAS

arshat Pinchas *(Numbers 25:10-30:1) begins with Hashem bestowing His blessing of peace and priesthood on Pinchas, Aaron's grandson, for slaying a prince of the tribe of Simeon and a Midianite princess while they were engaged in a public licentious act (at the end of last week's Torah portion). Pinchas' zealous response saves the Jewish people from a plague which had broken out in the camp. Hashem commands Moses and Elazar (Aaron's son and successor as Kohen Gadol) to conduct a new census of the entire nation, the first one taken in almost thirty-nine years. The Torah then relates the claim issued by the five daughters of Tzlaphchad for a portion of inheritance in the land of Israel, since they had no brothers and their father had died in the desert. Hashem responds in the affirmative, and in the merit of these righteous women many of the laws of inheritance are taught. After Hashem shows Moses the land of Israel from the top of a mountain, Moses is commanded to pass on his mantle of leadership to Joshua by resting his hand upon Joshua's head, since Moses would not be entering the land. The Torah portion concludes with a lengthy description of the special* korbanot *to be brought on the various festivals throughout the year, above and beyond the regular* korban tamid *brought every morning and afternoon. These sections are also read from the Torah throughout the year on the appropriate holidays.*

To Be Continued. . .

by Benyamin Cohen

At the end of last week's Torah portion, we were told of the Midianite women's attempt to lure the Jewish men to worship *Ba'al Peor*, a hideous pagan idol. Their strategy to seduce the men was succeeding and had already led to the deaths of 24,000 people by a Divinely dispatched plague. The story climaxes when Zimri, a prince of the tribe of Simeon, is seen having illicit relations with Kazbi, a Midianite princess, right in the middle of the Israelite camp. Pinchas, the grandson of Aaron, responds by taking a spear and piercing it through the stomachs of both sinful parties, thereby ending the plague.

And so we begin this week's Torah portion which is named after Pinchas for his courageous deed. Here we read about Hashem's reward to Pinchas – a blessing of peace and eternal *Kehunah*, priesthood. Strangely, even though this discussion only occupies part of one short section of the Torah portion, nevertheless the entire portion is named after Pinchas. Not only that, if a Torah portion is going to be named after somebody, it would seemingly make more sense to include the entire episode of Pinchas – from his heroic action to Hashem's reward – all in one portion. Why was his courageous deed discussed last week in Parshat Balak and his reward described this week in Parshat Pinchas?

Perhaps, the Torah's division of the episode into two portions is an attempt to teach us a lesson. Pinchas killed Zimri for one reason and one reason only – he knew it was the right thing to do. Somebody had to take action and stop the Midianite women from causing the death of the entire Jewish nation. Pinchas' action was motivated on the highest level. Pinchas did not act for self-gratification. He did not do it because he wanted to get a Torah portion named after him. He did it solely for the sanctification of Hashem and His people. By separating Pinchas' action from his reward, the Torah is teaching us that Pinchas did not foresee, or even care about, receiving a reward from Hashem. His action stood alone, on its own merit.

How often do we find ourselves doing something not because it's the right thing to do, but because we want to receive some type of reward? How often do we do something just to boost our own ego? What the Torah is teaching us through Pinchas is that we should try most diligently to do things simply because we know that it is right. Our reward will come in its proper time. We should not do good deeds just to see our name in lights.

⌒ How to Become a Priest
by Matthew Leader

This week's Torah portion could more accurately be called "Post-Pinchas" in that the opening narrative really is a continuation of, and primarily focuses on, last week's portion's events. We begin Parshat Pinchas with a description of the reward that Pinchas receives for his rather pointed opposition to the sin of a prince of the tribe of Simeon with a Midianite princess. We know that as a rule, heavenly rewards are doled out on a *midah k'neged midah* basis. Since Hashem rewards Pinchas with the blessing of priesthood, it can therefore be assumed that the main thrust of his action must have been actively connected to the idea of priesthood. But how?

First, we must understand that Pinchas was not merely acting as a "religious zealot" wildly attacking sin. He was fighting an ideological battle, one which is disturbingly relevant to us today. Midian had introduced the Children of Israel to *Ba'al Peor*, a grotesque form of idol worship, and they were beginning to be led astray. What was it about this particular idolatry that was so enticing that the Jewish people could descend to such a depraved level that a tribal prince would commit a public act of immorality with a Midianite woman?

Our sages express to us the whole philosophy of *Ba'al Peor*. The Midianites worshipped this idol by utterly debasing it through defecating upon it. The total theme of the *Ba'al Peor* worship was one of freedom – freedom from any rules or restrictions, both socially and morally. The worship was not one of a god, but a worship of anarchy, chaos, and an <u>absence</u> of Hashem. Obviously, this kind of philosophy can be very inviting, especially to those who value themselves as smart and independent. The Midianites, however, realized that the Jewish people are the direct antithesis of this concept. From the moment we defined our national identity with the words *"na'aseh v'nishma* – we will do and we will listen"*, every action of our lives has been proscribed by a higher authority to which we knowingly and voluntarily bend our will. Our creativity, uniqueness, and individuality stem from the way that we each operate <u>within</u> the system, not from the ways that we can find to reject it.

So too do we find with the action of Pinchas. Rashi tells us that before killing the offending parties, Pinchas asked Moses to rule on what to do in this case. In sharp contradistinction to other "zealots" the world over, Pinchas was not possessed by wild, unchecked emotion, but by a basic analytical assessment of the situation and its appropriate response. His action was a defense not only of the honor of Hashem, the Torah, Moses, and the nation, but of our very religious composition.

Therefore, we can now understand why Hashem chose to reward him by making him part of the priestly line. Other heavenly rewards such as prophecy, long life, great wisdom, or wealth are appropriate for acts of individual devotion or piety. Pinchas' action, however, was in defense of the order and system decreed by Hashem. What better way to be rewarded than by becoming the highest personification of that order – a *Kohen*, servant to the system he defended and upheld.

PARSHAT MATTOT

attot *(Numbers 30:2-32:42) begins with a dis-cussion of the laws regarding vows (nedarim) and oaths (shevuot). The Torah then describes the Jewish people's battle against and victory* over Midian, followed by a detailed account of the distribution of the spoils of war. In anticipation of the upcoming entrance into the land of Israel, the tribes of Reuben and Gad step forward to request that their inheritance be on the eastern side of the Jordan River rather than in the Holy Land proper, since the eastern bank would be more suitable for their abundant livestock. After some discussion, Moses agrees, but only on the condition that they assist the rest of the nation in conquering the entire land of Israel before returning to settle their inheritance.

∽ Heartless Murderer
by Ranon Cortell

Two portions ago, at the end of Parshat Balak, a staggering and decimating plague swept the Children of Israel as a result of the sins incited and assisted by our formidable foes, the Moavites and Midianites. In the same portion, our entire existence was also dangerously threatened by a crafty and powerful gentile sorcerer, Bilam, who was enlisted by the joint forces of Midian and Moav to curse the Jewish people, hoping to render them defenseless prey to their ravaging enemies. Yet, in this week's portion, when Hashem decides that it has come time to avenge the honor of Israel and destroy its enemies, He commands Moses to destroy only the Midianites while allowing the Moavites to escape scot-free.

Why, one asks, were the Midianites chosen for destruction while the Moavites, who led the rank intrusion, were spared?

To answer this question, Rashi explains that the Moavites acted purely for self-defense reasons against a looming and potent enemy on their borders, while the Midianites had engaged in a dispute that did not concern them, for they were not threatened by the Jews since they lived far away from the route to the land of Israel. It was for the Midianites' action of baseless hatred that Hashem took His vengeance. The Rosh explains that such a hatred and involvement in other people's disputes is especially dangerous spiritually because even when the quarreling parties arrive at a settlement, the hatred of the unaffected outsider will retain its vigor since, after all, it was not based on anything to begin with.

This message is especially crucial to our generation for whom baseless hatred is one of our most outstanding faults and challenges. The Talmud (Tractate Yoma 9b) exhorts us that for the unbearable sin of baseless and futile hatred of a fellow Jew, one's wife and children are caused to die, Heaven forbid. Rashi explains that this punishment is *midah k'neged midah*, for just as one has failed to love others, the ones that love him may be taken away from him. Therefore, we must view this terrible sin of baseless hatred as a heartless murderer and combat it fervently.

Rabbi Yechiel Weinberg relates a conversation he had with the Alter of Slabodka. One day the Alter was talking about the "Three Weeks", the period of Jewish mourning for the destruction of the Temples in which we are currently immersed. In summary, he explained that the reason for the institution of this period of mourning was to awaken us from our rut of sin and spur us to repentance, so that we should be deserving of the rebuilding of the Temple. The first Temple was destroyed due to the Jewish people's involvement in murder, idol worship, and immoral relations, and yet the exile lasted only seventy years. The second Temple, on the other hand, despite the Jews involvement in Torah and good deeds, was razed mainly because of the menacing sin of baseless hatred, and alas we still have not been worthy to see it rebuilt.

Beware, the Alter commands, this sinister influence still lurks among us, and unfortunately we lack the level of good deeds and Torah that encompassed our forefathers. Honestly, he asks, how many of us, upon seeing a colleague elevated to a position of honor which we thought we deserved, would not seethe at the horrible insult and wonder why our friends did not jump forward to defend our honor? And yet how many of us simply go through the motions and laws of this time period without acting upon its essential message – to eradicate the baseless hatred from our hearts?

How true the words of the Alter ring and reverberate in our innermost hearts. We must instill this crucial message within us, repent for our past sins, and learn to practice baseless love. Once we achieve this, and with the help of Hashem, the Temple will be rebuilt speedily in our days.

∽ Common Sense
by Michael Alterman

Consider for a moment the exhilaration which the Jewish army must have felt as they returned from their convincing victory over the Midianites, described in this week's Torah portion. Fresh from their battle and triumph, they must have been extremely excited as they stood poised, after almost forty years in the desert, to finally cross the Jordan River into the land of Israel. They had seemingly fulfilled Hashem's command to the letter of the law – to wipe out the Midianites, a nation which had been a debilitating thorn in the sides of the Children of Israel on more than one occasion by causing the Jewish people to sin and actively seeking their destruction.

As the Jewish army returned to their camp, however, they probably were quite surprised to see Moses coming out to greet them – not with a congratulatory smile on his face, but instead upset and saddened. "You let the women live?" Moses rebuked them (Numbers 31:15).

A primary purpose of the attack, claimed Moses, was to punish and kill the Midianite women who had enticed the Jewish men into idolatry and illicit relations, inducing a plague which resulted in the deaths of 24,000 Jews. Moses was dismayed to see that the officers had not only allowed the women to remain alive, but even stood idly by while the people brought them back as captives. It certainly sounds like Moses had a good reason to be upset.

However, if we scan through Moses' instructions to the army before they left for battle, we will find that he never actually commanded the army to kill the women. As a result, it would appear that the returning officers had a valid excuse for their supposed misdeed. Since the regular procedure in battle was to kill only the men while sparing the women and children, Moses should have explicitly told them to kill the women if that was what Hashem wanted. If so, what right did Moses have to be incensed at the officers for not following orders which were never given?

In answering this question, the Sh'lah learns from this event an important lesson which is a fundamental tenet of Judaism. Hashem blessed Man with a highly developed brain capable of achieving the greatest levels of wisdom and understanding. However, Hashem did not bestow upon us this wonderful gift for free. He expects us to make use of it in everything that we do. Being given these faculties demands our acting responsibly and sensibly.

It should not have been difficult for the officers to recognize that if anybody from the Midianite camp deserved to be punished, it would be the parties that were the most guilty. It was those licentious Midianite women who had caused most of the trouble, and they should have been the first to be killed. Moses therefore should not have needed to tell the army something which was so obvious; that the women deserved punishment was clear and unmistakable. Since the officers should have understood this on their own, they were held responsible for not killing the women, as if they had violated a direct command.

By blessing Man with an advanced intellect, Hashem obligated us to continually use our conscience and common sense to challenge, sharpen, and fine tune our perspectives on life. Rabbi Moshe Chaim Luzzatto states that Hashem created us with the sole purpose that we should rejoice and derive pleasure from the splendor of G-d's presence. When we fail to educate ourselves and determine what our unique purpose is in this world, we miss out on the key to achieving the greatest pleasure possible, and that is the ultimate tragedy. When we hide behind ignorance, nobody loses out except for ourselves.

PARSHAT MASEI

arshat Masei (Numbers 33:1-36:13) opens by summarizing the entire route traveled by the Jewish people over their forty years in the desert, beginning with their exodus from Egypt and concluding with their arrival at the banks of the Jordan River. After commanding the people to drive out all of the Holy Land's inhabitants, the Torah delineates the exact boundaries of the land of Israel. Since the Levites would not be receiving a regular portion, special cities were to be set aside for them, some of which would also serve as cities of refuge for accidental murderers. In certain circumstances, somebody who unintentionally killed another person would flee to one of these cities of refuge to seek sanctuary and avoid retribution from a close relative of the victim, and he would be required to remain there until the death of the present Kohen Gadol. After setting the guidelines for the various categories of murder, the book of Numbers concludes with further information regarding the daughters of Tzlaphchad and the laws of inheritance.

⌘ The Road Less Traveled
by Rabbi Yonason Goldson

The Jewish people are unique in that they are truly one, not a collection of individuals coming together to form a nation, but a single collective soul divided up into separate entities. Each one has an identity defining his unique role as an integral part of the whole. Just as the human body will not function properly unless every component part is performing its job, so too does the collective Jewish *neshamah* fall ill when the individuals who compose it do not fulfill their responsibilities. And when the body is not well, all of its parts suffer.

The power and responsibility entrusted to us by Hashem is awesome, and the consequences of our failures are potentially cataclysmic. The Creator, in His infinite wisdom, understood that most of us would inevitably stumble from time to time in our passage through life in this world, so He built into His design of creation a contingency plan: Where one person stumbles, another may catch him; when one Jew damages the universe through wanton or careless acts, another Jew may repair that damage.

Those *tzadikim*, the righteous who immerse themselves in the study and practice of Hashem's Torah, are the repair crew. By achieving ever greater levels of understanding and observance through their sensitivity to every nuance and intonation of the Torah's words, they rectify the mistakes made by the rest of us and guide us towards a greater understanding of ourselves, so we should not err again.

In the words of this week's Torah portion lies a subtle allusion to these ideas. When one recounts his travels, he will normally say that he traveled to a certain place and stayed there. The Torah, however, in its recounting the travels of the Children of Israel, employs an awkward phrasing, reporting that they journeyed from one place and encamped in the next, without mentioning their arrival at all. Furthermore, the list begins by stating, "And Moses wrote their goings forth to their journeys. . .and these were their journeys to their goings out" (Numbers 33:2); aside from the apparent inconsistency and redundancy, the simple meaning of the verse is elusive.

The words of this verse contain the following allegorical meaning: In our journeys through life, as with the Children of Israel's journeys through the desert, sometimes we "journey" away from the path that Hashem has prepared for us, and we become lost in a spiritual wasteland. At such moments, the righteous among us "go out" to rectify what we have done; through their personal diligence in Torah study and practice, they guide us back to the proper path by the example they set. Thus, after we "journey" away from one place, they "encamp" at the next, meaning that they reestablish the supernal balance of the universe and restore the direction of the Jewish people to its correct orientation.

Who are these *tzadikim*, these righteous ones? No one should be satisfied with his achievements, our sages tell us, until he has attained the level of our fathers Abraham, Isaac, and Jacob. Is this not an impossible task? Daunting, perhaps, but not impossible, for the sages intended with their words to convey to us that just as the Patriarchs developed themselves by realizing the full potential Hashem had given them, so too will we be like them if we develop our own potential to the maximum. Thus, we ask Hashem three times a day in our prayers to "place our lot with them – the righteous – forever," that He should guide us and help us develop ourselves to the limit of our potential so that we may be counted together with the righteous in this world and in the next.

Adapted from Sefer Noam Elimelech.

❧ 2000 Years and Counting
by Rabbi Yossi Lew

In Parshat Masei, the instruction is given to delegate "cities of refuge" to which a person who accidentally killed someone can flee from pursuers and avengers. If it is determined that the killing was accidental, the killer remains in the refuge city until the death of the *Kohen Gadol*, at which time he may return home. This sojourn is regarded by our sages as "*galut*", for although he is safe from attackers, the person is now relegated to live in a strange and foreign place, sequestered and isolated, "exiled" from family and friends.

The Torah discusses the cities of refuge in three other places. It is interesting that the Torah prefers to record the specific instructions pertaining to *galut* in a portion which is read during a period in the Jewish calendar that is a sad time for the Jewish people – the "Three Weeks". These three weeks begin on *Shivah Asar B'Tammuz* when the walls around Jerusalem were breached by our enemies, and culminate on *Tishah B'Av* when the Temple in Jerusalem was destroyed. Both of these days are marked by fasting and praying. The breaching of the walls and eventual destruction of the Temple were the beginning of the exile and suffering that has lasted for almost two thousand years, until the present day.

To be honest, this notion of fasting and mourning for the downed walls seems somewhat perplexing. Let's face it, the broken walls around Jerusalem seem like a mere detail in a long line of grievous misfortunes that has befallen the Jewish people. After the many tragedies and troubles that we have incurred throughout the past two thousand years – just think about the Holocaust, or that we are still threatened by evil terrorists who imperil our very existence – and after the rebuilding of a home for the Jewish people in the land of Israel, and with wonderful Jewish communities throughout the world, wouldn't it make more sense to fast and pray for the likes of world peace, elimination of hunger, abolishing illness, and so forth?

We can understand this by first examining the concept of *galut*. This lengthy *galut* which we mourn does not exclusively refer to the removal of the Jewish people from our homeland, or to all of the other terrible calamities which have befallen our people throughout these years. Rather, it is something much more meaningful and serious. What we are really mourning is the destruction of the Temple and what it stood for. The Temple exemplified the revelation of Hashem to His people and to this world. The destruction of the Temple personifies the removal of this revelation and Hashem going into "hiding" so to speak. This is the real tragedy.

To illustrate this, we can use the example of a king who had a favorite son who was banished from the empire. While in exile, the young prince, having been removed from the shelter and protection of his home, experiences all kinds of torments and miseries. The smart prince would utilize every iota of ambition and energy to only one single end – to return home to his father the king where he could revel in the majestic glory of the monarchy. Once back home, all other distressing afflictions and worries would automatically disappear. The same is true with us, the Jewish people. Our whole focus and attention should be the ability to get back home, back to Hashem's home, our Holy Temple, and to experience that Divine revelation once more, when Hashem will welcome us back into His kingdom. Once that happens, there will automatically be no more trouble.

So, this three week period gives us a chance to rise above the ongoing troubles of the *galut*, and reflect upon the real issue and meaning of *galut*. The breaching of the walls around Jerusalem and the ensuing destruction of the Temple is a core problem, not a mere detail in our sea of troubles. Our prayers and thoughts should therefore be focused towards the main solution, that Hashem should immediately send us our righteous *Mashiach*, and consequently herald in a time of peace, tranquillity, and goodness. As we ask of Hashem in the daily *Shemoneh Esrei* prayer, we need to see *"b'shuvcha l'tzion b'rachamim* – when Hashem will return to Zion in mercy." We have been "sequestered" far too long in *galut*. We must be allowed to come home.

DEUTERONOMY

PARSHAT DEVARIM

 his week we begin the fifth and final book of the Torah, Sefer Devarim *(Deuteronomy)*, which is known in rabbinic literature as Mishneh Torah, *the review of the Torah. Its contents were* spoken by Moses to the Jewish people during the final five weeks of his life as the people prepared to enter the land of Israel. In it, Moses explains and elaborates upon many of the mitzvot which had been previously given, some of which were already mentioned explicitly in the Torah and others which appear here for the first time. He also continuously warns them to remain diligent and faithful to Hashem's laws and teachings.

Parshat Devarim (Deuteronomy 1:1-3:11) begins with Moses' veiled rebuke in which he makes reference to the many sins and rebellions of the past forty years. He then continues by recounting several of the significant incidents which occurred to the Jewish people in the desert, shedding light on the Torah's earlier accounts. Moses spends a significant amount of time discussing the failed mission of the spies: Ten of the twelve men sent to scout out the land had returned with a bad report, and because of the people's lack of faith, Hashem condemned the entire nation to forty years of wandering in the desert during which time the generation of the exodus died out. Moses then skips forward to discuss the Children of Israel's conquest on the eastern bank of the Jordan River, and the Torah portion concludes with words of encouragement for Moses' successor, Joshua.

∞ The Riddler

by Yoel Spotts

"These are the words which Moses spoke to all of Israel beyond the Jordan River, in the desert, in the Aravah, opposite Suf, between Paran and Tofel, and Lavan and Chatzerot and Di-Zahav" (Deuteronomy 1:1).

Although this verse may represent the opening and introduction to *Sefer Devarim*, at first glance the verse appears laden with problematic passages and phrases. The astute observer will immediately notice that not only were the Jews not located in the desert as the verse seems to suggests (they were actually in the plains of Moav), but nowhere in the Torah do we find mention of places such as Paran, Tofel, and Lavan. Rashi solves the puzzle with the explanation that in reality this verse has no intention of informing us of the location of the Children of Israel. Rather, these phrases are actually allusions to events and serve as a continuation of the first half of the verse. Thus, the verse should actually be read, "These are the words [of rebuke] which Moses spoke to all of Israel," with the verse proceeding to delineate the various sins committed by the Jews in the desert, each "place" referring to a different evil.

However, we are immediately presented with another difficulty: Why should Moses have to cloak his words of admonition in a shroud of disguise? Why not just come straight out and clearly delineate the crimes of the Jewish people? Once again Rashi comes to the rescue, explaining that Moses chose to hide his rebuke in hints and allusions so as not to risk insulting or offending a fellow Jew. If one were to spend only a moment of deliberation on Rashi's words, he could easily dismiss them and move on. However the time invested to delve a bit deeper into Rashi's interpretation is well worth it, as it reveals a remarkable treasure.

The book of Deuteronomy represents Moses' final achievements as leader of the Children of Israel. He has guided the Jews through the desert for forty years, acting at times as their parent and at other times as their mediator and negotiator. He has seen it all. Now the time has come for Moses to deliver his final words of rebuke and encouragement. It's now or never; if the Jews don't get the message now, they never will.

Certainly, it should be expected that Moses would want his intentions to be made as clear as possible, so as not to leave any room for misunderstanding. However, we find the exact opposite in this verse, as Moses cloaks his message behind a veil of cryptic allusions and references. And for what reason? So as not to offend or embarrass a fellow Jew which might lead to disunity among the Jewish people. Moses is willing to take the risk that his last words of admonition might be misconstrued and misapplied, in order to maintain harmony in the camp of Israel. The demand for peace is so great that it even overrides Moses' significant message in his final speech.

In fact, we find the same idea in the words of our sages concerning the reign of Achav, one of the most wicked kings Israel ever had. The Talmud (Yerushalmi Tractate Pe'ah) teaches that although the practice of idol worship had engulfed virtually the entire Jewish population in Israel at that time, the armies of Achav nonetheless were able to defeat their enemies in war. Why? Because the unity and harmony that prevailed then among the Jews overshadowed even the grave sin of idol worship.

The message is clear – the necessity for peace and solidarity among the Jewish people is of utmost importance. Even Moses' last will and testament, or the evil of idol worship, cannot undermine the significance of unity. Although we certainly must be cognizant of this reality at all times, the period that we currently find ourselves in begs us to pay the matter even more attention. This interval between *Shivah Asar B'Tammuz* and *Tishah B'Av*, known simply as the "Three Weeks", commemorates the events leading up to and including the actual destruction of the two holy Temples on *Tishah B'Av*. The Talmud (Tractate Yoma 9b) teaches that the destruction of the second Temple was brought about by the evil of unwarranted hatred towards others. It was the failure of the Jews of that time to recognize the importance of respecting and honoring the needs of their fellow Jews that led to the fateful destruction of the Temple. It is up to us to rectify their omission by taking to heart the important lesson concealed in Rashi's words on this week's Torah portion. For just as the Temple was destroyed due to unwarranted hatred, so too it will be rebuilt through unwarranted kindness.

∽ Repeat After Me
by Benyamin Cohen

The book of Deuteronomy, which we begin to read today, contains Moses' parting address to the Children of Israel; essentially it is a summary of the first four books of the Torah. In fact, the word "Deuteronomy", taken from the Greek word *Deutronomion*, actually means "Second Law", basically a repetition of the Torah. It makes you wonder. What was the point? Why did Hashem include in the Torah an entire fifth book which primarily consisted of review? Were the first four books not enough?

Conceivably we can derive a significant lesson from the inclusion of this fifth, and seemingly superfluous, book. Perhaps, the following perplexing statement as told in the Talmud can shed a bit of light on the situation. The Talmud points out that when a person is reviewing something, he should review it 101 times. What is the difference between 100 and 101? The commentaries on the Talmud explain that, from a psychological standpoint, a person will review a concept 100 times simply to achieve such a lofty goal. The actual reviewing is overshadowed by the person's acclaimed achievement. Simply put, 100 is a nice round number. To review something 101 times shows the supreme nature of the character of the person involved. While reviewing 100 times says, "Ah, I've completed my mission. I can go out and play ball now," reviewing 101 times says that you are going above and beyond the natural call of duty.

How often do we find ourselves at the end of a lecture saying, "Wow, that was incredible. I'm going to take these lessons and apply them to my everyday life." How many times do we learn something in a class that really inspires us? How often do we read an article in *Torah from Dixie* thinking how illuminating it was? Yet, just a day later, the lessons and inspirations have simply disappeared. Jumping back into our jobs and daily routines erases what we learned just a day earlier. If we would only take the short time necessary to review, imagine how much more of a lasting impact these lessons would have. By implementing even the slightest regimen of review, we can use the lessons that we learn in a class or read in a book to actually catapult us to higher levels of Torah observance and practice without us even realizing it. Think of the consequences!! Think of the results!! It's literally mind-boggling.

For purposes of review, please read this article again!

PARSHAT VA'ETCHANAN

a'etchanan (Deuteronomy 3:23-7:11) continues the Torah's recounting of Moses' final speech to the Children of Israel. He tells the people that he had implored Hashem to allow him to enter the land of Israel, but Hashem refused his request. Moses then continues to exhort and warn the people to obey the Torah and its commandments, neither adding nor subtracting from its mitzvot. They are told to always remember the incredible Revelation they experienced at Mt. Sinai, passing that memory on from generation to generation. Moses warns the Jewish people of the prolonged exile that they will experience if they forsake the Torah, and how Hashem will eventually bring them back to the land of Israel. After setting aside the three cities of refuge on the eastern side of the Jordan River, Moses repeats the Ten Commandments and further describes Hashem's Revelation at Mt. Sinai, while at the same time continually warning the Jewish people to maintain their observance of Hashem's Torah. Moses teaches them the first paragraph of the Shema, the fundamental passage which we recite twice a day expressing our belief that Hashem is one and stating our commitment to love and serve Him. Once again, Moses exhorts the people to trust in Hashem and remain faithful to the Torah, and to beware of the pitfalls of prosperity and success. After commanding the Jewish people to teach their children about the miraculous exodus from Egypt, the portion concludes with some further commandments and warnings concerning the forthcoming conquest of the land of Israel.

⊙ Instant Torah
by Rabbi Elie Cohen

This week's Torah portion, includes the first of the three paragraphs of the *Shema* prayer. The second paragraph of the *Shema* is found in next week's Torah portion, Eikev, and in many ways mirrors the first paragraph. Much can be learned by comparing and contrasting these two sections of the Torah. The following is one example:

The Torah states in the first paragraph, "And these words [of the Torah] which I am commanding you today, shall be upon your heart" (Deuteronomy 6:6). The second paragraph begins with the verse, "And it shall be, if you will surely listen to My commandments which I am commanding you today . . ." (Deuteronomy 11:13). In both sections, the phrase, "which I am commanding you today" is employed. What is the significance of this seemingly superfluous phrase?

In his interpretation of the phrase in the first paragraph, Rashi explains that the Torah is teaching us that its words should not be viewed simply as a stale and out-dated dogma to which a person does not attach any importance. Rather, they should be considered like a newly-written enactment which everyone excitedly runs to greet. The Torah uses the phrase, "which I am commanding you today," to teach us to always view the words of the Torah as fresh and new.

Rashi also interprets this phrase in the second paragraph. There he simply writes, "The words of the Torah should be new to you, as if you heard them today." Although this appears to be merely a reiteration of his own comments on the first paragraph, a careful analysis reveals that this is not the case. In interpreting the phrase in the first paragraph, Rashi mentions "running" to greet an enactment. In the second paragraph Rashi omits this "running". In addition, Rashi speaks in the second paragraph as if the reader of his commentary has already heard the Torah's words, and he directs the person to view them as if he received them today.

What emerges is clear. The first paragraph is referring to the student of Torah <u>before</u> he has actually learned the material. He must approach those words of Torah by running with enthusiasm to greet them – for the first time. The second paragraph gives us an even greater challenge – that even <u>after</u> we have learned a part of the Torah, we should maintain a special verve for it, as if we had learned it for the first time today.

∽ # All Mitzvot Are Created Equal
by Benyamin Cohen

If you had to choose only one *mitzvah* to perform, which one would it be? Imagine a prisoner who is granted a one day reprieve on which he can fulfill any *mitzvah* he wants. Should he choose *Rosh Hashanah* so that he will get a chance to hear the resounding sound of the *shofar*? Or perhaps he should choose *Yom Kippur* so that he can pray in synagogue to Hashem for mercy and forgiveness? Maybe he should choose *Shabbat* so that he can recite the *kiddush* and bask in the innate holiness of the day?

This perplexing case actually occurred in the 16th century and was brought before the Radvaz, the chief rabbi of Egypt who wrote a classic collection of *halachic* responsa. Quite surprisingly, he answered that the prisoner should choose the first available day – regardless of whether it would be a holiday, a *Shabbat,* or merely a weekday. His reasoning was based on a statement in *Pirkei Avot* (2:1): "Be as scrupulous in performing a 'minor' *mitzvah* as you are with a 'major' one, for you do not know the rewards given for *mitzvot.*" The sages are teaching us not to discriminate between the *mitzvot.* We must be as scrupulous with a "difficult" *mitzvah* as we are with an "easy" one. We therefore cannot treat one *mitzvah* as having priority over another one.

Where do we find this concept in the written Torah itself? The Torah strongly veers from ever attaching a reward to a specific *mitzvah.*

If each *mitzvah* had a corresponding reward, it would be very easy and convenient for us to be selective in our actions, simply choosing to perform the *mitzvot* which we want to do. Therefore, the Torah only mentions a reward for two specific *mitzvot*. In this week's Torah portion, we read the filial fifth commandment to honor one's parents, about which the Torah in Parshat Yitro stated that the reward is long life. The other *mitzvah* – to shoo away the mother bird before taking her eggs – is also linked to the reward of longevity.

What is so significant about these two *mitzvot* that there is an explicit reward attributed to them? The Talmud teaches us that honoring one's father and mother is the most difficult *mitzvah* to properly perform. It recounts numerous illustrations of rabbis trying to fulfill this *mitzvah*. One story tells of Rabbi Tarfon who would bend down and allow his mother to step on him every time she climbed into bed. Even that, the Talmud states, did not fulfill even half of his obligation!

What is the easiest *mitzvah* to fulfill? Imagine yourself walking down the road and you see a mother bird perched on top of some eggs. The Torah commands us to shoo the mother away before taking her eggs. That is so easy to fulfill – it is just a simple wave of the hand. It takes no effort at all. It doesn't cost us anything. As the Talmud in Tractate Chulin succinctly states, it is the easiest *mitzvah* to fulfill.

These two *mitzvot* are the only ones mentioned with a specific reward because, in effect, they encompass all of the remaining 611 *mitzvot*. By telling us that the reward for both the simplest and most difficult *mitzvot* are one and the same, Hashem is teaching us that all *mitzvot* are created equal in that there is a reward given for both of these *mitzvot* and every one in between. If we had to choose one *mitzvah*, which would it be? The first one that comes our way. Don't miss the incredible opportunity.

For a more elaborate discussion of this fundamental topic, please see <u>*Understanding Judaism: The Basics of Deed and Creed*</u>; *Rabbi Benjamin Blech, (Jason Aronson Inc, N.J., 1991).*

PARSHAT EIKEV

ikev (Deuteronomy 7:12-11:25) begins as Moses continues to encourage the Children of Israel to trust in Hashem and in the wonderful rewards which He will provide them if they keep the Torah. Moses assures them that they will successfully defeat the nations of Canaan, at which point they must remove every vestige of idol worship remaining in the Holy Land. Moses reminds them about the miraculous manna and the other wonders which Hashem provided for them throughout the past forty years, and he warns the Jewish people to beware of the pitfalls of their own future prosperity and military prowess which can cause them to forget Hashem. He further reminds them of their transgressions in the desert, retelling the story of the golden calf at length, and describing Hashem's abundant mercy. Moses stresses that the generation of the desert had a special responsibility to remain loyal to the mitzvot because of the many miracles which they had personally experienced. After detailing the many virtues of the Promised Land, Moses teaches the people the second paragraph of the Shema which stresses the fundamental doctrine of reward and punishment based upon our performance of the mitzvot. The Torah portion concludes with Hashem's promise once again that He will provide the Jewish people with protection if they observe the laws of the Torah.

∞ Head Over Heels
by Rabbi Lee Jay Lowenstein

The name of this week's Torah portion, Eikev, literally means "heel". A simple translation of the opening verse would therefore be: "And it will be on the heels of your observing the commandments . . . that Hashem will keep His covenant and His kindness which He swore to your forefathers." Rashi cites a *Midrash* which offers an alternative reading of the verse. The *Midrash* states that if you will be careful to observe the commandments which individuals normally trample under their heels, then the Almighty will fulfill His promises to you.

At first glance one would instinctively say that the *Midrash* means that if you are so careful to keep <u>even</u> the minutiae of the Torah, then Hashem's boundless rewards are yours. However, careful scrutiny reveals what is intended: The reward comes for observing the "lesser" *mitzvot* and for drawing <u>no</u> distinction between them and those deemed more "serious". This raises several difficulties. Why shouldn't we distinguish between them? Is it fair and just to suggest that reward comes for performing the "lesser" *mitzvot* in the same way as it does for doing the more "serious"? Furthermore, what is the definition of a *mitzvah* which one would "trample under the heel"? Finally, why do our sages select the heel as opposed to naming the entire foot as the culprit who so mercilessly stomps upon the word of Hashem?

Back in the Garden of Eden, Man failed the greatest test of all time. The matter of eating from the Tree of Knowledge was not merely an issue of Man looking for the most exotic food to excite his taste buds. It was about existence itself and who is pulling the strings. Hashem, in His infinite knowledge, knew that it was best for Man not to partake from the tree at that time. Yet Man felt that he knew better; he determined that he alone is the one who controls his destiny and is capable of doing everything properly. Perhaps to express this on a deeper level: Man thought that he deserved to exist, that he had a right to be, and that he was duly ordained to exercise this right by becoming the sole master of his destiny. After his fall when he, his wife, and the snake were cursed, Hashem stated that there will be enmity between the snake and Mankind; the snake shall bite at his heel and he shall crush its head (Genesis 3:15). The once great, potentially eternal Man would now become a perpetual victim of the snake; and where specifically would his "Achilles heel" be, but the heel itself. Why?

In English there is a phrase which describes one's firm resolve on a position – "he is digging in his heels". The heel represents Man staking his claim upon the earth. As the verse says, "The heavens belong to Hashem, but the earth was given to Mankind" (Psalms 115:16). Man claims that the earth is his turf and therefore he is granted the right to control it, to master it. Connection to the earth via the heel emboldens Man. Observe how many wars have been fought over territorial stakes! The more Man "digs into" the earth, the more power he thinks he wields, and the more rights he feels he has, the further he distances himself from a meaningful relationship with Hashem. Ironically, the very same force which gives Man so much perceived strength is the very source of his downfall – the heel. It is no surprise, then, that this is the striking zone at which the snake will always have the vantage point.

The Hebrew word for shoe is "*na'al*". Etymologically this may stem from the Hebrew word "*no'el*" which means "to lock" or from the word "*aliyah*" which means "to go up". Either way, the connotation is that shoes sever our ties with the ground and insulate Man from the earth's fierce pull. In doing so, they give us an *aliyah*, a spiritual lift, because they remove us from the force which seeks to drag us down and away from Hashem – the earth.

We have little difficulty understanding philosophically that the Torah was created by Hashem for the betterment of Mankind. Obviously there must be some master rule book which governs the universe and lays down a standard of values and desirable behaviors. However, what is really our approach to Torah? Do we observe the *mitzvot* because we want what is best for ourselves and a Torah lifestyle fits that bill? Do we feel that we have a right to decide for ourselves what is true and just? Or, perhaps, do we remove ourselves from the equation and say that a human being cannot know independently what is best for himself and we must therefore relinquish total determination of right and wrong to the Torah?

The Maharal explains that the *mitzvot* which tend to be trampled upon are those which we perceive as not meriting great reward. If our approach to Torah is purely utilitarian, that we have the right to choose what is best for ourselves and we therefore choose Torah, one can readily understand how those *mitzvot* which do not provide the greatest benefits can be "swept under the rug" in favor of the "big ones". Why shouldn't I choose what is best for me? However, if we understand that we do not have any rights at all to choose which *mitzvot* we do or do not like, and we recognize that Hashem has blessed us with the opportunity to serve Him by observing His Torah and that His will is correct no matter what we may think, then we will grab the opportunity to fulfill any *mitzvah* regardless of its perceived "worth". Therefore, what becomes evident is that the "lesser" *mitzvot* become the litmus test whereby we demonstrate what our true attitude towards Torah is.

If we pause to consider that the freedom to choose does not mean a freedom of choice, we will instantly know what true humility is. Then we would really be head over heels!

👁 Blessings All Around
by Mendel Starkman

It is a common scenario: You are in your kitchen, reaching into the refrigerator, and you pull out a large, juicy apple. You raise the apple to your lips and take a big bite, enjoying every morsel of this G-d given gift. Suddenly, you realize that you have forgotten an essential part of this apple's enjoyment: You have forgotten to recite the appropriate blessing, thanking the Creator for this wonderful gift.

In this week's portion, the Torah states that when the Children of Israel come to the land, they will "eat, be satisfied, and bless Hashem" for the wonderful land that He has given them (Deuteronomy 8:10). From this verse, the sages derived the commandment of *Birkat HaMazon*, to thank Hashem by reciting the appropriate blessings after eating meals. However, points out the Sefer HaChinuch, this concept of blessing Hashem begs explanation, for we know that Hashem does not really need our blessings. After all, Hashem has all the honor and everything that is good, He is omniscient and omnipotent, and has all the blessings already. The actions and words of people, whether good or bad, will not add or detract from Him at all. So what is the purpose of reciting blessings?

The Sefer HaChinuch explains that Hashem only wants the best for His creations. However, He wants them to be worthy before He gives them His blessings. From this stems our need to recite blessings to Him. Through the blessings that we recite, we awaken within ourselves the idea that Hashem is the one Who bestows blessings upon us, and through this recognition we become worthy of receiving His blessings. It is essentially a snowball effect. Through our blessing Him, we become worthy of His showering blessings on us, for which we must bless Him even more, for which He gives us even more blessings, and so on and so forth.

This week's Torah portion also mentions another idea that can be applied in a similar way. We are told that when we come to the land of Israel and conquer it, we may eventually become caught up in ourselves and say that the strength and power of our hands brought us our fortune (ibid. 8:17). But how could we ever make such a mistake? Having a nation coming from slavery and untrained in the ways of war, defeating the military power of seven mighty nations could only possibly have taken place through intervention from above. How could Hashem's participation be overlooked?

Yet we see that with time, it is possible to become enthralled with the idea that these victories only took place through our own accomplishments and not with the help of Hashem. This is why Moses continued, verse after verse, to admonish us to remember that our victories took place through the merit of our forefathers, and not only because of us and our accomplishments.

Similarly, Rabbi Yisrael Salanter gave advice how to counter feelings of pride and arrogance. When it seems that we have accomplished something wonderful, we must remind ourselves of our deficiencies and shortcomings, and not just give ourselves a pat on the back. Reflecting in this way will prevent us from succumbing to arrogance, allowing us instead to recognize that it is Hashem and not ourselves Who is the moving force behind our successes, and thereby realizing the gratitude that we owe to Him. This realization, along with the idea that He is the one Who blesses us, will culminate in a single opportunity – an opportunity to make a blessing to Him, which will only serve to help us later when the circle continues and He showers more blessings upon us.

This is what Reb Aharon HaGadol meant when he pointed out to his student, "You make a blessing so that you can eat the apple, while I eat an apple so that I can make a blessing." He felt so strongly the love for blessing Hashem, that he would literally go out of his way to find opportunities to make blessings.

Now we understand two of the reasons why we recite blessings. Firstly, they are for us to recognize Who it is that blesses us, and secondly, to show our gratitude for what Hashem has already given us. So the next time we are in our kitchen and we take a bite of an apple, how will it be possible for us to forget to recite a blessing? And when we do remember to utter the holy words, we must remember to think about what we are saying and to Whom it is directed, for the benefits are so great.

PARSHAT RE'EH

n Parshat Re'eh *(Deuteronomy 11:26-16:17)* Moses continues to exhort the Jewish people to follow the ways of the Torah and to trust in Hashem. Moses begins by unambiguously putting the mitzvot into perspective, stating that the Jewish people will be blessed if they observe the Torah and cursed if they do not. He then begins a lengthy review of various mitzvot comprising the major part of the book of Deuteronomy, first discussing some of the commandments that are relevant to the people's imminent conquering of the land of Israel, enjoining them once again to remove every vestige of idolatry. After teaching them some details about the offering and consumption of korbanot and other foods, the Torah commands that the Jewish people refrain from imitating the nations around them. They are told to beware of false prophets and other people who might cause them to stray from Hashem, and they are taught the laws of the Ir Hanidachat, a Jewish city which has become so corrupt that a majority of its citizens have succumbed to idolatry and are therefore given the death penalty. The Torah then reviews which animals are Kosher to eat and which are not, followed by the laws of ma'aser sheni – the "second tithe" which is consumed by its owners, but only in the city of Jerusalem. After commanding that all debts are to be canceled at the end of every seventh (Shemitah) year, and that we should be warm-hearted and charitable to our fellow Jews, the Torah

repeats the laws relating to the Jewish servant. He is to be unconditionally freed in the Shemitah *year and showered with generous gifts by his former master. Parshat Re'eh concludes with a brief description of the three pilgrimage festivals –* Pesach, Shavuot, and Sukkot – *when everyone would ascend to Jerusalem and the Temple with their offerings to celebrate their prosperity.*

⌘ Individual Importance
by Ranon Cortell

This week's Torah portion begins with Hashem's dramatic exhortation: "See, I present before you today a blessing and a curse" (Deuteronomy 11:26). As to the nature of this blessing and curse, we are informed by the sages that it refers to the holy Torah and its *mitzvot* which, depending on our observance of them, will provide for us either a blessing or a curse. However, if one examines the grammatical content of the statement, one is struck by a stark contradiction in the tenses used in the verse. First, in the singular tense Hashem tells each individual "*re'eh* – see". Then, the verse describes the blessing and curse as being said to a plural audience, "*lifnaychem* – before you" (or as we say in the South, y'all) referring to the entire Jewish nation. Several explanations have been proffered by our eminent sages to resolve this most peculiar differentiation.

Rabbi Moshe Alshich suggests that this contradiction reveals the nature of Hashem's mission for the Jewish people in our unfortunately corrupt world. An average monarch, when assigning a gargantuan task to his nation, would not be concerned with each individual's progress as long as the work is completed by the end of the deadline. However, this is not true of the King of king's mission for His sacred nation. Each and every individual has full responsibility to observe everything included in the boundaries of the Torah. For this reason the verse uses the contradictory tenses, to inform us that although the Torah was given to the nation as a whole, every single Jew must strive to perform the duties imposed upon him by Hashem.

A second explanation of the dichotomy of the verse revolves around the concept that every Jew is responsible for his neighbor's observance of the hallowed Torah. In direct consequence of this concept we may be punished or rewarded for our friend's actions. Therefore, the verse uses the singular and plural tenses to teach us that by placing the responsibility of keeping the Torah upon each individual Jew, Hashem is also imposing upon us the responsibility of making sure our friends and family maintain its sacred laws as well.

As a result of these insightful nuances from a simple textual contradiction, we can derive that we must constantly remember that the weighty but joyful responsibility of Hashem's Torah is incumbent upon each and every one of us. Additionally, we must also be constantly concerned with the welfare and growth in observance of our fellow Jews.

The Wayward City
by Rabbi Ariel Asa

Scene 1: The prosecuting attorney concludes his presentation of the evidence and rests his case. He has proven beyond a shadow of a doubt that the inhabitants of the Jewish city were indeed guilty of mass idol worship, and should therefore be sentenced to death.

Scene 2: The defense attorney, realizing that the evidence is stacked against his clients, assesses the situation and chooses his strategy carefully.

He peers at the jury and then, with an emotional hushed tone, begins describing the importance of being merciful and of ingraining this attribute into the Jewish nation in every possible way. "By destroying this entire city," he claims, "there will be an upsurge in violent tendencies throughout the land of Israel."

He has the jury's attention as he begins listing the relatives of each of the defendants. "Imagine their reaction when they hear how their loved ones were obliterated. We could be dealing with riots of major proportions."

The defense attorney takes one more look at the jury as he concludes in a crescendo: "We all know the population statistics. Our greatest need, at present, is to populate the country, and a guilty verdict would set us back several years. Think of the consequences of your decision."

Scene 3: The jury has finally emerged and is ready to declare its verdict in the case of "*Ir Hanidachat* vs. The State". The foreman of the jury comes forward and quotes a remarkable promise from a verse in this week's Torah portion, answering all three of the defense attorney's claims at once: "And Hashem will give you [the attribute of] mercy, and they [the relatives] will be merciful towards you, and Hashem will increase you just as He promised to your forefathers" (Deuteronomy 13:18).

"Guilty as charged!"

Based on the commentary of the Netziv.

CO Opportunity Knocks
by Kevin Rodbell

Knock, knock. Nearly swallowing whole the bite of chicken and rice that he had just put into his mouth, Josh Levenson quickly pulled back his chair from the kitchen table and started toward the door. Glancing at his wife who was cutting their youngest son's food, he stopped for a moment and said sternly, "Kids, eat your broccoli."

Ding, Dong. Josh shouted, "Just a second. Who is it?" as he walked toward the door. His children still had not touched their vegetables, they remained seated before their plates of grilled chicken, brown rice, and steaming broccoli. Faced with the command to ingest stalks of the hideous green vegetable, they seized the mealtime interruption as yet another opportunity to stave off the unpleasant inevitability. Forks and mouths fell motionless and all eyes turned to the door, curious who had arrived. But Josh knew who was calling even before looking through the peep-hole. Only one type of visitor frequented his door at dinner hour – *tzedakah* collectors.

Jews have always supported their needy along with the many other worthy causes of their communities. In tribute to Jewish philanthropy, Rambam records, "We have never seen or heard of a Jewish community that does not possess a *kupah* (an agency for providing money to the poor for their basic needs)" (Laws of Gifts to the Poor, Chapter 7). But the Jewish people stand apart even more in their attitude toward giving. When commanding the Children of Israel to give *tzedakah*, Hashem beseeches us in this week's Torah portion: ". . . you shall not harden your heart or close your hand against your destitute brother" (Deuteronomy 15:7). The Ibn Ezra comments: "You should comfort his heart with pleasant words."

The task of collecting money can be very unappealing. Aside from being the recipient of unkind looks and sometimes even snide remarks, a person charged with raising funds for himself or an institution must trudge through all weather, going from house to house, hoping to make ends meet. Often he must bear the disappointment of not meeting his goals. These circumstances make him especially sensitive to any sort of unwelcome reception. The Ibn Ezra addresses this issue: Empathizing with the one collecting and raising his spirits is part and parcel of the *mitzvah* to give charity. And by training ourselves to empathize, we further our purpose as creations "in the image of Hashem," because Hashem has ultimate empathy – for anyone who cries out to Him sincerely.

Josh turned the doorknob. "Please, come in. I'm sorry it took so long – I was busy with the kids." The kids watched attentively as a man and his tattered briefcase entered the living room.

Dinner hour interruptions are not always appreciated. But when viewed in perspective, the dinner hour seems like a most appropriate time to encounter charity collectors. With their eyes, ears, and forks focused on the man at the door, the Levenson kids have a chance to digest much more than their broccoli. Watching their father interact, they can absorb the experience of how to treat those who are in need – with dignity and understanding. And which nutrient provided by broccoli could possibly be more essential to their growth?

PARSHAT SHOFTIM

hoftim *(Deuteronomy 16:18-21:9) deals
primarily with the commandments
regarding the establishment of a system
of leadership in the land of Israel, begin-
ning with the appointment of courts, judges, and officers in
every city. After delineating the process of prosecuting an idola-
ter, the Torah teaches that the death penalty shall be imposed
upon any scholar who renders a decision against the Great
Sanhedrin (High Court of 71 judges) in Jerusalem, no matter
how important or great the disputing scholar may be. The
Jewish people are commanded to request a king once they
have settled in the land of Israel. Some of the special gifts
which are to be given to the* Kohanim *are listed. After
describing the nature of prophecy, the Torah repeats the laws
of the* Ir Hamiklat, *city of refuge for accidental murderers,
and describes the special judicial case of* Edim Zomemim,
*conspiring witnesses. The Torah then deals with several
aspects of the nation's conduct in war, telling them not to be
afraid of the enemy, and listing those people who are exempt
from army service. The enemy must first be given the
opportunity to make peace, and the Jewish people must be
careful not to destroy any fruit trees in battle. The Torah portion concludes with the case of the unresolved murder and
the ritual of the* eglah arufah, *the axed heifer, which serves
as an atonement for the people of the neighboring cities for
not preventing the murder.*

◌ The Fox and the Fish
by Rabbi Daniel Cohen

A demographic study of the cities of refuge described in this week's Torah portion reveals a surprising element in their population. One would assume that the cities would be comprised solely of the Levites who maintained their permanent residence there and of any individuals who killed accidentally and were seeking protection from their pursuers. However, there is another group – rabbis. The Talmud (Tractate Makkot) explains that any individual who fled to the city of refuge must take his rabbi with him (not his lawyer, accountant, or doctor). By analyzing this law, we can gain a deeper appreciation of the primacy of Torah in one's life.

This obligation emerges from the verse, "He [the accidental killer] must flee to one of the cities and <u>live</u>" (Deuteronomy 19:4). Physical sustenance alone does not enable the killer to "live". Only when it is coupled with spiritual sustenance (i.e. his rabbi) can he truly live. An uncharacteristic comment by Rambam supports this notion. Although Rambam's style in his legal magnum opus is to elucidate Jewish law, he adds a revealing comment when articulating the requirement to bring one's rabbi to the city of refuge. He writes that wise individuals devoid of Torah knowledge and study are considered devoid of life. The Torah infuses life.

A story told in the Talmud about Rabbi Akiva crystallizes the indispensability of Torah. Rabbi Akiva lived during the period of Roman persecutors who forbade Torah study. Despite the ban, Rabbi Akiva continued his studies and was captured and sentenced to death by the Romans. When asked by his students why he took such a risk, he shared with them the story of the fox and the fish. A clever fox offered a fish a wonderful proposal: "Come onto land and you will be saved from the fisherman's net!" The insightful fish responded, "While in the water, there is a possibility that I may live by evading the fisherman's net. However, on land I am sure to die." Without the potent waters of the Torah, we too cannot survive.

Upon leaving this world, one of the questions that Hashem will ask each human being is whether he set aside time to study Torah every day (Talmud Tractates Sanhedrin 7a and Shabbat 31a). The Torah is not merely a legal guide to life. Through learning the Torah, we deepen our appreciation of the *mitzvot* and reinvigorate our relationship with Hashem. As we approach *Rosh Hashanah*, let us make a commitment to immerse ourselves in the sea of Torah and may we be blessed by its living waters each and every day.

⌒ No Bribes Allowed

by Michael Alterman

The Torah commands, at the beginning of this week's portion, that it is forbidden for a judge to accept any bribes because, as the verse explains, "The bribe will blind the eyes of the wise and make crooked the words of the just" (Deuteronomy 16:19). Rashi comments further that this injunction applies at all times in all cases, even if the judge still plans to adjudicate the case properly. Such a law, however, seems difficult to comprehend, for if a person is totally confident that the bribe he is accepting will have absolutely no adverse effect on his judgment, then why should he not be permitted to accept a gift from a litigant? What is wrong with making some extra money on the side?

To answer this, the Talmud (Tractate Ketubot 105b) offers a profound insight into human psychology. Our sages teach that once a person accepts a bribe, his opinions automatically lean towards that litigant's argument to the extent that it becomes virtually impossible to remain unbiased and emotionally detached. In effect, the judge and the litigant become one person as their opinions and thought processes are intrinsically bound together. Suddenly, the judge is unable to hear the other side of the argument as he has become personally involved in the case. As a result, even if the judge genuinely intends to rule properly, since he is unable to view <u>himself</u> as being guilty, he will find it much more difficult to rule against the one who paid him the bribe. The judge has been blinded.

At first glance, one may find all of this to be quite interesting yet totally unrelated to everyday life and the common decisions made by regular people. One may think that only judges and those of great influence need to be concerned with such lofty problems. However, nothing could be further from the truth. When we attempt to make decisions in our own lives, we are faced with similarly debilitating biases which blind us from entertaining new ideas which run counter to what we have been doing until now. We fail to consider whether or not we are acting correctly since it is always easier to maintain the status quo. In this self-destructive manner, our comfort with the status quo "bribes" us into deciding not to make any improvements in our character traits and behavior, even before we have given the idea any serious thought.

We have just entered *Elul*, the Hebrew month immediately preceding *Rosh Hashanah*. It is a period designated for introspection and *teshuvah*, a month in which we must carefully consider what we have accomplished in the past year and what we hope to achieve in the future. It is a time for us to open our eyes in search of the truth, to remove all of the biases and deterrents which prevent us from thinking clearly. With this in mind, we will be properly prepared to begin anew in the upcoming year and be able to strive far beyond the "bribes" which so drastically constrict our spiritual growth.

Based in part on the writings of Rabbi Eliyahu Dessler.

◯ Truth & Consequences
by Rabbi Herbert J. Cohen, Ph.D.

"Cast the first stone" is the directive given to the witnesses who testify in a case of capital punishment. In this week's Torah portion, we learn that if a person gives testimony which warrants imposing the death penalty of stoning, then the witness himself becomes the executioner (Deuteronomy 17:6-7). He carries out part of the death penalty by throwing the first stone. Why is this so?

The answer perhaps lies in our understanding of how a Torah Jew is supposed to think and act. Jewish law tells us that if someone has evidence in a capital crime case, he is duty bound to come forward to the court and say what he knows. However, his evidence must be incontrovertible. He must be absolutely sure of the truth of his observations because not only will his words convict, but he will also have to <u>act</u> on the basis of his testimony.

Therefore, the witness is inwardly compelled to weigh his words carefully, to be certain that what he <u>says</u> represents what he <u>saw</u>. The witness will not be able to give testimony and then walk away, oblivious to the consequences of his remarks. He needs to understand in his heart of hearts how his words will have a ripple effect far beyond the courtroom.

What the Torah is implicitly telling us is that we have to be extremely careful before we accuse someone of doing wrong. Our sages tell us to "be deliberate in judgment" (*Pirkei Avot* 1:1). They encourage us to be slow to condemn. Do not pass judgment quickly, for an ill-considered statement on our part may cause irreparable harm to someone else. Let us resolve to be extremely careful as to the truth of what we utter and consider the consequences of our statements.

PARSHAT KI TEITZEI

 i Teitzei *(Deuteronomy 21:10-25:19) begins by discussing the intriguing case of the* eshet y'fat to'ar, *the beautiful gentile woman captured by the Jewish soldier in battle. For the rest of the portion, the Torah continues with a listing of various* mitzvot *covering a wide range of topics. After speaking about a firstborn's special inheritance rights, the case of the wayward son, and the importance of respecting other people's property, the Torah commands us to shoo the mother bird from the nest before taking her young, and that* shatnez *may not be worn. The case of the defamation of a married woman is then discussed, followed by the prohibition of adultery and other forbidden marriages, and the command to maintain the Jewish army's camp as a sanctified place. After briefly mentioning divorce and the requirement of a* get *(bill of divorce), the Torah discusses kidnapping, the* mitzvah *to pay workers in a timely fashion, and the concept of an individual's responsibility for his own actions. The Torah then discusses the special consideration which must be given to an orphan and a widow, the punishment of lashes, the levirate marriage (called* yibum *and* chalitzah *in the Torah), and the* mitzvah *to be honest in business. This power-packed Torah portion concludes with the exhortation to remember the atrocities which the nation of Amalek committed against us upon our exodus from Egypt.*

∽ Prisoner of War

by Yoel Spotts

At first glance, the section recorded at the beginning of this week's Torah portion regarding the *eshet y'fat to'ar* seems entirely out of character with the overall message of the Torah. Throughout the five books of Moses we read about laws emphasizing restraint and self-discipline, responsibility and control. Yet, in this week's Torah portion we discover the case of the *eshet y'fat to'ar*, when a soldier, in a time of war, is permitted to discard those lofty ideals and surrender to his desires. What message is the Torah trying to convey by apparently allowing Jewish soldiers to seize captive women at will without giving any thought to self-control?

However, before we pass judgment too quickly, we must first examine more carefully the verses which relate the proscribed course of action, as the Torah's consent to this rendezvous with a captive woman does not represent the end or even half of the story. In Deuteronomy 21:12 we learn that shortly after their initial encounter, the woman must shave her head and let her fingernails grow, certainly not an attractive sight. Verse 13 further explains that she must cry incessantly over her dead parents for a full thirty days, all in full view of her captor. Only <u>after</u> this month of mourning may they resume normal relations as man and wife. Surely after such a display, almost any man would become quickly uninterested in the very same woman who, only a short time ago, had so greatly stimulated his interest. Indeed the Torah, expecting such a response, proscribes the proper action which will cause the man to no longer desire this woman as his wife. Obviously, the Torah's apparent sanction of such carefree behavior is not so clear-cut; clearly, there is a deeper message here.

Let us consider for a moment the plight of the soldier in a time of war. Torn away from his wife and family for months on end, he is subjected to the harsh conditions of brutal confrontation. If that weren't enough, he must endure the temptations of the gentile women who have come to parade before the Jewish soldiers in their most alluring attire in order to divert their attention from the battle at hand. (In fact, for this reason the Torah requires that the "abducted" woman change out of her clothes of war upon entering the soldier's house.) The Jewish soldier in this predicament may find himself unable to control his emotions and consequently becomes ensnared by the traps set by the gentile women. What shall happen to this soldier – will he be condemned to eternal damnation for his crime?

Judaism says no. Hashem created Man as a physical being in a physical world with physical desires. Of course Man's mission in this world is to overcome his evil inclination which drives him to act upon those desires. However, a person cannot be expected to conquer his emotions overnight. It is a lifelong battle. Thus, the Torah is willing to concede that a person may find himself unable to restrain himself from the evils of sin. Nevertheless, he must not allow himself to remain in this depraved state. Granted he has failed this time, but he must take the proper precautions to ensure success the next time. Thus, the soldier must shave the woman's hair, allow her nails to grow, refrain from having relations with her, do anything to make the woman as despicable as possible. Hopefully, after thirty days have passed, his desire for her will also have passed.

Although most of us have never been faced with the exact same circumstances as the Jewish soldier described in this week's Torah portion, we nonetheless have had to endure our own share of temptations. Nobody can be expected to successfully deflect his cravings every time. King Solomon declared that long ago when he said, "There is no man so wholly righteous on earth that he always does good and never sins" (Ecclesiastes 7:20). Everybody will at one point succumb helplessly in the face of his desires. The real question then becomes: What happens next? Will he surrender to his weaknesses, resigned to the notion that Man has no hope in the war against his evil inclination and that all is lost? Or will he arise with new resolve, determined that although he may have lost the battle, he can still win the war? Will he truly learn from his mistakes and take the proper precautions to ensure future victories? How one answers these questions determines whether one will allow himself to be held hostage by his emotions, or will be able to set himself free from the bonds of the evil inclination. With the commandment of the *eshet y'fat to'ar*, the Torah has provided us with the prescription for effectively treating the post-sin syndrome. Now it is up to us to make sure we take our medicine.

◯ Fruit by the Foot
by Rabbi Lee Jay Lowenstein

A few weeks ago in Parshat Eikev, I discussed the dangers associated with becoming too entrenched in the earth. The act of "digging in one's heels" was viewed as a rebellion against Hashem, wherein Man states that the earth is his turf and that he possesses an inalienable right to decide for himself what is right and wrong. We may expand upon this theme through one of the fascinating *mitzvot* that we encounter in this week's Torah portion.

In one of the final sections of the Torah reading, we are commanded regarding the *mitzvah* of the levirate marriage, known in Hebrew as *yibum*. The Torah stipulates that if a brother should die childless, one of the remaining brothers shall marry the wife of the deceased and have children with her, thus guaranteeing the continued memory of his departed sibling. Should the surviving brother(s) reject this opportunity, a substitute ceremony called *chalitzah* (literally, removal) is performed. This act requires the wife of the deceased to remove the living brother's shoe and to spit upon the ground in his presence. To spit at someone is the ultimate demonstration of disgust and, in this case, she rightfully displays her feelings towards him for his lack of sensitivity to his own deceased brother. However, of what significance is her removal of his shoe? What does this have to do with his denial of offspring for his late brother?

Our vocabulary is full of anthropomorphisms. "Mother Nature" and "Father Time" are just two examples of our affinity for such expressions. The term "Mother Earth" bears a unique interpretation which sheds light upon human nature and the essence of our struggle for perfection. Simply understood, the earth nurtures and provides for us like a loving mother, offering every raw material imaginable for achieving our many dreams. However, the term carries far greater significance than this. The Torah tells us that Man was created from the earth itself. Hashem assembled Man from the dirt of the four corners of the globe, molded it into a form, and breathed life into him. The physical side of Man was "born" from the womb of the earth. In Hebrew, the word for "grave" and "womb" are identical, *"kever"*, thus drawing the comparison full circle.

Our sages present an interesting interpretation regarding the creation of the trees. Hashem commands, "Let the ground bring forth fruit trees which give fruit" (Genesis 1:11). The sages understand the term "fruit trees" to be a qualitative description of the type of tree to be borne. Not only was the tree to bear fruit, it was also commanded to be a fruit tree (i.e. edible from the branches down to its roots!). The earth, however, chose to "disobey" Hashem's decree and instead issued fruit-bearing trees with an inedible bark (ibid. 1:12). The earth selfishly reasoned that if it adhered to the strict letter of the command, its trees would be devoured into oblivion. Later, after the sin of Adam, the earth is punished for its "defiance" with a blistering curse: ". . . the earth will be cursed on your account; in sorrow you shall eat from it all the days of your life, thorns and thistles shall it bring forth . . ." (ibid. 3:17). Rashi addresses the question why the earth is not cursed until Adam sins, instead of when the earth itself "sinned" three days earlier. Says Rashi: "This is comparable to one whose child has strayed from the norms of society; when people wish to curse the son they also curse the mother who nurtured such a child."

If the earth gave birth to Mankind, then the same "genetic code" which is present in the parent must have passed to the child. When Man displays selfishness as he did in the act of eating from the Tree of Knowledge, there can only be one source for such egotism: Mother Earth.

The *mitzvah* to marry your brother's widow is not as simple as it may sound. On the surface, it would seem that the Torah requires the living brother to serve as a surrogate father. In reality, this process of *yibum* demands one of the greatest sacrifices a human can make – the sacrifice of personal identity. Imagine marrying a woman, moving into her house, and having to adapt to someone else's lifestyle. You wear her dead husband's clothes, follow his routine, eat his breakfasts, use his shaver, etc. One would say that such a life is more an imprisonment than freedom. This is what in theory, if not in practice, the Torah expects of the living brother. He must allow his identity to be subsumed into his deceased brother's, in essence to become his brother. Why? In order to produce children who will carry on the family heritage.

The earth refused to yield of itself in order to be more fruitful; the brother who refuses to perform *yibum* has chosen to preserve himself at the expense of another. The widow removes his shoe as if to say, "You are connected to the earth and are just as selfish as it is!"

True growth only comes when we cut the umbilical cord of greed and materialism which anchors us to the physical source of Man's personality. Fortunately for us, Hashem is our "other parent" who has imbued us with an eternal soul, one which is capable of the greatest virtues known to Man. As we prepare for the High Holidays, let us reflect upon which parent deserves more of our attention so that next year will be a fruitful one in every way.

∽ # People are People Too
by Mendel Starkman

Every *mitzvah* in the Torah can be placed in one of two categories. Namely, *mitzvot bein adam laMakom* – commandments between man and G-d (i.e. eating Kosher, keeping *Shabbat*, and reciting blessings) which have no direct effect on other people; and *mitzvot bein adam l'chaveiro* – commandments that involve interaction with other people. Many times we become very involved in the first kind, yet we seem to lose sight of the second. At several points in this week's portion, though, we see the sensitivity that is necessary for those *mitzvot* involving man and his fellow.

The Torah tells us that if a person wishes to take eggs or chicks from a nest, he must first shoo away the mother bird (Deuteronomy 22:6). The Ramban explains that one of the reasons for this commandment is so that we do not act with a callous, unmerciful heart by causing the mother bird the discomfort of witnessing the taking of her young.

The Torah also commands us not to plow with an ox and a donkey together (ibid. 22:10). The Da'as Zekeinim explains that one of the reasons for this prohibition may be the fact that an ox chews its cud, whereas a donkey does not. Imagine the pain which the donkey would feel if, laboring side by side under the yoke, he would turn his head to see the ox chewing its cud. "When did he get food," the donkey would be thinking, pained by the fact that the ox has food and he does not.

In both of these scenarios, the Torah teaches us an incredible lesson regarding the sensitivity that we must have in recognizing and preventing the distress and discomfort of others. If the Torah can be so demanding about how sensitive we should be to these animals, how much more so must we be sensitive to other people.

Rabbi Paysach Krohn focuses on this idea and tells the following true story which exemplifies how far we must go to prevent another person's discomfort: There was once a man who always carried around a roll of quarters. After he passed away, someone revealed the reason why. At the place where this man prayed, poor people would often come around, asking for contributions. This man realized that if he were to take out a dollar and then ask for change, the poor person would feel a momentary surge of excitement at the prospect of being given a whole dollar. Then, when change would be requested, that excitement would revert to disappointment. In order to avoid the poor person's momentary discomfort, this man would walk around with a roll of quarters, so he would always have the proper change when it was needed.

This story serves as an example of how sensitive we must be to the feelings of others, constantly striving to prevent them from experiencing any unnecessary discomfort. When someone needs a helping hand, no matter how big or how small, it is our duty to offer it. For if the Torah can be so concerned about a donkey's temporary discomfort, we are certainly expected to go out of our way to help a person in need. And if we must be so careful to prevent someone from suffering, even from the momentary disappointment of a poor person who realizes that he will only receive a percentage of what he anticipated, how much more so must we not be the source of that discomfort by humiliating, ridiculing, or disparaging others.

Through this awareness, may we be able to fulfill all of the *mitzvot* – both those between Man and Hashem and those between people – with the proper sensitivity and respect for one another.

PARSHAT KI TAVO

arshat *Ki Tavo (Deuteronomy 26:1-29:8)* begins by describing the annual mitzvah for the farmers of Israel to bring their bikurim, or first fruits, to the Kohen in the Temple, at which point the farmer acknowledges the important role Hashem played in providing his sustenance. After exhorting the Jewish people once again to remain faithful to Hashem Who specifically selected them as His chosen people from amongst the nations of the world, Moses teaches two special mitzvot which they are to perform upon entering the land of Israel to reaffirm their commitment to the Torah. First they are to inscribe the entire Torah on twelve large stones, and then they are to recite blessings and curses in the valley between Mt. Gerizim and Mt. Eival which will apply respectively to those who observe and defy the Torah. Following a recounting of the wonderful blessings which Hashem will bestow upon the Jewish people for remaining faithful, Moses gives a chilling prophecy of what will befall the Jewish people for not following the Torah. Known as the tochachah *(admonition),* Moses graphically describes the horrible destruction which unfortunately came to pass when we strayed from Hashem's mitzvot. The Torah portion concludes as Moses looks back at the wondrous miracles which Hashem performed over the past forty years, reminding the people of the tremendous debt of gratitude that they owe Hashem for His loving care.

↺ Land of Opportunity
by Stuart Werbin

"Grandpa, can I have twenty bucks to go to the Braves game?"

"What's that, Davey? You want to waste my hard-earned money on some frivolous activity?! In my day, we didn't get to do fun things. We worked 18 hours a day in the hot, boiling sun, with 20-pound packs of books strapped to our backs, and then we had to walk three miles to school in two feet of snow – uphill both ways."

Many of us have parents, grandparents, or great-grandparents who came to America, with little or no money and possessions, in search of a better life. Many were very successful, thank G-d, and we reap the benefits of their toil.

In this week's portion, the Torah lists many curses that will unfortunately befall the Jewish people if they do not follow in the ways of Hashem. The Torah stipulates, "You will be a sign and an example [of a downtrodden people] because you did not serve Hashem while you were in a state of happiness and satisfaction, and had everything that you needed" (Deuteronomy 28:46-47). The Torah is talking about a time when we will be blessed with much material wealth. During this time, the Torah says, people may decide to use their wealth in ways contrary to what Hashem intended.

Most of our ancestors came here from Europe in hope of a better life, free of the poverty and persecution of the *shtetl*. Many of them also came for a different reason – they wanted to live in a place where they could practice their religion freely, where they could find the economic means to be able to perpetuate more Torah learning and *mitzvah* observance. There are countless stories of Jews who were told by their employers, "If you don't come to work on Saturday, don't bother coming in on Monday," and they still stubbornly refused to work on *Shabbat*. These immigrants were filled with a simple belief in their Creator, a faith which was born and nourished by their experiences in the beautiful Jewish societies of Europe.

Their self-sacrifice can be an inspiration to all of us. If they made room for Judaism in their lives at such great personal cost, surely we can study and observe more Torah because, thanks to their efforts, our sacrifices are so much less. Let us take this lesson to heart as we approach the High Holidays: Become more active in our synagogues, attend classes in Torah learning, and say to the world, "I am an affiliated Jew and there is meaning and purpose in my life." In this merit, may Hashem take away the curses from our lives and only bestow blessings upon us.

∽ All in the Heart
by Kevin Rodbell

The single short chime of his digital watch announcing the time, 4:30 P.M., startled and awakened Jon from his daydream. The glass of Coke slid quickly off the tray and landed straight on the floor. It smashed against the black and white tiles, shattering glass in all directions. Dark liquid quickly spread over eleven tiles, forming a slippery puddle of soda right next to the table Jon was waiting on. "Man, I'm sorry sir – I just don't know where my mind was."

Indeed, Jon was not concentrating on balancing the tray. Of course, with his face flushed red, he was now fully focused on the situation at hand. Jon's summer job as a waiter began at 9:00 every morning and ended at 5:00 every afternoon. Usually by 4:30 he was anxious to leave; today was no exception. Although his hands, eyes, and ears were always busy serving juicy hamburgers, greasy fries, and ice-cold soft drinks, Jon's mind would constantly wander to the night's upcoming baseball game. Summer baseball was Jon's favorite pastime. He loved the excitement and camaraderie so much that visions of sliding squarely into home and racing after high pop flies constantly filled his mind. Jon focused on hitting home runs rather than serving meals. Today he faced the consequences with a mop instead of a Louisville Slugger.

Everybody is familiar with this feeling of "my mind is elsewhere". Certain things which we consider more important – whether it is paying the electric bill or taking a much deserved vacation – tend to draw our attention away from balancing the tray or whatever else we might be doing. Indeed, people can spend most of their day performing necessary tasks that are not of primary interest, as evidenced by their daydreaming about other matters. Jon, for one, spends nearly two-thirds of his waking hours in the restaurant, but his major occupation in terms of hours doesn't indicate his heart's true focus.

Similarly, many Jews spend long hours at work, but this time allocation of Jewish professionals does not reflect what should be their ultimate aspiration in life, the aspiration that we express twice daily when reading the *Shema* prayer: "You shall love Hashem with all your heart." Despite all of the time we spend doing seemingly mundane activities, the heart of a Jew truly yearns to grow in Torah and to build a relationship with his Creator.

Rabbi Moshe Feinstein highlights this concept in a perplexing statement that Moses makes to the Jewish people in this week's Torah portion: "You have seen everything that Hashem did before your eyes in the land of Egypt . . . the great trials that your eyes beheld, those great signs and wonders. But Hashem did not give you a heart to know, or eyes to see, or ears to hear until this day" (Deuteronomy 29:1-3).

The Jews had complained on ten separate occasions about the inhospitable desert conditions in which Hashem had placed them, but never did they acknowledge all of the great miracles which Hashem performed for them in Egypt and in the desert over the past forty years. Hashem constantly proved His dedication to the Children of Israel, but they always responded with rebellion and dissent. Finally, on that day, at the end of their journey in the desert, Moses perceived that the Jews were ultimately dedicated to Hashem.

One particular event swayed Moses' opinion about the Jewish people. At the very end of his life, Moses copied over the Torah and attempted to give the scroll to the family of Levi; they, more than any other tribe, were to dedicate their lives to studying and teaching Hashem's precious book to the Jewish people. Rashi relates that the rest of the Jewish people joined together and said to Moses that they had also been present at Mt. Sinai when Hashem gave the Torah. They claimed that presenting this special Torah scroll to the Levites could one day cause them to say that the Torah was given to them exclusively.

Rabbi Moshe Feinstein explains that, in reality, the family of Levi would never make such an audacious claim; of course the whole Torah, even the laws specifically applying to the Levites, were given to the entire Jewish people. Rather, the other tribes suspected something more subtle. Non-Levites, who must spend long hours at work earning a living, feared that the Levites, who have the opportunity to spend their entire day immersed in Torah, would claim exclusivity in the areas of teaching Torah and resolving complicated matters of Jewish law. The non-Levites wanted to assure a place for themselves among the experts in Torah.

By demanding an active role in perpetuating the Torah, the Jewish people displayed their hearts' true focus and reassured Moses that they had their priorities straight. Income is a definite necessity, but no matter how much effort we rightfully devote to other endeavors, Jews must remember that the Torah and our relationship with Hashem remain our true life goal.

PARSHAT NITZAVIM/VAYELECH

itzavim (Deuteronomy 29:9-30:20) begins as Moses gathers together every member of the Jewish people for the last time in his life to initiate them into the eternal covenant with Hashem. Moses warns them not to be tempted by the evil ways of the idolaters who live around them, and to avoid rationalizing inappropriate conduct by saying that Hashem will forgive them, for maintaining such a belief is the ultimate source of our destruction and exile. Although they will sin, eventually the Jewish people will repent and return to the Torah, and Hashem will usher in the Messianic era, when we will all return to the land of Israel and the Torah's many wonderful blessings will be fulfilled. Moses tells the people not to fear that they will be unable to live up to the Torah's expectations, assuring them that the mitzvot *are neither distant nor inaccessible; a life of Torah is well within everyone's reach. The portion concludes with an exhortation to choose the Torah and life over the dismal alternative of evil and death.*

Parshat Vayelech (ibid. 31:1-30) opens with Moses walking through the Jewish camp on the final day of his life to bid farewell to his beloved people. After Moses teaches them the mitzvah *of* hakhel, *the once in seven years gathering of the entire nation to hear the king read certain passages from the Torah, Hashem addresses Moses and Joshua (who will be taking over the mantle of leadership) in the Tent of Meeting, commanding*

them to copy over the Torah and to continue teaching it to the
Jewish people. The portion concludes with Moses' concern that
the Jewish people will stray from the Torah after his death, causing
them to be punished.

CB Soul Responsibility
by Rabbi Lee Jay Lowenstein

With prophetic accuracy, Parshat Nitzavim continues to detail the
travails which will befall the Jewish nation over the course of its history.
The devastation of the land, the mind-boggling number of misfortunes,
and the fury of the Almighty all will cause the nations of the world to
wonder in amazement, what evil the Jewish people could have done to
deserve such a tragic fate (Deuteronomy 29:23). Yet, miraculously, the
Jewish people will survive. Downtrodden and oppressed, the Jewish
nation will examine its past and see how it has been the beneficiary of
a multitude of Divine kindnesses. This reflection will be the genesis of
a wholesale return to the values of the Torah and to the strengthening
of the bond between the Jewish people and Hashem.

According to Ramban, the Torah explicitly guarantees the ability to
rejuvenate ourselves through earnest repentance in this week's portion.
The Torah instructs us: "For this commandment that I charge you today
– it is not hidden from you and it is not distant. It is not in the heavens
that you should ask who will go up and fetch it for us. . . . Rather, it is
very close to you indeed – within your mouth and your heart – to
perform it" (ibid. 30:11-14). *Teshuvah* is indeed a very human responsibility, one which requires participation of both one's heart and mouth.

Although Ramban's understanding of the verses to be referring to
teshuvah fits well within the story line of the Torah reading, it is extremely
difficult to understand in light of a fascinating ruling issued by the Talmud. The Talmud (Tractate Baba Metzia 59b) relates the episode of a
major dispute between Rabbi Eliezer and the sages of Israel with regard

to the ability of a particular vessel to become *tamei*. The Torah itself lays down the fundamental principle that in cases of dispute we must rule in accordance with the majority. Rabbi Eliezer was vastly outnumbered, yet he refused to concede his position. So convinced was he that the law followed his opinion that he began to solicit supernatural means to consolidate his view. He declared, "If the law is like me, let this river flow backwards!" Sure enough, the river changed its course and the water ran upstream. The rest of the sages coolly rejected this display, pronouncing, "One does not cite legal proof on the basis of streams!" Rabbi Eliezer continued to bring supernatural proofs, all of which the sages dismissed in the same manner. Finally, in desperation, Rabbi Eliezer said, "If the law is like me, let a voice come from the heavens to confirm it is so!" As if on cue, a heavenly voice was heard saying, "Why do you argue with Rabbi Eliezer? He is surely right!" At that point, Rabbi Yehoshua (the leading force behind the dissension) rose to his feet and proclaimed, "The Torah is no longer in the heavens (referring to the verses quoted above); it is entrusted to the sages of Israel, and we, the majority, rule that the *halachah* is in accordance with us."

The rabbis of the Talmud understood the verses in our Torah portion to have major *halachic* ramifications: The Torah is now under the sole proprietorship of the sages of Israel and their collective wisdom. How are we to justify this position in light of the reading of Ramban which is, in fact, the simplest translation of the verses? What does the fact that the Torah is the property of the Jewish people, as the Talmud reads the verses, have to do with our ability to repent, as Ramban reads them?

There are two basic motivations which inspire an individual to repent. The most obvious is the fear of accepting the consequences of sin. The Torah is replete with references to the horrible tragedies which will befall the Jewish people should they stiffen their necks and turn away from Hashem. *Teshuvah* of this sort is more an act of "saving one's skin" than an attempt to correct a wrongdoing. There is, however, a more profound impetus, one which lies at the heart of the Jewish soul and is where the real power of *teshuvah* rests.

How do we explain the Talmudic dictum that the Torah is no longer in heaven? How could it be that we can argue with the word of the Almighty Himself and be correct in our application of *halachah*? There can be only one solution: The Jewish people are not merely servants of Hashem; we are partners with full responsibility to preserve and determine the applications of the eternal principles of the Torah. As with any partnership, there must be a common denominator which binds us together, forming the basis of the relationship. In this instance, it is the unique quality of the Jewish soul. The soul of a Jew is referred to by Kabbalistic sources as a spark of the Divine. There exists within us a fragment of eternity. It is this holy fire which empowers the Jew, it inspires his desire to control his environment and propels him toward the greatest success life can offer. This very same soul enables us to "mimic" Hashem's Divine qualities and makes us suitable trustees of the absolute truths of the Torah.

To be authorized to set policy, interpret the Torah, and apply it according to the prescribed methods which were transmitted to Moses, attests to the lofty nature of the Jewish people. We are Divine creatures and have the power to shape reality according to our collective wisdom. Moreover, if Hashem has entrusted us with His Torah, His most precious gift, it is proof of the powerful love that He feels for us. One does not entrust a servant, no matter how loyal, with his most prized possession. Only to a child or beloved friend is one willing to bequeath the very object of one's passion.

Understood on this level, sin is not only heinous because of its affront to the Creator, it is also equally damaging to us on a personal level. Surely the chain smoker, who is wasting away with lung cancer, must feel at least a tinge of regret for all the years of self-inflicted harm. How much more so should the sinner feel remorse when reflecting upon the enormous damage his sins have caused. It should make one wonder: "How can I, a spark of the Divine, have acted in so disreputable a manner as to do such and such? I owe it to myself to be a better person, to live up to the role Hashem has created for me; to be His beloved partner in the greatest story of all time, the story of my life and the history of the Jewish people!"

May it be Hashem's will that this year we view ourselves in a different light. Instead of approaching the High Holidays with feelings of anxiety, let us think about who we really are and how we owe it to ourselves to improve. After all, what kind of story would our lives reflect if they never amounted to anything more than reruns?

∽ Choose Life
by Ranon Cortell

As *Rosh Hashanah* approaches, many of us sense a bit of heaviness in the air, the uncomfortable manifestation of an upcoming, relentless storm. Slowly, the misdeeds of our past seem to scroll through our haunted minds, and we feel frightened because of the impending and scrutinizing examination of our lives. But, thank G-d, there is a way to find reconciliation with our King. We can simply demonstrate regret for our immeasurable transgressions by asking for forgiveness and resolving not to commit the grievous sins again.

Unfortunately, this procedure is not as simple as it appears. It requires a will of iron and an almost inhuman ability to suppress the surging and despotic demands of our evil inclination. However, Parshat Nitzavim presents the perspective necessary for achieving such a drastic turnabout. With impressive drama, Hashem exhorts us: "I have set life and death before you, blessing and curse. Choose life so that you may live" (Deuteronomy 30:19). It is so apparent and clear; after all, nobody wants to die. If only we would delve deeper into the recesses of our hearts and vanquish the evil inclination, then everything would become transparently clear. Recklessly following our physical desires only increase them, and as a result of the ensuing dissatisfaction we are removed from the joys of this world. Only by choosing the path of following Hashem's ways will we ever achieve a meaningful and enduring joyous life.

Rabbi Moshe Feinstein points out the operative word in the first verse of the section: "See that I have placed before you <u>today</u> life and goodness" (ibid. 30:15). Our decision as to which direction our life is heading is never fixed and immovable; it is a constant day-to-day determination. Never despair, the Torah entreats us, it is never too late to follow the path to eternal tranquillity. One must by no means become overly confident in one's spiritual status. The Torah warns us here that each day we must again make the decision to follow in the true path of life and ultimate happiness.

Rashi explains Hashem's directive "choose life" by comparing Hashem to a loving father who takes his most cherished son aside and tells him to select for himself the best of his estate as an inheritance. Not only that, the father even shows his son the field which is the most fruitful and tells him to choose this one. Rabbi Eliyahu Dessler explains that Hashem loves us so greatly and wants us to experience the ultimate pleasure of life so strongly that He even hints to us when we have done something wrong and thereby nudges us to embrace His ways. Hashem accomplishes this by giving us that sense of nagging guilt and apprehension after we make an incorrect decision which is a blessed compass implanted in our hearts, constantly guiding us to faithfully serve our Creator.

Behold, the path diverges before us. One side is filled with thorns, thistles, and endless gloom, and the other is bathed in sunshine with delicious fruit, trees, and flowers encompassing the pathway. Choose life, and with the help of Hashem we will all be judged favorably by our loving Father.

PARSHAT HA'AZINU

a'azinu *(Deuteronomy 32:1-52) is comprised primarily of Moses' "song" about the horrible tragedies and supreme joy which will make up the Jewish people's future history. Not your classic piece of rhyme and music, Moses' "song" is nevertheless comparable to a great work of art in that it blends together otherwise disparate ideas into a beautiful symphony of thought. It expresses the recognition that every aspect of Creation and everything that Hashem does – past, present, and future – somehow fits together in a perfect harmony, although with our limited human understanding we do not always recognize it to be so. Moses calls heaven and earth to bear witness that if the Jewish people sin and display ingratitude to Hashem for the many wonderful favors He bestowed upon us, we will be punished, while if we remain loyal to the Torah and Hashem we will receive the greatest blessings. Even though the Jewish people will stray, Hashem guarantees our survival and ultimate redemption. The portion concludes with Hashem's command to Moses to ascend Mount Nebo, where he will view the land of Israel and then pass away.*

⌒ Hitting Rock Bottom
by Rabbi Elie Cohen

At the end of Parshat Ha'azinu, Hashem commands Moses to ascend Mount Nebo to view the land of Israel and then he will pass away.

Hashem reminds Moses that because of his sin of hitting the rock, he will not be permitted to actually enter the Promised Land. Hashem thus states, "On account of the fact that you did not sanctify Me in the presence of the Children of Israel [you may not enter the land]" (Deuteronomy 32:51). The implication of the verse is that Moses' sin with the rock was the missed opportunity to sanctify Hashem.

Rashi explains the verse as follows: Hashem had commanded Moses to <u>speak</u> to the rock so that it should give forth water. Instead, Moses <u>struck</u> the rock twice. If Moses would have spoken to the rock, as he was commanded, and the water would have emerged, the Jewish people would have learned an important lesson. If a rock, which is not subject to reward and punishment, follows the command of Hashem, certainly we, who are subject to reward and punishment, should comply with Hashem's will. Had Moses spoken to the rock, Hashem would have been sanctified and elevated in the eyes of humanity.

It is interesting to note that this is not the first place where Rashi interprets this missed opportunity for "sanctification". When the incident with the rock actually occurs and is recorded in the Torah in Parshat Chukat, Hashem tells Moses and Aaron, "Since you did not trust in Me to sanctify Me before the eyes of the Children of Israel, therefore you shall not bring this congregation to the land which I have given them" (Numbers 20:12). There too, Rashi explains the missed "sanctification", but in slightly different terms. Rashi states that if Moses would have spoken to the rock, causing it to produce water, the Jewish people would have said that if this rock, which does not speak nor hear and does not need sustenance, fulfills the word of Hashem, certainly we who do speak and hear and do require sustenance, should fulfill the Divine word.

At first glance, Rashi seems to be saying basically the same thing in both places, notwithstanding the slight change. However, after studying his commentary in the original, one gets the strong impression that Rashi is very exacting in his word choice. In fact, one can find many instances throughout Rashi's commentary where in two very distant places he interprets a particular concept using the identical phrase. Thus, it is highly unusual to find such a discrepancy – that in this week's Torah portion Rashi describes the rock as an entity which is not subject to reward and punishment, whereas in Parshat Chukat Rashi refers to the rock as an entity which neither speaks nor hears and does not need sustenance.

In order to resolve this difficulty, we should analyze our own relationship with Hashem. We understand that there is more than one way in which we relate to the Almighty. He is our Creator and the Sustainer of our existence. Above and beyond that, He is our Judge, Who rewards and punishes based upon our actions.

Now we can understand the two comments of Rashi. When the event first occurs, Rashi is referring to Hashem as the Creator and Sustainer; thus he points out that we, who need to turn to Hashem for the very abilities to speak, hear, and receive sustenance, should follow G-d's word. After all, He gives us everything that we have and are. In this week's portion, however, Rashi explains that the lesson can be understood on a different level – realizing that Hashem is our Judge. We are rewarded and punished by Him for our actions, and as such we should listen to His directives.

The Talmud states that Man was created and judged on *Rosh Hashanah*, the Day of Judgment. The Talmud also states that during the Ten Days of Repentance between *Rosh Hashanah* and *Yom Kippur*, Hashem is more readily available for us to relate to Him. Let us take advantage of this opportunity to relate to our Creator and our Judge, to be inspired in our actions and thereby to sanctify Him.

PARSHAT V'ZOT HABRACHA

 'zot HaBracha (Deuteronomy 33:1-34:12), read on Simchat Torah, *describes Moses' last words to the Jewish people. After praising the entire nation for accepting the Torah, he bestows* specific prophetic blessings on each of the tribes according to their national responsibilities and individual greatness, and then blesses the entire nation as a whole. The Torah concludes with Moses' death on Mount Nebo, and a tribute to his greatness and unique level of prophecy, the highest ever achieved by a human being.

∽ **Time & Again**
by Yitzchak Saltz

Now that we have arrived at the end of the book of Deuteronomy, it is time to look back and reflect on what we are about to complete. The rabbis refer to this book as *Mishneh Torah*, an explanation and review of the Torah, since Deuteronomy includes many *mitzvot* which were already taught earlier in the other books of the Torah. We may wonder, why was it necessary to review so many things again?

Rabbi Samson Raphael Hirsch explains that the narrative in Deuteronomy occurred at the end of the Jewish people's forty-year sojourn in the desert. They had witnessed many open miracles as Hashem provided for their every need: They never had to work the land in order to produce food; Hashem provided them manna on a daily basis. The well of Miriam provided water at all times and the Clouds of Glory protected them day and night. Standing on the banks of the Jordan River, the Jewish people were poised to enter the land of Israel where they would no longer be the recipients of so many obvious miracles. There would no longer be manna – they would have to plant, plow, and harvest the land in order to sustain themselves. The well and clouds would also depart – reality would now govern their lives.

A student, who has a final exam on everything he studied the past year, must review what he has learned. Similarly, the Jewish people had spent years in the wilderness learning the Torah and developing their close relationship with Hashem. As they prepared to enter the land of Israel and once the miracles of the wilderness ceased, it was necessary to review, in readiness of successfully and adequately meeting the varied challenges of this new stage in their lives.

Upon completing a Tractate of Talmud, very often the first step is to develop a system to review. Now that we have embarked on a new year and begin again our cycle through the Torah, let us not forget everything we have learned in the past.

JEWISH
FESTIVALS

ROSH HASHANAH

🐚 Discovering Ourselves
by Michael Alterman

The court is now in session. The heavenly books of judgment lay open and our deeds of the past year are being examined by the Judge. In addition to an evaluation of the Jewish people as a whole, on *Rosh Hashanah* every one of us will pass before Hashem individually, as the rabbis describe, like sheep being herded through a small opening in the gate of the corral, <u>one by one</u>, to be counted (Talmud Tractate Rosh Hashanah 18a, *Netane Tokef* prayer). No longer can we hide in comfort amongst the masses, concealing ourselves from the penetrating Divine scrutiny. Today we must come face to face with ourselves, standing before our Creator.

While this process transpires above, we will also be looking inwardly, rendering judgment on ourselves, determining whether we are traveling down the proper path of life, or perhaps floundering on a side road leading nowhere in particular. Are we living up to our vast potential in our relationships with those around us; in our relationship with Hashem; and regarding what we can accomplish with our talents, strengths, and virtues? These are the questions which will comprise our self-examination. And like someone staring into a perfectly polished mirror, trying desperately to uncover even the slightest facial blemish or imperfection so that it can be carefully corrected, we will examine our inner selves and compare our desired conclusions with our present reality so that we can make the necessary improvements.

Unlike every other species, the human race was created as an individual – Adam. With this singular act of creation, Hashem taught us a tremendous lesson – that all of creation, an entire world of vibrant life and beauty, was even worthwhile for just one person. Similarly, the *Mishnah* (Tractate Sanhedrin 4:5) states that every one of us is required to view ourselves as that one individual, to inculcate the principle that "for my sake was the entire world created" into our innermost beings. The question immediately presents itself: What are the rabbis trying to convey? Is this meant to provide us with an over-inflated, conceited and egotistical view of ourselves?

The sages understood that every person comes into this world for a unique purpose, to fill a need which cannot be accomplished by anyone else. Each of us is imbued by Hashem with the perfect combination of raw talents and character traits with which to fulfill our role. We are expected to accomplish nothing less than that. When we develop those talents and use them properly, we justify all of creation; when we don't, it's as if we have caused the destruction of an entire world. Life is a wonderful opportunity . . . and an enormous responsibility.

Even before we are born, the *Midrash* says, Hashem forms a heavenly image representing what we can eventually accomplish with our lives. When we enter this world, we embark on a mission to attain that level of achievement, to make our physical earthly selves equal to that lofty heavenly image. Perhaps this idea is best conveyed by the events which occurred one *Rosh Hashanah* more than 3,500 years ago. When our Patriarch Abraham raised his knife to slaughter his beloved son Isaac, fulfilling Hashem's difficult command and thereby passing his tenth and final trial, an angel of Hashem called out his name twice: "Abraham, Abraham" (Genesis 22:11). At that moment, the *Midrash* comments, Abraham had finally made it, for after 137 years of struggle, the two versions of Abraham – his earthly real person and his heavenly image – were perfectly equal. At last, Abraham had achieved his purpose on earth.

Rosh Hashanah presents us with a special opportunity to start fresh as we set our sights on fulfilling our unique mission. However, in order to effectively continue on our journey, we must take the time to evaluate our talents and to render judgment on ourselves. We must not forget that our potential is immeasurable;

we must not sell ourselves short. May this Day of Judgment, ushering in a new year, serve to propel us one step closer to our Divine image in heaven.

☙ New Year *Express*
by Daniel Lasar

You board a train bustling with activity. People are coming and going in all directions. A voice booms out over the loudspeaker: "All aboard, welcome. Please find your seat and enjoy the ride."

Rosh Hashanah is the time of the year when we are at a heightened state of awareness concerning our mortality. Moreover, it is a time when our degree of self-introspection is especially augmented. We take stock as to how we have chosen to live our lives. With the knowledge that our time in this world is finite, comes the human urge to "seize the day". This concept of *carpé diem* surely flows amidst the adrenaline surging within us and accompanies our every glance at the inspiring words of the *machzor*: "On *Rosh Hashanah* we will be inscribed and on *Yom Kippur* we will be sealed, how many will pass from the earth and how many will be created; who will live and who will die. . . ."

In many ways, life resembles a train ride. A person boards and embarks upon a journey for a limited period of time until arriving at a final destination. At stops along the way, different people enter and exit – for some it is the beginning of the journey, for others it is the end. Over the course of the voyage, one may have encountered many different people. Similarly, every *Rosh Hashanah* represents one of these train rides, when the coming year may bring new people into our lives, while others may depart from us.

Additionally, this pause allows us to reevaluate where our lives are headed. We can rechart the course we are on, if we want. A subtle behavioral modification in one area can have a pivotal effect, such that our "destiny" is significantly recalibrated. The key question is: Will we be courageous and honest enough with ourselves to make even a non-dramatic, though important change in our lives? Commitment to being a better spouse, parent, child, or teacher is perhaps difficult, but can impact lives tremendously. Dedicating oneself to lighting *Shabbat* candles or going to the *mikveh* requires much fortitude and commitment, but reaps great spiritual reward.

Unfortunately, after the excitement of the High Holiday season subsides, it is only natural that the momentum generated by the experience abates. For many of us, as each year passes by, so is another year of potential improvement transformed into a year of missed opportunity. In Parshat Eikev, the Torah states that the land of Israel is "a land that Hashem seeks out; the eyes of Hashem are always upon it, from the beginning of <u>the year</u> to <u>year's</u> end" (Deuteronomy 11:12). Rabbi Yoel Teitelbaum offers an interesting interpretation of this verse. The Torah omits the Hebrew letter "*hey*" (which means "the") regarding the end of the year, designating that time period as simply "year's end – *acharit shanah*". This contrasts with the Torah's choice of language in reference to the beginning of the year, where the "*hey*" is included (*reishit ha'shanah*). Rabbi Teitelbaum explains that this verse serves as a warning to avoid a common pitfall. People commonly resolve that the coming year will be <u>the</u> year for spiritual rejuvenation, only to realize twelve months later that it was just <u>another</u> year, another missed opportunity to alter our lives' course. The Torah is telling us to capitalize and build upon the inspiration of the season so that the upcoming year will truly be one of growth.

May this year truly be <u>the</u> year, for each and every one of us. A year of increased commitment to the Torah, heightened acknowledgment of the purpose of our existence, and renewed vigor to serve our Creator. The time is now, the choice is ours. Seize the day!

And when the voice blares out over the loudspeaker, "Last stop. All passengers must exit the train," will you think to yourself, "Is this where I really wanted to end up?"

YOM KIPPUR

∽ Day of Atonement?
by Rabbi Daniel Estreicher

The Talmud (Tractate Yoma 85b) states that *Yom Kippur* serves to atone for sins which a person commits directly against Hashem. However, *Yom Kippur* does not atone for sins between man and his fellow until he has actually attained the forgiveness of the injured or insulted person.

On *Yom Kippur* we stand in judgment before Hashem and ask forgiveness for our sins. There is one group of sins, however, that involves almost all of our activities for which no forgiveness is being offered. This is the area known as "*bein adam l'chaveiro* – between man and his fellow man," personal relationships, for which judgment is passed but for which atonement cannot be achieved until the wronged party is placated.

Unfortunately, we often overlook this critical area in our relationships. Many of us, as the great masters of *mussar* (Jewish ethics) have pointed out, are very careful concerning our relationship with Hashem. If we do something wrong, we truly regret having committed that sin. Yet, when it comes to our relationships with our fellow human beings it is a completely different story. As a great sage so appropriately stated, "We are extremely careful about what comes into our mouths, but not with what comes out." We fail to realize that speaking against someone else is wrong. It is our way of life – everybody does it. What we must seriously understand and appreciate, especially on *Yom Kippur*, is that this is the wrong attitude. Our relationships with our fellow human beings are just as important as our relationship with Hashem.

Let us try to make an effort in our dealings with each other to be more sensitive, kind, and understanding. Through this merit, Hashem will deal with us in a similar manner.

SUKKOT

℘ Sukkah Security
by Ranon Cortell

Leaning back in his relatively comfortable folding chair, David wraps his bulky winter jacket more snugly around his trembling shoulders, and with teeth chattering to the drum beat of winter, he lowers his face perilously close to the boiling chicken soup, inhaling its wholesome steam. As the *s'chach* (the *Sukkah's* makeshift roof) rustles with the chilling October winds and his breath hovers in visible white clouds before being carried away on unseen wings, David wonders what is the crucial lesson that he is supposed to take to heart from his forced relocation to this temporary shelter. What message is Hashem conveying to us by telling us to leave the security and protection of our homes and go into the *Sukkah*, exposing ourselves to the harsh elements? To understand this we must first discuss the source of this holiday and the significance of some of its complex and intricate laws.

The Talmud (Tractate Sukkah 11b) states that the huts in which we dwell on the holiday of *Sukkot* serve as a poignant reminder of one of two things – either the huts that the Jewish people dwelled in as a nation during our wanderings throughout the sultry tracts of desert after the exodus from Egypt, or of the Clouds of Glory which Hashem provided for us during our sojourns in the desert which protected us from the perilous weather, our powerful enemies, and any harmful desert creatures that threatened to sting or bite us. Every moment of our existence in that scorching desert was lived in a miraculous state. Our water was supplied by a mobile well, food fell from the heavens, our clothing never wore out, and our most powerful enemies were crushed effortlessly before us. Hashem's hand was a constant visible force.

But soon, the Jewish people would enter their homeland, and Hashem's discernible hand and dazzling miracles would eventually become invisible to the non-discerning eye. For this reason, Hashem commanded us to exit our comfortable heated houses and come under the flimsy *s'chach*, to remind us that we are still completely reliant on G-d's mercy, just as we were in the desert. Despite the apparent security of our homes and our control over our fortunes, we are all, in a sense, living in a *sukkah*. We are protected only by the unceasing and loving devotion of Hashem, just as the Children of Israel were protected by the constant presence of the Clouds of Glory.

The Talmud states that although the roof of the *sukkah* must be made of flimsy earth-grown materials, the walls can be completely enclosing and made of any substance. Rabbi Samson Raphael Hirsch explains that the *sukkah's* walls illustrate this crucial concept – that even though the rich man's walls may be built of metal and the poor man's of two flimsy wooden boards, they both ultimately rely on the same source of protection – Hashem. When one looks around at the comfortable and reliable world he has created for himself, one is tempted to doubt Hashem's handiwork in all aspects of existence and instead attribute his successes and failures to his own strengths and abilities, to natural forces, or simply to luck. Through the *mitzvot* of the Torah, Hashem reminds us that all of these suppositions are false and that only through His great kindness do we possess the affluence surrounding us.

The Sefer Akeidah teaches that the reason the *s'chach* must provide more shade than open space is to exhort us to trust in Hashem – represented by the *s'chach* – rather than place our faith in the numerous stars whose radiance fills the minute open holes and are a supposed source of luck. The Talmud also states that we may not use a *sukkah* that was erected thirty days before the holiday, but rather we must build a new *sukkah* every year. Rabbeinu Bachya explains that this reminds us that the world, represented by the *sukkah*, is not simply governed by natural laws, but is recreated every moment and is therefore new and not to be taken for granted.

Lastly, many commentators ask why it is that the 15th day of *Tishrei* was chosen, from all days of the year in which the Children of Israel wandered in the desert, to celebrate *Sukkot*. The Rashbam explains that it was at this time of year that all the harvests had just been gathered in the land of Israel, and amidst the abundant piles of grain the farmer might gloat and pat himself on the back with the assurance that <u>he</u> brought forth this grain by the sweat of his brow and the strength of his hands. Therefore, it is precisely at that moment that he must enter the *sukkah* and be reminded that it is Hashem alone Who bestowed upon him this blessing, whether it be through the rain or his good health, all amply provided by Hashem.

David leans back peacefully on his cold metal chair. He now hears the unheard voice of the *sukkah* calling out to him plaintively and reminding him to trust in Hashem. It is not by your hands alone that abundance has come, the *Tishrei* winds howl. It is not the immutable laws of nature, his newly-cut *s'chach* whispers. Nor is it the forces of luck, his overabundance of bamboo poles warns. And although these voices may be difficult to accept, they also provide the greatest of comfort and joy; that no matter what situation we find ourselves in, Hashem is constantly there, albeit in the misty background, protecting us from harm and showering us with His abundant kindness.

CHANUKAH

∞ Beauty or Beast
by Rabbi Dov Ber Weisman

On *Chanukah* we celebrate our liberation from Greek sovereignty. One of the many lessons we learn from *Chanukah* is the Jewish outlook towards culture and "beauty". Greece is a direct descendant of Yefet, the oldest son of Noah, and is known for its remarkable appreciation and cultivation of beauty. In fact, the name "*Yefet*" in Hebrew means "beauty". The Greeks were famous for their art, theater, culture, and the glorification of the fair form of the human body. And why not focus on these things, since they are all talents and features with which Hashem blessed Man and should therefore be appreciated.

However, the beauty of "beauty" can only be properly appreciated if it is connected to its source. In the words of the Kotzker Rebbe, "Many things in the world appear beautiful. However, their beauty does not endure. After one has seen them often, their grandeur and desirability fades. Only things that pertain to Hashem, Who endures forever, have eternal beauty."

Therefore, Noah blessed his son Yefet "to dwell in the tents of Shem [the ancestor of the Jewish people]" (Genesis 9:27). The physical beauty of Yefet, if taken and placed in the tents of Shem – if used to enhance Torah and *mitzvot* – becomes part and parcel of the spiritual and endures eternally. As phrased by the sages, since Man is more susceptible to the dictates of his heart and senses than to his mind and soul, the gift of Yefet to perceive and create beauty must "dwell in the tents of Shem". If not, the danger exists that Yefet's beauty is not only wasted, but is even destructive, since beauty for its own sake degrades Man.

External grace and beauty covering corrosive emptiness – this was Greece. Culture must be guided by a higher ideal, one which is external to Man's feelings and senses, and this is the role of Shem. As bearers of the Torah, we must utilize that which has beauty and physicality in order to enhance our spirituality.

PURIM

ᗡ Cheap Shot
by Rabbi Shimon Wiggins

When examining the first confrontation between the Jewish people and the nation of Amalek (Exodus 17:8-16) about which we read on *Shabbat Zachor*, the week before Purim, two basic questions come to mind. Firstly, why did Amalek attack the Children of Israel without provocation? The verse merely relates that Amalek attacked the Children of Israel in a place called Rephidim, but what motivated this attack? Secondly, why did they deserve this sudden punishment?

The first question is compounded by the *Midrash* which compares the Jewish people upon leaving Egypt to a tub of boiling water. Just as nobody would dare jump into a pot of boiling water out of fear that they would be scalded to death, so too the Jews were seemingly invincible after their miraculous exodus, when the nations of the world reacted to them with fear and awe. No one would dare attack the people who had G-d on their side – except Amalek. Once they did attack, and even though they lost, they managed to cool off the hot water so that other nations could also jump in without fear of being burned. What gave Amalek the strength to attack us?

Rabbi Yitzchak Hutner develops the answer to the first question from another *Midrash* which compares Amalek to a *leitz* – a person who mocks and ridicules everything in life. Such a personality seeks every opportunity to undermine and belittle that which is important and valuable in society. Amalek is the quintessential *leitz*.

The Ten Plagues, the splitting of the Red Sea, the destruction of Egypt, the manna falling from Heaven – all of these events which had created a sense of awe and trepidation in the other nations towards the Jews, making the tub hotter and hotter, only increased Amalek's desire to be the first people to jump in. To Amalek, the classic *leitz*, this boiling tub of grandeur, nobility, and spirituality had to be cooled, regardless of the consequences.

Let us now return to our second question. Why did the Jews deserve to be attacked by Amalek? The key to understanding this particular failing is the name of the location where Amalek attacked us – Rephidim. Although on a simple level this name is merely a geographical location, the *Midrash* tells us that it is an acronym for *rafu y'dayhem min haTorah* – the hands of the Jewish people were weak in their support of Torah. What does this expression mean? The usual term for lack of Torah study is *bitul Torah*, neglecting the study of Torah. What then is the idea behind their hands being weak in their support of Torah?

Rabbi Yitzchak Hutner explains that this expression refers to a weakness in recognizing and appreciating the importance and relevance of the Torah in our lives. When we fail to realize how vital Torah is to our very existence and to the existence of the entire world, we are inviting Amalek into our midst.

Not only should we be concerned with how much Torah we learn, but also with how much value and importance we attribute to the Torah which we study. Do we realize that Torah is Hashem's wisdom? Do we realize that Torah sustains the entire world? Do we realize that the ultimate perfection of the world can only come through Torah? May Hashem help us to increase our time to study Torah and appreciate its greatness.

Pesach

⌒ ## Spring Cleaning
by Benyamin Cohen

The holiday of Passover is fast approaching, and if we're not too careful it might pass right over us. Year after year, Passover seems to come over the horizon as we begin our spring cleaning and find out which relatives will be coming to town. One of the main features of this pre-Passover rush is the inimitable search and removal of *chametz*, those leavened food products which are forbidden to us on Passover. We take our magnifying glasses and search every nook and cranny of the house, making sure that no remnant of *chametz* remains. In trying to keep up with the Schwartzes we all want to have the cleanest and most impeccable home for Passover. But perhaps we are all forgetting something – something that is very crucial.

In our search for the physical bread crumbs which may be scattered in our homes, we tend to forget to clean the most important part – our soul. The *mitzvah* to search for *chametz* should not only be taken literally, but we must also realize that we all have *chametz* within ourselves – those bad habits which contaminate our Jewish soul. Therefore, each and every one of us must search within ourselves: What have I done wrong this year? How can I be a better Jew? Before it is too late, we must eradicate our inner *chametz*. We need to take an inventory of our deeds and dust away those which are not proper. It is a race against time. Will we be ready?

⌒ ## Recipe for Success
by Rabbi Shlomo Freundlich

The Talmud (Tractate Berachot 17a) relates that the great sage Rabbi Alexander would append to his daily prayers the following words of supplication: "Master of the world, it is clearly revealed to You that our desire is to comply with the Divine will. However, it is the yeast in the dough which prevents us from doing so." Our sages cryptically used the metaphor of "yeast in the dough" to characterize the evil inclination within us. What is it about the concept of *chametz* which thwarts one from finding spirituality?

Rabbi Chaim Friedlander explains that the leavening of dough is essentially a natural process. Adding yeast or other leavening agents simply expedites the chemical change. When flour and water are mixed and a given amount of time naturally passes, a chemical change will occur rendering the mixture *chametz*. The leavening process has been set in motion simply by allowing nature to take its course on this mixture. On the other hand, *matzah*, although comprised of identical ingredients, is produced by human intervention. It is a hurried process that achieves its objective by careful and strictly supervised manipulation of the ingredients within a specific time frame. Our initiative and creativity, not the natural course of passing time, produces the intended result.

Chametz, therefore, is symbolic of *tevah*, nature. The notion that nature governs our existence and propels us through life is antithetical to a Torah-minded Jew. Conversely, *matzah* suggests a Divine force above and beyond the natural course of events that subjugates nature to its will and produces an intended result to facilitate the Divine plan for Man.

The Zohar relates that when the Jewish people left Egypt they were confused regarding certain issues of faith. Hashem exclaimed that they should take their medicine and their spiritual uncertainty would disappear. The medicine was the *matzah*, and upon eating it the Children of Israel were cured of their spiritual malaise.

When eating *matzah* at the seder this Passover, rather than remarking on how crunchy or soggy it is, why not focus on the message of the *matzah* which urges us to reaffirm that Hashem orchestrates all of life's events and that our actions impact on how He relates to us. Nature doesn't determine our destiny – our commitment to Torah and *mitzvot* do.

∽ Mental Captivity

by Yoel Spotts

"And if Hashem had not taken our forefathers out of Egypt, we, our children, and our children's children would still be enslaved to Pharaoh in Egypt" (*Passover Haggadah*).

Many commentators wonder how the writer of the *Haggadah* could be so bold as to predict that if Hashem had not taken us out of Egypt more than 3300 years ago, then we would still be there today. After all, no nation, no matter how powerful, can reign forever. Certainly, somewhere during the thousands of years, the Egyptians would have been overthrown, allowing the Jewish people a window of opportunity to escape from their slavery. How then are we to understand this seemingly unrealistic claim that we would still be slaves had Hashem not taken us out at the time of the exodus?

A fascinating solution to this difficulty is presented by the Beis Halevi in his classic commentary to the *Haggadah*. The explanation of the troublesome passage centers around the realization that there are, in fact, two levels of enslavement – slavery of the body and slavery of the mind – and that a person may find himself in a situation when he is not enslaved on both levels at the same time. It is possible for one to be in a state of physical freedom, in total command of his body, yet mentally find himself absolutely bound by outside forces which leave him without any control over his own mind. Such a person will have great difficulty leading a normal life. Indeed, we read of the great obstacles encountered by the freed slaves of the South following the Civil War, for although they had been physically emancipated, they nonetheless were plagued by the "slave mentality".

The Jewish people were enslaved in Egypt for 210 years. The conditions which they experienced proved to be so harsh that the Egyptians succeeded in controlling not only their bodies, but their minds as well. The Jewish people felt so overpowered by their Egyptian masters that they could in no way fathom serving another master, namely Hashem. Thus, even if the Jewish people could have successfully freed their bodies sometime over the centuries, their minds would have nonetheless remained entrapped in Egypt.

For this reason, Hashem intervened and provided the ultimate escape, the miraculous redemption, which allowed the Jews to regain control of their minds as well. Now they could become Hashem's people. Now they could accept Hashem's laws. The redemption from Egypt, therefore, proved to be <u>the</u> precondition for the most momentous event in Jewish history – the receiving of the Torah. Thus, the *Haggadah* is in fact stating the undeniable truth: If Hashem had not taken us out of Egypt, we would still be slaves. For although our bodies might be free, nonetheless we would remain mentally and spiritually enslaved to Pharaoh with no hope of becoming Hashem's chosen people.

With this profound insight, we can readily understand another perplexing statement in the *Haggadah*: "In every generation, one must view himself as if he himself left Egypt." Thank G-d, we live in a country where we may practice our religion as we please. We are neither persecuted nor oppressed. We appear to be free men. How then are we to simulate the experience of leaving bondage?

In reality, we may think that we are free, but this freedom represents only half of the equation. Although we may have full command of our bodies, our minds unfortunately are not totally under our control. Stress from family, friends, and work, as well as other environmental pressures wreak havoc on our mental well-being, diverting us from serving Hashem properly. Our minds remain cluttered with everyday worries and concerns, leaving no room to think about the performance of the *mitzvot*. Passover is the time to leave all of our problems behind. Passover represents the opportunity to liberate ourselves from the mundane and elevate ourselves to higher mental and spiritual plateaus. In this way we can feel as if we ourselves have left Egypt, freeing our minds from bondage and enslavement.

SHAVUOT

⊙ For Scholars Only?

by Rabbi Shlomo Freundlich

As we begin the reading of the fourth of the five Books of Moses, we must take note of a very interesting calendrical phenomenon. The holiday of *Shavuot* <u>never</u> occurs before the Torah portion of Bamidbar is read. Why is this so? Tosafos remarks (on Talmud Tractate Megillah 31b) that this is no mere coincidence. It was an arrangement instituted by our sages to ensure that the holiday of *Shavuot*, a day when the vitality of the fruit trees is judged in the heavenly courts, should not be juxtaposed to the last portion in the book of Leviticus which recounts the horrible curses that will one day befall the Jewish people.

Rabbi Moshe Feinstein offers another reason which also serves to help us better relate to and appreciate the essence of the holiday of *Shavuot*. He notes that *Shavuot*, which marks the anniversary of the Revelation of Hashem and His Torah to the Jewish people at Mt. Sinai, can be very sobering and overwhelming to an individual with limited ability to comprehend or study Torah. After all, when such a person is told of the breathtaking scope of the Torah and senses that as much as he tries he has only scratched the surface in his personal understanding of the classic texts, isn't it expected and even natural for him to wonder what connection he really has to that great historic moment at Sinai? Can such a person even minimally feel the spiritual ecstasy of being a member of the nation to which Hashem has given His Torah? Would it be wrong or misplaced for such an individual to wonder if the inspiration to be drawn from the holiday of *Shavuot* is reserved for the scholar, while the less scholarly and the beginners should just watch curiously and respectfully from the sidelines?

The answer, claims Rabbi Feinstein, is expressed in our reading the Torah portion of Bamidbar as a precursor to *Shavuot*. In Parshat Bamidbar, Moses is charged with counting the Jewish people, the purpose of this census being to bring to light the idea that the Jews are now a unified, cohesive, and spiritual force whose collective mission is to fulfill the word of G-d. Everyone of age is counted. They <u>all</u> stand before Hashem equally, each with his unique talents and abilities. <u>Every</u> Jew's life has a precious purpose in the eyes of Hashem if he or she employs Torah as the blueprint of life.

The Talmud (Tractate Baba Batra 10b) relates an incredible incident. Rabbi Yosef the son of Rabbi Yehoshua fell gravely ill and lapsed into a deep coma. Eventually, Rabbi Yosef awoke from the coma and his father, sensing that he had undergone some otherworldly experience, asked him what he had perceived. Rabbi Yosef responded, "I saw the important people given low stations in the next world and the less significant people were assigned positions of distinction."

Rabbi Yisrael Salanter explains that in this world we regard our rabbis, scholars, and authors of Torah works as people of distinction and great worth, whereas the simple Jew is relegated to a more insignificant role in shaping the destiny of the Jewish community. But in the next world, the World of Truth, a crushing and haunting reality sets in. We are judged not according to our accomplishments, but rather according to our ability. If the one who enjoys a position of prominence in this world has failed to expend <u>all</u> of his G-d given ability, then he has, in a sense, failed and does not enjoy the same position of prominence as the simple unlettered Jew who strained himself to the utmost to understand even one page of Talmud.

As we celebrate the beautiful holiday of *Shavuot*, we can all rejoice before Hashem with the realization that serving Him faithfully and being true to our historic calling does not entail becoming a superstar. Rather it requires tapping into the ability and potential with which Hashem has blessed us.

∾ Torah Talk

by Kevin Rodbell

Entering the high-ceiling, table-lined *beit midrash* (study hall) at 4:37 AM, Jason was simultaneously overwhelmed by the thick smell of coffee and the roar of hundreds of people learning Torah at the top of their lungs. The room was simply pulsating with activity. He shuffled through the maze of tie-clad individuals, placed a thick, well-worn Talmudic text next to his third cup of Maxwell House, and reached over to pull his seat out from under the table.

As his hand grabbed the back of the white plastic chair he remembered the rule of the night – sitting meant sleeping. He returned the chair and moved toward the left in the direction of a wooden lectern. He and 200 others had been learning intently in the *beit midrash* since 9:00 the previous evening – more than seven hours straight – and they still had two hours until sunrise. Exhausted as he was, Jason felt determined to immerse himself in that Talmudic text until dawn. Caffeine would provide an artificial boost of energy (and blood pressure), but ultimately, Jason realized that his desire to learn, his sheer perseverance, would bring the long night to a successful culmination.

Like Jason, tens of thousands of Jews all over the world will spend the entire first night of *Shavuot* studying Torah. The all night learning experience of *Shavuot* really serves as a model for the entire year: Hashem commands, "This book of the Torah is not to leave your mouth; you shall contemplate it day and night" (Joshua 1:8). This translates into one of the most fully encompassing *mitzvot*. A Jew must designate time <u>every</u> day to the study of the Torah – ideally, lots of time – and, regardless of the number of hours, the Torah must remain the ultimate goal of a Jew. Hashem demands our utmost dedication of time and energy to the pursuit of truth through the Torah because the more effort we expend in studying the Torah, the more it becomes a part of us and the more it strengthens our relationship with Hashem.

In *Pirkei Avot* (2:17) Rabbi Yossi galvanizes us, saying, "Prepare yourself to learn Torah, for it is not [effortlessly attainable] for you [like] an inheritance." The harder we work to improve our character and the more diligently we pursue the depths of Torah knowledge, the more Hashem rewards our efforts in this world and in the next.

Rabbi Chaim of Volozhin emphasizes this concept by citing two sources that seem to contradict it. In the course of blessing the Jewish people before his death, Moses describes the Torah as being "the eternal heritage for the congregation of Israel" (Deuteronomy 33:4). The Hebrew word "*morasha*" used to mean heritage, also connotes inheritance, something that comes automatically and without effort. This would suggest that there is a guarantee of automatic success in Torah study and growth. Similarly, the Talmud records that for any family with three generations of Torah scholars, Hashem guarantees that the chain of Torah scholarship will continue in future generations, as the Talmud homiletically summarizes, "The Torah always returns to its familiar place of lodging." This family has welcomed the Torah for three generations, so, analogously, the Torah becomes a loyal return customer. However, while this may sound well and good, how is it consistent with the passage in *Pirkei Avot* which states that Torah knowledge can be attained only through diligent pursuit?

Rabbi Chaim answers that the passage in *Pirkei Avot* was carefully crafted to dispel the false notion that the Torah can be attained effortlessly. We must translate the verse more precisely: Hashem promises that the Torah is the inheritance of the <u>Jewish people</u>, the "congregation of Israel", and will always exist amongst them as a living, dynamic entity. But each <u>individual</u> must prove himself worthy of its acquisition.

Likewise, we must follow the analogy drawn by the Talmud to its logical conclusion: The Torah will return as a faithful guest to its familiar place of lodging with the family of Torah scholars. However, as the manager of any hotel knows, if paint is peeling from the walls and the rooms smell moldy and uninviting, customers will lose their loyalty very quickly and not return. Ultimately, it is up to the individual to demonstrate that <u>he</u> deserves to continue the tradition of scholarship and piety established by his father, grandfather, and great-grandfather. Only then is he worthy and his family history will come into play.

Growth in Torah is the most meaningful and longest lasting accomplishment that an individual can achieve, and the more effort we put into it, the more we receive in return. Indeed, on *Shavuot* and every other night, for that matter, it is our obligation and privilege to dedicate ourselves to personal development through Hashem's Torah.

ROSH CHODESH

∽ **Moonlight**
by Rabbi Lee Jay Lowenstein

Jewish tradition tells us that at the conclusion of each *Shabbat* Torah reading, a second scriptural reading called the Haftorah is added. This selection from the Prophets is not chosen arbitrarily; rather its theme is meant to complement the primary topic of the Torah reading or be germane to some unique event associated with the particular *Shabbat*. When *Rosh Chodesh*, the beginning of a new Hebrew month, falls out on Sunday, we depart from the normal selection associated with the weekly Torah portion and in its stead read from the book of Samuel I (20:18-42) about the relationship of David, the future king of Israel, and Jonathan, son of King Saul. Presumably, this choice was made due to the reference of the impending new month found in its opening verse: "And Jonathan said, 'Tomorrow is the New Month.'" However, it is odd that a single minute reference should be sufficient to justify its selection for this occasion. Is there, perhaps, some message within the story of the friendship between David and Jonathan which exemplifies the theme of the onset of the new month?

The Talmud (Tractate Chullin 60b) addresses a difficulty with regards to the creation of the two primary heavenly bodies, the sun and the moon. One part of the verse in the creation story states that the Almighty fashioned <u>two</u> great luminaries, yet the second half identifies one of them as the "great luminary" and the other as the "small luminary" (Genesis 1:16). Our sages explain that initially the sun and the moon were created as equals. The moon approached Hashem and complained, "Master of the Universe! Is it possible that two kings may share the same crown?" To which Hashem responded, "Moon, go and diminish yourself so that you will only reflect the light of the sun." To appease the moon Hashem offered several consolations:

The Jewish people will use a lunar calendar to measure time, and the righteous Jews will bear the appellation of "the small one" (a symbol of humility), comparing them to the moon. It is the way of our sages to speak metaphorically of great ideas. What is the underlying message they seek to impart with this fantastic story?

Let's address one final question which requires our analysis of the relationship between David and Jonathan as seen through the eyes of our sages. In *Pirkei Avot* (5:19) our rabbis declare, "All love which is based upon external factors will never last. Only love which is truly selfless has the power to endure." To solidify this message, they cite the relationship of David and Jonathan as the paradigm of selfless love. Isn't it unusual that in the entirety of Jewish literature the only example they felt was effective at conveying this point was the friendship between these two? Why not select an example of a relationship between a man and woman to serve as a guide? After all, such a relationship is far more prone to fall prey to external considerations!

A man and woman enter into a relationship because they have a deep-down need to feel whole and complete, a need which this union brings to fruition. In a man to man friendship, however, each party potentially feels threatened by the other. A man senses that all men are his competitors and life is an uphill struggle to be number one. For a man to admit that he needs the assistance of another is to blow a gaping hole in the armor of his defenses. A man literally spends his life wondering "How can two kings share the same crown?"

Perhaps no one sensed this more than Jonathan. He was the crown prince of Israel, successor to the illustrious King Saul. However, Saul had fallen from Hashem's favor and was to be replaced by the budding David. Saul senses this; Jonathan knows it too. In the Haftorah, Saul lashes out at his son, "Do you not know?! As long as [David] lives upon the earth, you and your kingdom shall not be secure!" (I Samuel 20:31). Yet for the sake of friendship Jonathan gives it all up. He makes himself small in David's presence. The result of this is not only a powerful bond of friendship, but the very future of the

Jewish people is paved as David, the progenitor of the Messianic dynasty, is given his rightful place. Certainly, there cannot be a more definitive example of selfless love, of one giving up his own rights for the sake of another, than was evidenced in this friendship.

The destiny of the Jewish people is intertwined with the moon. Just as the moon waxes and wanes, we too have times of great success and failure. Just as the moon continuously "renews" itself, we take our cue from it and renew our relationship with the Almighty. In the last few moments of the "old" moon, as it wanes seemingly out of existence, we read about the selflessness of Jonathan and how he guaranteed a brighter future for the Jewish people. The moon teaches us that if we are to establish a relationship with Hashem, we too need to be willing to diminish ourselves occasionally. Sometimes giving up of ourselves is not a loss; it is a stepping stone to greater opportunity. And behold, only moments after vanishing, the moon again is "reborn" to shine in all of its brilliance!

Isaiah prophesied that the moon will one day be restored to its original grandeur. May it be the will of the Almighty that He quickly restore us to our original splendor that we may proclaim, "King David (the *Mashiach*) of Israel lives on" as we are led back to our homeland once again.

TISHAH B'AV

◌ Here Comes the Bride
by Benyamin Cohen

After a little hustle and bustle, all of the guests settled down and finally took their seats. At last, David and Karen's wedding was ready to begin. Months of preparation were about to culminate in the happiest day for the young couple. Arrangements of flowers lined the center aisle and adorned the windows of the main sanctuary. The afternoon sun shone brightly through the synagogue's skylight. The rabbi, regal and poised, stood just in front of the ark waiting patiently for the ceremony to begin.

A hush fell over the room. The orchestra began playing as David's nieces and nephews strutted down the aisle before him, cameras flashing from every direction. One by one, David's immediate family preceded him down the aisle, marching in perfect cadence to the rhythm of the music. Finally, it was David's turn. His father on one side and his mother on the other, David held their hands tightly as a single tear began rolling down his cheek. This was the happiest moment of his life.

Jerusalem, 9 Av 70 C.E. - The Romans had taken control of the outer courtyard of the holy Temple. During the morning hours, the Jews tried unsuccessfully to ward off the Romans, only managing to scare off a few soldiers. The Jewish faction, tired and weary, retreated in haste to the inner sanctum of the Temple and slammed the doors shut behind them. Their fate was sealed.

David arrived at the wedding canopy and now Karen's family was making their way down the aisle. Karen's two younger sisters walked ahead of her, tossing rose petals onto the sanctuary floor. Karen, in all her glory, appeared at the entrance. The guests rose in unison as if they were welcoming a royal princess. Veil upon her face, parents on each side, Karen regally glided to the front of the room and took her place beside David under the wedding canopy. The guests sat down, the music stopped playing, and the rabbi stepped forward.

The sun had set and the early evening darkness descended upon the Temple Mount. In the blackness, the Jews still huddled inside the inner sanctum of the Temple, praying to the Almighty in hopes of a miracle. Just outside, a fire had broken out. The Roman soldiers threw their torches over the innermost walls of the Temple, adding more force to the fire. The flames burst high into the air with brilliant strength.

"We are gathered here today," began the rabbi, "to bear witness to the holy act of marriage." The rabbi went on to describe the sanctity brought about by the union of two people in marriage. He spoke of the tremendous *kiddush Hashem* (sanctification of G-d's name) that occurs when two such kind and generous individuals as David and Karen, are wedded in soulful bliss. David removed the golden ring from his suit pocket. In the afternoon sunlight, the ring glistened with a celestial glow. Karen sniffled as she held back a tear. "Behold, you are consecrated to me by means of this ring, according to the ritual of Moses and Israel," David recited as he carefully slid the ring onto Karen's finger.

The blazing inferno continued, gaining strength as it consumed the wooden structure of the Temple. The Jews gathered around the altar, praying for their lives, praying for their holy sanctuary. The density of the smoke was unbearable and, one by one, the bodies of our Jewish brethren began piling on top of each other.

Karen's uncle, a rabbi of a small synagogue in Wilmington, ascended the stairs to the wedding canopy and read the *ketubah* (marriage document) in his booming cantorial voice. A box of tissues was passed amongst the relatives who were emotionally affected by the proceedings. A smile broke across David and Karen's faces as each of the seven marriage blessings were recited. With each passing blessing, the glint in the young couple's eyes grew brighter.

The Romans began throwing spears and arrows over the Temple wall, randomly murdering the Jews still trapped inside.

As the wedding service came to a close, the rabbi placed a crystal glass on the floor beneath David's foot. For close to two thousand years, it has been a Jewish tradition to shatter a glass at the end of every wedding service to symbolize that despite this moment of sheer joy, our happiness will never be complete until our Temple is rebuilt.

If the smoke and endless barrage of shooting arrows hadn't already overcome them, the remaining Jews were left to be slain by the Roman soldiers. Others were simply crushed in the nighttime panic.

David raised his foot up high and, with full force, stomped down on the glass, crushing it into dozens of tiny pieces.

A river of blood flowed across the cold stone floor of the Temple and slid down the eastern steps.

Tishah B'Av is the anniversary of so many dark chapters in our history. The saddest events have occurred on this fateful day – both of our holy Temples were destroyed; the fortress of Beitar fell, followed by the subsequent defeat of Bar Kochba and massacre of his men; as well as the ploughing up of Jerusalem by Hadrian in 135 C.E. Also, on this date in 1290, King Edward I signed an edict expelling all of the Jews from England. In 1492, 300,000 Jews were expelled from Spain, per the decree of Ferdinand and Isabella. The *Kitzur Shulchan Aruch* (Code of Jewish Law) warns us of the perils of entering into a business contract or a court case during the month of *Av*, for this entire month is fraught with danger for the Jewish people.

What brought about such terrible destruction? According to our sages, one of the main impetuses for our downfall was our callousness and our failing regarding one particular character trait. We were (and are) guilty of *sinat chinam*, baseless hatred amongst the Jewish people. Imagine the magnitude and significance of this one character trait if it was the cause of such horrible disasters!

We observe *Tishah B'Av* every year, but how can we alleviate this unfortunate situation into which we were cast? We are nearing the end of a three-week period of mourning, a time when we are supposed to examine our actions and bring our souls in for a spiritual "dry cleaning". The key is to not stop there. Once *Tishah B'Av* is over, if we can take those lessons and the improvements which we recently made and incorporate them into our daily routine, then we will be one step closer to eradicating baseless hatred amongst our brethren. If we can only stop ourselves the next time we are about to spread gossip about another Jew or before we show disrespect for the feelings of others, then we will surely be on the road to the ultimate redemption when our holy Temple will finally be rebuilt. At that time we will herald in the *Mashiach* and see Hashem in all of His glory, like a bride walking down the aisle to join her groom.

ᗧ **Glossary**

akeidah/akeidat Yitzchak – binding of Isaac

Av – eleventh month of the Jewish calendar

Ba'al Peor – a grotesque form of idol worship

Bamidbar – book of Numbers

Beit HaMikdash – the holy Temple in Jerusalem

beit midrash – *yeshiva*/synagogue study hall

Bereishit – book of Genesis

Birkat HaMazon – Grace After Meals

brit milah – circumcision

chametz – leavened products

Chanukah – the festival of Lights

cherub/cherubim – angel-like figure(s) formed out of the top of the holy Ark in the *Mishkan*

chesed – loving-kindness

chok/chukim – *mitzvah/mitzvot* whose ultimate rationale is beyond human understanding

Chumash – Pentateuch, the Five Books of Moses

derech eretz – proper behavior or manners

Devarim – book of Deuteronomy

Elul – twelfth month of the Jewish calendar

erev rav – the "mixed multitude" of gentiles who joined the Jewish people in the exodus from Egypt

galut – exile

gaon – genius

gevurah – strength, restraint

Haftorah – weekly reading from the Prophets

Haggadah – basic text of the Passover seder

halachah/halachic – Jewish law

Hashem – colloquial term for G-d

Ir Hanidachat – a Jewishly-populated city of idolatry

kaddish – prayer sanctifying the name of G-d; special prayer recited by mourners

kedushah/kadosh – holiness/holy

ketoret – incense offered on the altar in the *Mishkan*

kiddush – prayer recited on wine at the beginning of *Shabbat* and festival meals

kiddush Hashem – sanctifying the name of G-d

kippah – skullcap

Kodesh HaKedoshim – Holy of Holies

Kohen Gadol – High Priest

Kohen/Kohanim – priest(s), descended from Aaron

kollel/kollelim – institution of higher Jewish education for adult men

korban/korbanot – offering(s)

korban Pesach – Paschal lamb

korban tamid – daily communal offering, brought once in the morning and once in the afternoon

lashon hara – evil speech or slander

lechem hapanim – show bread displayed in the *Mishkan*

M'arat HaMachpelah – the burial tomb of the Patriarchs and Matriarchs purchased by Abraham and located in Chevron

Ma'ariv – evening service

ma'aser – tithes given to the Levites

machzor – holiday prayer book

Maggid/Maggidim – circuit speaker(s) of *mussar* topics

mashgiach – spiritual advisor and mentor

Mashiach – the Messiah

matzah – unleavened bread eaten on Passover

melu'im – the consecration service of the *Mishkan*

menorah – candelabra

metzora – person suffering from the disease of *tzaraat*

mezuzah – parchment inscribed with two paragraphs of the *Shema* and attached to the doorpost

midah k'neged midah – measure for measure, the principle that Hashem rewards and punishes us according to our specific actions

Midrash – rabbinic interpretations and/or parables of *Tanach*

mikveh – ritual bath

Minchah – afternoon service

minyan – quorum for prayer, a minimum of ten men

Mishkan – portable tabernacle built by the Jewish people in the desert

Mishnah – the basic text of the Talmud

mitzvah/mitzvot – commandment(s)

musaf korbanot – additional offerings unique to each holiday

mussar – Jewish ethical teachings

nazir – individual who willingly vows to abstain from consuming wine/grape products, hair cutting, and contact with a dead body

nefesh – soul

nes – miracle

nese'im – princes

neshamah – soul

nisayon – test/trial from Hashem

Nissan – seventh month of the Jewish calendar in which Passover is celebrated

parah adumah – red heifer, used in purifying those who are *tamei*

Parshat – the Torah portion of

Pesach – the holiday of Passover

Pirkei Avot – Ethics of Our Fathers

Purim – holiday celebrating Jewish victory over the wicked Haman recorded in the book of Esther

rachamim – mercy

Rosh Chodesh – the first day of each Jewish month

Rosh Hashanah – Day of Judgment/ Jewish New Year

Rosh Yeshiva – dean of an institution of higher Jewish education

s'chach – branches placed on the top of a *sukkah*

sanhedrin – great Jewish court

sefer – book

sefirat ha'omer – the *mitzvah* to verbally count the days between the holidays of *Pesach* and *Shavuot*

Shabbat – the Sabbath

Shabbat Zachor – the *Shabbat* before Purim

shatnez – mixture of wool and linen which Jews are prohibited to wear

Shavuot – the Festival of Weeks, commemorating the giving of the Torah at Mt. Sinai

Shema – Torah passage recited every morning and night, reaffirming basic beliefs of Judaism

Shemittah – Sabbatical year when the earth in Israel must lie fallow

Shemoneh Esrei – the focal prayer of every service

Shivah Asar B'Tammuz – the 17th day of the Jewish month of *Tammuz*, observed as a fast commemorating the breaching of Jerusalem's walls leading to the destruction of the Temple

Shmot – book of Exodus

shofar – ram's horn

shtetl – village

shulchan – the table in the *Mishkan*

sotah – a woman who has been accused by her husband of being unfaithful

sukkah – booth in which we dwell on the holiday of *Sukkot*

Sukkot – the Festival of Booths

taharah/tahor – purity/pure

talit – four-cornered prayer shawl with *tzitzit* attached to each corner

talmid chacham – Torah scholar

Tanach – the Bible, consisting of the Pentateuch, the Prophets, and the Writings

tefillin – small leather boxes containing passages from the Torah, worn by Jewish men every day

teshuvah – the process of repentance

Tishah B'Av – the ninth day of the Jewish month of *Av*, saddest day on the Jewish calendar, observed as a 24-hour fast commemorating the destruction of the Temples in Jerusalem

Tishrei – first month of the Jewish calendar, containing the holidays of *Rosh Hashanah*, *Yom Kippur*, and *Sukkot*

tochachah – rebuke of the Jewish people by Hashem, found in the Torah in Parshat Bechukotai and Parshat Ki Tavo

Torah – the fundamental scriptures of Judaism, written by G-d and given to Moses on Mt. Sinai

tumah/tamei – ritual impurity/ritually impure

tzadik/tzadeket/tzadikim – righteous man/woman/people

tzaraat – a disease that is the physical representation of a spiritual malaise, contracted primarily by someone speaking *lashon hara*

tzedakah – charity

tzitzit – fringes worn on four-cornered garments

vav – the sixth letter of the Hebrew alphabet

Vayikra – book of Leviticus

yeshiva/yeshivot – institution(s) of higher Jewish education

Yom Kippur – Day of Atonement

Yovel – Jubilee (50th) year

∽ Biographies of Commentators

Abarbanel, Rabbi Yitzchak (1437-1508) – Great philosopher, statesman, and leader of Spanish Jewry during the time of the Expulsion. He wrote a classic commentary on nearly all of *Tanach*.

(Reb) Aharon HaGadol – A renowned Chassidic rebbe.

Alshich, Rabbi Moshe (1508-1593) – Author of a classic commentary on *Tanach*, *dayan* (judge) in Safed during its golden age

Alter of Slabodka – Appellation of Rabbi Nasson Tzvi Finkel (1849-1927), spiritual leader of the Slabodka Yeshiva which produced many of the great scholars and leaders of American Jewry of the past two generations.

Alter, Rabbi Shmuel – Compiled a digest of many commentaries on *Chumash*, entitled "Likutei Basar Likutei".

Beis HaLevi – Commentary on *Chumash* by Rabbi Yosef Dov HaLevi Soloveichik (1820-1892), one of the most brilliant Talmudists of the nineteenth century.

Blech, Rabbi Benjamin – A contemporary author and speaker.

(Rabbi) Chaim of Volozhin (1749-1821) – The leading disciple of the Vilna Gaon and founder of the renowned Volozhin Yeshiva, which became the prototype for the great *yeshivot* of Eastern Europe.

Chasam Sofer – Title of the books and appellation of Rabbi Moshe Sofer (1762-1839), the great *Rosh Yeshiva*, Torah leader, and *halachic* authority of Hungary.

Chiddushei HaRim – Appellation of Rabbi Yitzchok Meir Alter (1789-1866), founder of the Chassidic dynasty of Ger.

Chofetz Chaim – Appellation of Rabbi Yisrael Meir HaKohen of Radin (1838-1933), author of numerous basic works on nearly the entire range of Torah subject matter. He was known for his great piety and was acknowledged as the foremost leader of Jewry in his time.

Da'as Z'keinim – The commentary on *Chumash* by the Tosafist school of the twelfth and thirteenth centuries.

Dessler, Rabbi Eliyahu (1891-1954) – One of the outstanding *mussar* personalities and thinkers of the twentieth century, he lived in London and subsequently in Bnei Brak. His writings and discourses have been published in "Michtav M'Eliyahu".

Dubno Maggid – Rabbi Yaakov Krantz (1741-1804), the most famous of the Eastern European *Maggidim*, best known for his incisive parables in explanation of *Chumash*.

Feinstein, Rabbi Moshe (1895-1986) – *Rosh Yeshiva* of Mesivta Tiferes Yerushalayim in New York City and a foremost leader of Jewry and *halachic* decisor of our time. His comments on *Chumash* have been published under the title "Darash Moshe".

Firer, Rabbi Ben Zion – Contemporary Torah scholar in Israel.

Friedlander, Rabbi Chaim (1923-1986) – A prominent *mussar* personality who served as the *mashgiach* of the Ponovezh Yeshiva in Bnei Brak, Israel. His discourses have been published in "Sifsei Chaim".

Gifter, Rabbi Mordechai – The present *Rosh Yeshiva* of the Telshe Yeshiva in Cleveland.

Hirsch, Rabbi Samson Raphael (1808-1888) – Great leader of modern German-Jewish Orthodoxy and author of many significant works, including a renowned commentary on *Chumash*.

Hutner, Rabbi Yitzchak (1904-1980) – *Rosh Yeshiva* of Yeshiva Chaim Berlin in Brooklyn and a foremost leader of Jewry in his time.

Ibn Ezra, Rabbi Avraham (1089-1164) – Author of a classic commentary on all of *Tanach*, famous for its grammatical and linguistic analyses.

Kamenetzky, Rabbi Yaakov (1891-1986) – *Rosh Yeshiva* of Mesivta Torah Vodaath in Brooklyn and a foremost Torah scholar and leader of the past generation. His comments on *Chumash* have been published under the title "Emes L'Yaakov".

Kanievsky, Rabbi Yaakov (1899-1985) – Known as the Steipler Gaon, he was a Torah scholar of tremendous stature in Bnei Brak, Israel.

Kli Yakar – Classic commentary on *Chumash* by Rabbi Shlomo Ephraim Lunshitz (1550-1619) of Lemberg and Prague.

Kotzker Rebbe – Appellation of Rabbi Menachem Mendel of Kotzk (1782-1859), he was one of the outstanding early leaders of the Chassidic movement.

Krohn, Rabbi Paysach – A contemporary author and speaker.

Levovitz, Rabbi Yerucham (1874-1936) – A prominent *mussar* personality who served as *mashgiach* of the great Mir Yeshiva, his discourses on *Chumash* have been published under the title "Da'as Torah".

Luzzatto, Rabbi Moshe Chaim (1707-1746) – Often referred to by the acronym Ramchal, he wrote numerous works on Jewish philosophy, including the classical *mussar* text, "Mesillas Yesharim".

Maharal of Prague – Acronym for Rabbi Yehudah Loewe (1526-1609), one of the seminal figures in Jewish thought in the last five centuries and author of numerous works, including a classic commentary on Rashi entitled "Gur Aryeh".

(Rabbi) Meir Simcha HaKohen of Dvinsk (1843-1926) – A foremost Torah scholar of his time and author of "Meshech Chochmah" on *Chumash*.

Mizrachi, Rabbi Eliyahu (1450-1525) – Chief rabbi of the Turkish empire and author of a classic commentary on Rashi.

(Rabbi) Moshe Yitzchak HaDarshan (1828-1899) – The Kelemer *Maggid*, one of the most celebrated *Maggidim* of Eastern Europe, known for his "golden tongue".

Netziv – Acronym for Rabbi Naphtali Tzvi Yehudah Berlin (1817-1893), renowned *Rosh Yeshiva* of the famous Yeshiva of Volozhin in Russia and author of a commentary on *Chumash* entitled "Haamek Davar".

Ohr HaChaim – Commentary on *Chumash* by Rabbi Chaim ben Attar (1696-1743), a renowned Kabbalist and Torah scholar in Italy and Jerusalem.

Onkelos (c. 90) – A proselyte who authored the authoritative Aramaic interpretive translation on *Chumash*.

Otzar Chaim – A recent compilation (1960's) of commentaries on *Chumash*.

Rabbeinu Bachya (1263-1340) – Author of a wide-ranging classic commentary on *Chumash*.

Rabbeinu Yonah (d. 1263) – Author of numerous classic works on many Torah subjects, including a commentary to *Pirkei Avot* and a treatise on the laws of *teshuvah*.

Rambam (Maimonides) – Acronym for Rabbi Moshe ben Maimon (1135-1204) of Spain and Egypt, one of the leading Torah scholars and thinkers of the Middle Ages. His works include "Mishneh Torah", a comprehensive code of Jewish law; and "Moreh Nevuchim" (Guide for the Perplexed), a major work of Jewish philosophy.

Ramban (Nachmanides) – Acronym for Rabbi Moshe ben Nachman (1194-1270) of Spain, one of the leading Torah scholars of the Middle Ages and author of, among many other great works, a classic commentary on *Chumash.*

Rashbam – Acronym for Rabbi Shlomo ben Meir (1085-1174), a grandson of Rashi and author of a classic commentary on *Chumash.*

Rashi – Acronym for Rabbi Shlomo Yitzchaki (1040-1105) of France, considered the commentator par excellence on both *Chumash* and Talmud.

Reisha Rav – Title of Rabbi Aharon Lewin, author of "HaDrash V'haIyun" and a prominent Chassidic rebbe.

Rizhiner Rebbe (1797-1851) – A prominent Chassidic rebbe.

Rosh – Acronym for Rabbi Asher ben Yechiel (1250-1327), author of a classic *halachic* commentary on the Talmud.

Ruderman, Rabbi Yaakov (1900-1987) – Founder and dean of Ner Israel Rabbinical College in Baltimore, Maryland, and a renowned Torah scholar.

Salant, Rabbi Yosef – A great teacher of *mussar* in Jerusalem and author of "Be'er Yosef".

Salanter, Rabbi Yisrael (1810-1883) – Founder of the *mussar* movement which stressed morals based on the study of traditional ethical literature.

Schwab, Rabbi Shimon (1908-1995) – Rabbi of the renowned Breuer's community in Washington Heights, New York.

Sefer Akeidah – Commentary on *Chumash* by Rabbi Yitzchak Aramah (1420-1494), emphasizing deep and penetrating philosophical thoughts.

Sefer HaChinuch – A classic work explaining the 613 *mitzvot* by an anonymous thirteenth-century author.

Sefer Noam Elimelech – Discourses on *Chumash* by Rabbi Elimelech of Lizhensk (1717-1787).

Sfas Emes – Appellation of Rabbi Yehudah Leib Alter (1847-1905), the second Rebbe of the Chassidic dynasty of Ger, grandson of the Chiddushei HaRim, and author of many esoteric writings on *Chumash,* the Jewish festivals and *Pirkei Avot.*

Sforno, Rabbi Ovadiah (1470-1550) – Italian author of a classic commentary on *Chumash*.

Sh'lah – The great, all-encompassing work by Rabbi Yeshayah Hurwitz (1560-1630), including an exposition of the fundamental tenets of Judaism and a commentary on *Chumash*.

Shapiro, Rabbi Meir (1888-1934) – Great Torah scholar and leader, founder of the *Daf Yomi* program still in existence today in which many Jews all around the world undertake daily study of one identical folio page of Talmud.

Shmulevitz, Rabbi Chaim (1902-1979) – *Rosh Yeshiva* of the Mir Yeshiva in Jerusalem, he was one of the towering Torah figures of his generation. His popular *mussar* discourses attracted huge crowds of eager listeners.

Sifsei Chachamim – A popular commentary on Rashi compiled by Rabbi Shabsai Bass (1671-1718).

Targum Yonason – An Aramaic paraphrase and commentary on the *Chumash*.

Teitelbaum, Rabbi Yoel (1887-1979) – Leader of the Satmar Chassidim and a distinguished Torah scholar.

Tosafos – The commentary on the Talmud by the Tosafist school of the twelfth and thirteenth centuries.

Vilna Gaon – Appellation of Rabbi Eliyahu Kramer of Vilna (1720-1797). The appellation *Gaon*, by which he is referred, demonstrates his revered status, as he is considered the greatest Torah scholar in many centuries.

Weinberg, Rabbi Yechiel Yaakov (1884-1966) – A great German Torah scholar.

Wolkin, Rabbi Aharon (1865-1942) – A great Polish Torah scholar and commentator.

Yafeh To'ar – A classic commentary on the *Midrash* by Rabbi Shmuel Yafeh Ashkenazi (1525-1595).

Zohar – The basic work of *Kabbalah* (Jewish mysticism).

Zweig, Rabbi Yochanan – The present *Rosh Yeshiva* of the Talmudic University of Florida.